Praise for *Love in Any Language*

"This is a most fascinating book. LaTorre's excellent descriptive power, looking back on her youth, is refreshing with its innocence, courageous faith, and passionate energy as she follows her heart and builds a life for herself and Antonio back in the US. Her opening sentence says it all: 'I loved Peru.' Readers will love her candid story."

—**Kenneth Kelzer**, LCSW, author of *The Sun and the Shadow: My Experiment with Lucid Dreaming*

"The memoir includes all the challenges involved in merging two marvelous cultures and two individual lives. Evelyn manages her marriage while raising two children and pursuing career goals that include a doctorate. The reader experiences her amazing journey to become a successful career woman who has maximized her potential. A fascinating read."

—**Dr. Jackie M. Allen**, MFT, associate professor of education at the University of LaVerne and coauthor of *A Pathway to PDS Partnership: Using the PDSEA Protocol*

"Compelling and highly readable, this book gently tells of a cross-cultural marriage that might well have gone wrong—but instead lasted for five decades. Resolving clashes of ambition, personality, and values, the author and her Peruvian husband found a balance that worked. In an era of divorce and heartbreak, *Love in Any Language* offers hope."

—**Dori Jones Yang**, author of *When the Red Gates Opened: A Memoir of China's Reawakening*

T0300761

Love in Any Language

Love in Any Language

A Memoir of a Cross-cultural Marriage

Evelyn Kohl LaTorre

SHE WRITES PRESS

Published 2021
Printed in the United States of America
Print ISBN: 978-1-64742-195-3
E-ISBN: 978-1-64742-196-0
Library of Congress Control Number: 2021908863

For information, address:
She Writes Press
1569 Solano Ave #546
Berkeley, CA 94707

She Writes Press is a division of SparkPoint Studio, LLC.

All photographs were taken from the author's personal archive and enhanced by Tony LaTorre.

Map by Tim LaTorre

This book has been recreated from memorabilia, letters, and journal entries saved by the author for over fifty years. For the sake of readability and brevity, some separate incidents have sometimes been combined or presented in slightly altered timeframes. In some instances, the names of individuals have been changed, either at their request or the author's discretion.

When the author lived in Peru from 1964 to 1966, Cuzco was spelled with a z. City officials now spell Cusco with an s. The author has chosen to also use the Cusco spelling.

*For my husband who left all he knew to journey with
me through this adventure called life*

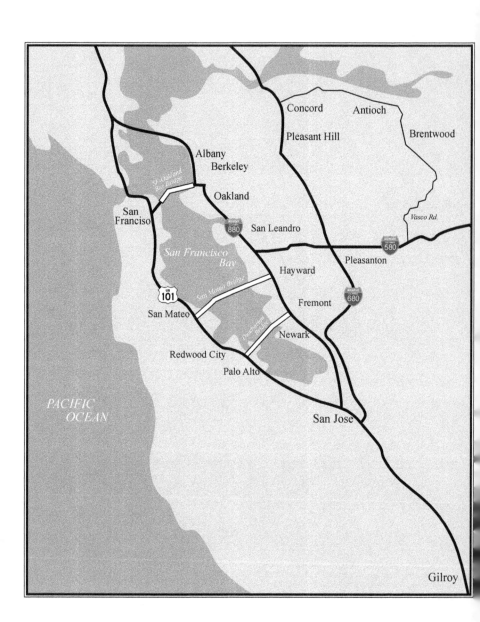

Contents

Rising from the Ruins

I loved Peru—the terrain, the cuisine, the artistry, and the people. I lived there for two years in my early twenties. The country captured my mind, body, and soul in 1965. And then there was Antonio, the university student who claimed my heart. Love and life in my Shangri-La was magical. Why would I ever leave?

The Andes mountains won me before Antonio ever did. Between my Peace Corps home in Abancay and the Incan capital of Cusco stood a string of seventeen-thousand-foot snow-capped peaks. Their white tops sparkled, too eye-watering to look at for long in the bright high-altitude sunshine. In the moonlight, the peaks gave off a mysterious, fascinating glow. Thoroughfares twisted through valleys that skirted the base of the expansive mountains and continued between Abancay and Cusco for 125 miles. My stomach fluttered each time I crossed the Apurimac River that flowed three thousand feet below a narrow bridge. The enormity and beauty of the soaring and plummeting natural forms made my body tingle, especially when I traveled the winding dirt roads with my dark-haired *novio*.

Scenery nourished my soul while Peruvian food filled my stomach. Peruvians flavored their meals with just the right amount of cumin, garlic, hot pepper, and other condiments to make any fare delicious. The spicy smells of the exotic traditional dishes of *anticuchos* (beef heart) and *cuy* (guinea pig), roasting over hot coals on Cusco's street corners and in its high-class restaurants, made my mouth water. I ate with gusto any dish made with one of the region's three thousand types of potatoes. *Papas a la huancayina,* potatoes smothered in a velvety cheese sauce, counted as both an appetizer and a main dish. I ordered the simpler *lomo saltado,* beef strips with potatoes and tomatoes, whenever available. The black, yellow, and red shades of the dish were as mouthwatering as the colors woven into the crafts I bought.

Intriguing Inca-design fabrics in sunflower yellow with sea-wave turquoise or tomato reds that faded into rosy pinks lured me into Lima's fabric stores the few times I visited the capital. A meter of the pink cotton material would make a size-ten sleeveless dress for me to wear in Abancay's warm summers. The muted color brought out my blue-gray eyes. The turquoise and yellow yardage went into my Peace Corps trunk for a future use. Blankets, sweaters, hats, and slippers made from alpaca wool exchanged trunk space with the dresses I'd sewn in California and brought to Peru in the fall of 1964. Local women asked to buy my homemade dresses when I departed Abancay for the States twenty months later. To the four trunks destined for California, I added a fluffy white stuffed alpaca and a baby-sized poncho, hat, and pair of socks. I wished I'd had room for more of the women's hats that I'd seen in the Cusco area. The varying types of headwear defined which village a woman came from. Unfortunately, I had room for only the *montera* style I liked best.

Ollantaytambo women wore bowler hats. In Chinchero women sported bright-red and indigo-blue flat *monteras.* Maras ladies wore tall, white stovepipe hats perched above thick, black braids that twisted down their backs. Bright multicolored outfits clothed the women, but not the men, who dressed in drab gray and brown knicker-type pants and regular shirts. Only their hand-woven alpaca ponchos displayed color. Stripes that ranged from orange to red brightened these capes that protected them from sudden downpours. Our neighbor in Abancay wove the blanket-sized wraps across upright sticks in our shared side yard.

The residents of Abancay and its outlying areas treated my roommate Marie and me like their own. Local ranchers and a friendly clergyman performed magic tricks for our entertainment. Physicians at the local hospital taught us basic medical procedures to provide first aid for residents in the isolated countryside we hoped to serve. Zoila and Zulma, unmarried sisters, made certain we had what we needed for our tiny storeroom house—a pot for cooking, a sewing machine, an iron. They helped us fit into our adopted town with invitations to movies and festival dances. Members of our girls' clubs taught us how to cook quinoa. And thanks were offered at every turn.

Our PE students expressed gratitude for training them to compete in Abancay's annual gymnastics drill competition. The local agricultural agency showered us with praise when our 4-H club president won the regional competition by demonstrating how to make potato pancakes with the secret ingredient of beer. Life in Peru had been good.

Much as I loved my Peruvian world, I couldn't live in the Andes forever. Antonio had asked me if I would, several times during the sixteen months we were falling in love. I always said no. One reason was that he had no plans for supporting a family.

Antonio was in his third year studying economics at the university. At the last minute, as I prepared to leave his glorious country, I agreed to marriage because I didn't want to leave him—and I was pregnant with his child. Because I couldn't see our future in Peru whenever I looked at the practical side of life and love, I suggested an alternate path—come with me to the US.

The same qualities I loved about the Andes made living there for the rest of my life impossible. Cusco's twelve-thousand-foot altitude hampered my digestion and breathing. Cold winters in the thin air felt even colder than the frigid seasons I'd survived as a child in Montana. The different holidays and the special foods made me homesick for the traditions and dishes of my country. I'd been away from California for two years and missed the climate and my family—especially now that I would soon have a baby to consider.

Life in the States would give my new husband and me a more secure future. Work and educational opportunities existed in greater abundance there. Though I hated to rob Peru of one of its intelligent youths, I believed we could have a better life together only if Antonio exchanged his country for mine.

All he knew of the US was from me and the movies. He spoke no English. He had little work experience. He had to finish college. My country demanded hard work, fluency in English, and an employable skill in order to earn a living wage. Nevertheless, he'd chosen to leave his home country for me. But love couldn't guarantee the life of security, excitement, and learning I wanted. I approached our future with trepidation. Could our love survive the pressures and faster pace in the US? Would I wonder if we should have remained in the land of the Incas where there had been adventure, passion, and love?

Leaving Peru

The wedding had been arranged in eight days. I strode down the center aisle of the sixteenth-century Spanish chapel in the Church of La Compañia on Antonio's arm that June 19, 1966. The Baroque-style church and the chapel stood atop Inca walls made of two-hundred-ton granite boulders that fit so tightly together they needed no mortar. The massive structures had withstood seven-point earthquakes since the fourteenth century. I hoped my marriage would be as indestructible as the church's foundation.

The invading Spaniards had rebuilt the church above the Inca walls more than once. Our courtship had been like La Compañia church— destroyed and rebuilt several times. Now we began married life on shaky grounds—no money and a child on the way. And we hadn't always seen eye to eye. I couldn't recall how many times we'd given up on a life together and broken off ties. But we could never stay apart for long. We were drawn together like two opposing magnets—even when we repelled one another. Something inside me said I needed this gentle and caring man as my husband. His thoughtfulness and facility to demonstrate affection made Antonio special—unique in my experience.

Our nuptials occurred the day after Antonio's twenty-third birthday and five months before my twenty-fourth. I thought I loved him, and he said he loved me. Throughout the time we'd been together, he'd demonstrated profound dedication to my wellbeing. I'd never before experienced such deep and sincere caring. No one had ever loved me as much as Antonio.

My body had slimmed the past month from bouts of morning sickness, but my heart beat strong. I committed to a life with Antonio, despite my doubts. Our future held responsibilities. How would we live? But on my wedding day, I pushed those doubts aside and walked arm in arm with him toward the altar.

Twenty of Antonio's assorted aunts, uncles, cousins, and university friends watched us kneel before the youthful priest. The parents and three younger siblings of my husband-to-be hadn't made the trip to Cusco from their home in Abancay. The valley's provincial capital was a day's bus ride west of Cusco, too far for his ill mother to travel and too costly for his stepfather to pay for. The presence of his extended family and friends was enough.

Antonio's youngest cousin took photos of us with my Instamatic camera. Our wedding pictures show a pale, blue-eyed, young American woman holding the hand of a light-complexioned, brown-eyed Peruvian youth in front of an ancient altar. The contrasts between us melted away in the solemnity of the occasion. I looked the part of a modern bride in my short-sleeved, knee-length, white taffeta dress and dainty net veil. Antonio wore a new black suit that matched his thick shock of wavy black hair. He stood a head taller than my five foot two inches in my two-inch heels, even with my light brown hair arranged on top of my head.

Padre Gálvez, Antonio's close friend from the university, officiated at our wedding mass. I stood in front of the prelate, pregnant—a condition I'd been cautioned to avoid both by priests who had taught my catechism classes and by my own father. Fortunately, I hadn't gone to confession with Father Gálvez, so this kindly priest didn't know I was with child. My flat stomach didn't betray me.

Over the past two years, I'd become fluent in Spanish. So I promised to love, honor, and obey in that language. We exchanged the

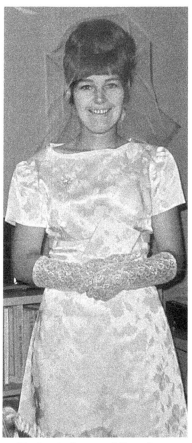

Evelyn in her wedding dress

wedding rings purchased by Antonio's stepfather. The priest pronounced us husband and wife. In an hour, we were an officially married couple.

After the mass, and with the photo-taking in the church concluded, we emerged laughing from the chapel. Hand in hand we ran down the centuries-old cobblestone street past sturdy granite Inca walls. Antonio's relatives threw handfuls of rice as we raced to a waiting Volkswagen Beetle. I was a stranger in a foreign dream world, now with a handsome husband. I thought I knew what I was doing, but a sudden bolt of surrealism hit me. Was this real? It didn't feel like reality.

Later that afternoon, I stood in the living room of the small Cusco apartment of Antonio's cousin Elsa, staring at my wedding cake. The *torta*, in a rectangular pan, sat flat, bumpy, and rutted like the dirt streets outside the rundown housing complex. Thoughtful Elsa had baked the confection for our wedding reception forgetting that cakes sometimes didn't rise in Cusco's twelve-thousand-foot altitude. I hoped the unpalatable mess wasn't an omen for my future.

Then Elsa brought out boxes of cream-filled waffle wafers. The cookies tasted fine with the champagne. She had solved the cake dilemma. Elsa's solution mirrored my philosophy—when things don't go as planned, find another way. Now eating for two, I gobbled up everything offered me.

No North American attended our wedding ceremony or reception. None of my family came. Not even Marie, my Peace Corps roommate and confidant. All were too far away. Most of my Peace Corps colleagues, like Marie, were traveling the world or had returned to the States. My parents and five younger siblings in California hadn't yet received the letter I'd sent two weeks earlier telling them I would be marrying the young man I'd written them about.

I didn't consider calling them. Phone calls, even between Peruvian cities, rarely connected. In my nearly two years living in Peru, I'd only phoned outside the country a few times. I'd called my mother at her Newark, California, police clerk job a few times over the shortwave radio of the American clerics in the town next to mine. But she'd been too preoccupied with her duties to talk about my life in Peru. Everyone in California was too busy with their own lives to consider mine.

My family couldn't have come to my wedding, even if I'd been able to call them. The trip was too expensive for my lower-middle-class parents. I had written them about a certain considerate university student who corrected my Spanish. But I didn't tell them I'd fallen in love with him. My father would be suspicious of any guy I married. Practical, devout Catholic Mom would be disappointed but work to make the best of the situation. My three sisters would be delighted and my two brothers curious.

The small number of attendees was just right. No one gave us any wedding gifts—just best wishes and hugs. Antonio's stepfather, Adolfo, paid for our gold wedding bands. My heart burst with gratitude that he'd found the money for our expensive jewelry. The cost must have been a financial hardship for him. Other than Adolfo's generous gesture, I didn't need relatives, friends, or gifts. I had much of what I needed in Antonio—someone who loved me enough to leave everything he'd known and settle in the States.

After the last handful of guests had left Elsa's apartment, I melted into one of her family's few wooden chairs. My taffeta wedding dress made a soft crunching sound as it wrinkled under me. I kicked off my scuffed white heels. Fatigue and peace swept over me after the previous busy week. Antonio's family had handled the wedding details just fine.

I leaned against the wall and watched Elsa and Antonio put away the leftover cookies and champagne. His slightly older cousin had the thick, wavy, black hair and smallish brown eyes characteristic of Antonio's maternal side of the family. Elsa was even the same height as Antonio, five foot eight, but with a more delicate frame. I hadn't gotten to know her well, but she seemed anything but delicate. She'd arranged our wedding reception in her family's small apartment with only a few days' notice. Antonio's family had been gracious and supportive, not critical and judgmental like my parents sounded in their letters to me.

Elsa lived in the modest three-bedroom apartment with her husband and two elementary-school-aged children. But there was little evidence of who lived here, just who cooked here. The kitchen–dining area had been cleared of everything save the table, to make standing room for the twenty chatting guests. Now, with the day's celebrations over, the invitees had all departed.

Antonio finished tidying up his cousin's sparse kitchen as I watched with interest. Maybe he'd make a helpful husband after all. Then he surprised me further with a plan. He had seldom planned anything.

My new husband ushered me into a taxi and told the driver to take us to the newest Cusco tourist hotel, the Savoy. I fretted at the cost. Antonio had no money. His stepfather, Adolfo, had arranged and paid for the room. Once again Adolfo had come to the rescue.

Antonio carried me across the threshold of our honeymoon suite. Not a typical Peruvian gesture. He must have seen the custom in American movies and wanted to please me. And please me he did. I was giddy with happiness knowing we'd have a lifetime in which to express our love. That night I had little need for the filmy powder blue negligee I'd purchased because it matched my eyes. My body quivered with joy and apprehension when I imagined being with Antonio forever. Guilt I'd felt for having had premarital sex with him vanished. Our officially married state now made our intimacy legal—and church-approved.

Our first night as a married couple concluded, we went to stay with Elsa's family. Our hosts slept in one bedroom, and the two children had the second. Elsa put us in Antonio's former small room—a stark contrast to the new, luxurious Savoy, but more affordable. Our suitcases covered the water stains on the wooden desk. We didn't mind accommodating ourselves in his twin-sized bed.

A few evenings at dinnertime, we joined Elsa and her husband after their workdays. Their son and daughter joined us if they weren't off at a soccer game with friends. The kitchen had returned to its original post-reception function. I marveled at how Elsa could serve such delicious dinners using two primus kerosene burners, a small refrigerator, and only cold running water. We bought a few groceries to help the family defray the added expenses of our stay. Most of the day we vacated the apartment, readying for our departure from the Incan capital.

I enjoyed Cusco during the city's annual major Incan ceremony of Inti Raymi, the Festival of the Sun. Antonio and I had attended the celebration together in 1965 when we were *enamorados,* committed to one another. A year later, we attended as husband and wife. I shivered with delight at the hope that we would view many future celebrations together.

The first day of the festival, proud indigenous residents came into Cusco from scores of outlying towns to parade around the capital's main plaza. They wore multicolored fire-red, jungle-green, and

Inti Raymi Parade

sun-yellow native costumes. Their pointy-nosed white masks were designed to ridicule the facial features of the Spaniards who'd conquered Peru in the 1500s. Their playful derision poked fun of the straitlaced Spaniards who'd replaced the more colorful Incan religion with serious Catholicism.

Revelers swayed in rhythm to five-note scale of the traditional marching music played on wooden flutes, dented trumpets, and stringed harps. The haunting flutes with their melancholy echoes permeated my soul. The trumpets made my feet move in time to the beat. The harps transported me to the heavens. I loved the music, bright colors, and my companion even more this year.

The next day, we walked a mile up a steep, dirt road outside Cusco, accompanying thousands of tourists from around the world. I heard snatches of German, French, and what I guessed was Italian. My head turned searching for the speakers when I heard English, but those pale revelers were never anyone I knew.

We followed the tourists and Peruvians up to the ceremony in the ancient Incan Sacsayhuamán fortress. There, two-hundred-ton granite boulders, like those under the plaza churches and along Cusco's streets, formed a quarter mile of imposing walls nineteen feet high. We witnessed selected locals dressed as Incan nobles, priests, and virgins of the sun replicate the ancient Incan ritual of sacrificing llamas.

In these modern times, *chicha*, a corn beer, flowed in excess, but not the blood of llamas.

Antonio announced that he had to return to Abancay to say good-bye to his family, who hadn't been able to attend our wedding. I hadn't expected that and tried to understand. He didn't speak much about his family, but I knew how much he loved his mother. He'd soon fly far away to live with me in California. Who knew when he'd ever see any of his family again?

I thought it my duty to go with him but didn't want to return to my former Peruvian home. I'd already bid a sad farewell to the many friends living in Abancay whom I cared about. A repeat of the heartache and tears would only add to my current state of unease. Traveling the curvy, mountainous road for eight hours would make my nausea worse. Antonio appeared fine with my choice. A week into our marriage, and we'd already made a decision that separated us. Though Antonio and I were officially a couple, we didn't act like we knew how to be partners. He went his way to take care of his business. And I didn't accompany him because my comfort came first.

At the end of June, after spending our mini-honeymoon among Inca ruins, my new husband boarded the bus in Cusco for the 125-mile trip to Abancay. I flew to the Lima home of Antonio's paternal grandparents, Francisco and Rosa LaTorre.

Antonio had revealed a bit about his origins during our courtship. Months before his birth, my husband's paternal grandparents had whisked Frank, Antonio's twenty-one-year-old biological father, away to Lima. They left behind Frank's sixteen-year-old pregnant girlfriend, Antonio's mother, Livia. I assume they didn't want their upper-class son to marry the farmer-class sixteen-year-old "Miss Cusco" beauty.

So Livia and her family raised Antonio with sporadic financial contributions from Frank. Still, the LaTorres had acknowledged Antonio as their grandson from the beginning.

He had seen his biological father three times in his young life: at ages two, twelve, and seventeen. The second time had been in 1955 when he and his mother had traveled to see his father, visiting from the US, in Lima. Three years before, Frank had immigrated to the US and settled in Ohio. In 1965, when Antonio and I yearned to be together forever, we had each written to Frank imploring his assistance. Would he help Antonio immigrate to the States? But his father set impossible conditions—fluency in English, an employable skill, and a job. Antonio couldn't begin to meet his father's demands while living in Peru. The message seemed clear to me. His father didn't wish to be a part of his son's life.

Antonio or his mother must have arranged my stay with the LaTorres in Lima. He expected to soon join me there. Upon his arrival, he would apply for his green card as the spouse of an American. I brought our marriage certificate to submit to the US embassy.

Surprise registered on tiny Grandma Rosa's wrinkled face when she opened the door at her house on Avenida Arequipa in Lima and saw me. Then she frowned with disapproval at not having been told earlier about her grandson's courtship or our wedding. More eyes widened when I introduced myself to two of the home's other residents, Antonio's Aunt Haydee and her twenty-year-old daughter, Patricia. Despite their astonishment, the family welcomed me with warm embraces. Grandma Rosa said they looked forward to greeting Antonio, whom they'd not seen in six years.

My concerns of rejection melted away, replaced by other discomforts. On a couple of evenings, Antonio's cousin invited me to lavish dinners at the country club where she introduced me to well-dressed young tennis players. Patricia seemed bent on either showing me off or finding me a mate—which she apparently forgot I already had.

The adults in the family instructed me not to use more gas or electricity than they deemed necessary. I suspected they weren't as well off as they wanted others to believe. The LaTorres' high-society charade outside the home clashed with what I observed inside. I'd just come from the poorer mountainous countryside with neither in-house plumbing nor consistent electricity, so I couldn't enjoy their faux lavish lifestyle.

"Turn off the gas," Grandma Rosa said as I fried an egg for breakfast. "And do it before you're finished cooking so you can use the last bit of heat from the stove."

"Switch off the iron before you finish pressing the last garment," Aunt Haydee cautioned when she saw me flattening the wrinkles of my only dining-out dress, "so you use all the heat."

These new coastal relatives pinched *soles* in their house as if they were poverty stricken, while appearing wealthy out in society. Antonio's family in Abancay was poor, but they didn't limit the use of the utilities they had. My family, too, had pinched pennies when we lived in southeastern Montana and again in California. But we'd never put on airs to seem richer than we were.

The frugality practiced within the grandparents' home contrasted with the expensive country club dinners. This Lima family placed value on status and material wealth, masquerading as well-to-do. And I wasn't used to their directives and didn't like being watched. Nevertheless, they cared about Antonio and extended that warmth to me.

I traveled daily to the American Embassy to complete my portion of the paperwork that Antonio needed to apply for his green card. But it was taking him too long to get to Lima. The Abancay to Lima trip normally took two days by land. Had his bus fallen off one of the high mountain cliffs? My worries increased at receiving no word of his whereabouts. Why didn't he call me?

Antonio had never phoned me in Abancay when we were dating.

Neither of us had phones. Now, the telephone lines between Lima and Abancay often didn't function when I tried to call him. The two times I reached him, he said he'd been delayed but didn't say why or for how long. I awaited his arrival, eager to reunite. My pregnancy made me feel more vulnerable than ever before. My husband should be with me.

After a week, I became impatient with wasting time in Lima. I should be in California arranging our future. Besides, I could no longer tolerate the weirdness of my hosts' household restrictions. I was out of place and lived in fear that my morning sickness would reveal my pregnancy. I'd hidden my secret well, not wanting these members of Lima society to judge me. Now I'd had enough.

On July 6, 1966, I stuffed $500 in *soles* into an envelope, addressed it to Antonio, and left it on the desk in my room. The amount would be sufficient for him to purchase his airfare to California. I wrote a note that explained my reason for leaving and enclosed a copy of the "Guarantee of Sustainability," that the US embassy required for Antonio's US visa. It read:

> I will assume support of my husband, Antonio, in the US. The cash on hand, in the form of a US government check, is for $536.20, part of a $1,638.20 total readjustment allowance earned as a Peace Corps volunteer. I will receive the balance upon my return to the US. This should be sufficient to live on for six months. My husband plans to begin work upon his arrival in California. I will also work. I have no other obligations or expenses.

Then, I said good-bye to the LaTorres and boarded a Pan Am plane bound for San Francisco, California. I didn't weep as the plane lifted off like I often did when departing from a beloved Latin American country. This time, I needed to be strong in order to forge ahead and begin the life I wanted for us.

Home Again

On the afternoon of July 7, my family—mother, father, three sisters, and two brothers—showered me with hugs at the San Francisco Airport. For nearly two years, they'd known about my life in a distant third-world country only through my letters. I hadn't been physically present to reassure them, answer their questions, or share my experiences. Now they expressed relief that I seemed healthy. Mom could stop worrying about my safety. My arrival confirmed that their prodigal daughter had returned intact.

I was also eager to resume my favorite sister status with my six-year-old brother, Randy. He had sent me sticks of gum and kisses marked with Xs in his letters to Peru. Now he looked at me and smiled, then withdrew. Randy wasn't certain who I was. Though disappointed, I tolerated losing my importance to him. Soon I'd have my own child.

Once more back in my former bedroom, I tackled emptying my suitcases and four trunks of the Peruvian articles I'd brought back—alpaca rugs, unique crafts, and the baby socks, hat, and poncho, bought before I knew I'd have use for them. My body warmed with anticipation, knowing that a more treasured part of Peru, Antonio, would soon join me. I cooked up some of the quinoa the Abancay 4-H girls' club had gifted me and served it mixed with cheese. The dish didn't have the same nut flavor as when I'd had it in Peru. My family hesitated to eat this strange foreign protein.

Baby clothes from the Cusco Market

In the land of plenty, I set about eating the things I'd missed for the past two years—pasteurized milk with Cheerios, Mom's buttermilk biscuits, and real hamburgers and hot dogs. The mellow taste of *café con leche* (coffee with milk), which I'd enjoyed in Peru, faded when I ate my dessert of apple crisp topped with whipped cream. This, after I'd downed my favorite home-cooked meal of fried chicken with mashed potatoes and "Evelyn gravy." No one seemed surprised that my stomach protruded a bit.

Neither of my parents thought my decision to marry had been a wise one, but they said little to me. My sisters told me that Dad had hit the ceiling when he'd read my letter from Peru saying I was marrying Antonio. He had remarked in front of them, "That guy just wants a green card." He didn't say that to me, now that I'd wed "that guy." I suspected they wanted more than an unemployed foreigner who spoke no English as their first son-in-law. My parents hadn't yet met Antonio, so they couldn't appreciate his qualities. They'd come to love him as I had—I hoped.

The man I'd known the longest had been my father. During my formative years in Ismay, Montana, he had earned $200 a month as a signal maintainer for the Milwaukee Railroad and hadn't been particularly ambitious. With the produce from our acre-sized summer garden, we five children didn't go hungry. However, the linoleum floor in our kitchen had had holes in it, and we sewed most of our own clothes, sometimes using the cloth from the twenty-five-pound sacks of flour we purchased. And Dad didn't allow us to buy sandals for summer. He would only purchase ugly, sturdy oxfords for our growing feet. He said it made no sense to pay for the open "holes" sandals had. But he'd always helped me make my special school projects, so I couldn't complain.

Mom often disapproved of my decisions when she thought them risky, like travel and relationships with foreign guys. But she always helped support the consequences. This time she had a pile of applications waiting to assist me with my job search. Mom had encouraged all her children to take written government tests for practice, even when we weren't looking for work. Before entering the Peace Corps, I'd spent days sitting in dingy gray exam rooms on uncomfortable chairs answering hundreds of multiple-choice questions for jobs I didn't want. My scores had ranked me high on lists for clerk, secretary, and juvenile hall worker. My name had remained frozen on county employment lists while I was in Peru. Now I notified the county to reactivate my name. I was available to work.

Mom's forethought paid off. My first week home, she presented me with a list of open positions in county agencies. I took a deep breath. I was employable.

Writing my name as "Mrs. Evelyn LaTorre" for the first time on the job applications jolted me into reality. My name had changed, but I hadn't. I felt like the same headstrong, determined woman I'd always been. Still, losing the last name I'd been born with felt like a familiar part of me had disappeared. Who was I now? How would I incorporate the man whose name I carried into my life in the US?

Being married and responsible for bringing Antonio from Peru to California brought out the social worker in me. I'd help him develop his potential. But having another adult depend on me made me uneasy and less free to do what I wished. This union would be another of my adventures.

Within two weeks of my return to the US, Alameda County called to offer me the night clerk position on the women's burn ward at Highland Hospital in Oakland—an ideal job for me. A month in a Montana hospital at age twelve with possible rheumatic fever and four months' training in Abancay's municipal hospital had left me with a deep admiration for the medical profession. But, after the freedom of the past two years, the thought of working a regular nine-to-five day made me shudder. The four-to-midnight shift, though still eight hours, seemed less confining. I smiled into the phone and accepted the evening position. However, I had to pass a physical examination before being hired.

A medical intern performed the assessment at Highland Hospital. I lay supine on the cold exam table feeling exposed in the white cotton hospital gown I'd tied in the front as instructed. The tall young physician-in-training slowly loosened the ties of my gown, bent over me with his stethoscope, and moved it over the bump in my abdomen. His eyebrows knit together with a look of concern. The exam over, he signaled me to sit up. I suspected what was wrong.

"You must realize," the young doctor said, "that you are around four months pregnant."

"I know," I said looking at the floor. Heat rose in my cheeks.

"How badly do you need this job?" he said softly.

"I really need this job," I said, worried I could lose this work opportunity.

The administration could deny employment to a woman who was

pregnant. He knew that but hesitated. Perhaps someone close to him had been in that situation, or like me, he thought the rule absurd. Either way, he seemed to have the courage and empathy the moment called for.

"Okay, I'll pass you," he said. "But be sure to see an obstetrician soon."

I thanked him and floated out of the examining room, relieved this compassionate intern hadn't written on my record that I'd be having a baby in five months and shouldn't be hired. I'd squeaked by.

ω

Antonio wrote that he'd arrived at his grandparents' home in Lima the week after I flew to California. He was heartbroken to find me gone. Every few days I received one of the prepaid aerogramme mailers I'd left him. He wrote that he missed me but understood why I hadn't remained longer with his grandparents. Their quirkiness irked him too. He was eager to join me. He tried to reschedule his required interview with US embassy personnel for an earlier date, but they wouldn't budge from his August 1 appointment.

I missed Antonio. We both longed to be together again soon. Between hunting for an apartment and a job, I wrote to him as often as time permitted. The week before I started my new job, I finally reached him by phone. I was thrilled to hear his strong, tenor voice again when he greeted me. Then I went straight to the reason I'd called.

"I need to buy a car to drive to work," I said.

"Don't buy one yet," he said. "We'll make that decision when I get to California."

"But I need to get to my new job in Oakland," I said, realizing he didn't yet have any idea of how transportation worked in my country.

"Can't you take the bus?"

"It's not as easy here as in Peru," I said, loving that he was interested in figuring this out. "It would take hours, and I work nights."

Antonio wanted to take some ownership of family decisions. But making those major choices together would delay the arrangements I needed to make immediately. Besides, I felt as independent as before my marriage. I preferred to do what I saw necessary. I didn't see a reason to cease resolving my own problems. I couldn't always honor his directives. Following my instincts shouldn't diminish Antonio's importance in our partnership. I listened to his idea about the car on the phone call with the same interest that I read Antonio's opinion in his letters of where I should go for graduate school.

The University of Wisconsin had accepted my application while I was still in Peru and instructed me to enroll in their graduate school of social work before September. Antonio wrote that I should take their offer. He was unfamiliar with US geography and didn't know how cold the northern states could be in winter. I calculated that a move to Wisconsin, so close to our baby's January birthdate, would be impractical. Graduate school wouldn't fit in with the added pressures of adjusting to life with a new husband and baby. I needed the support of my family in familiar surroundings. When the University of Wisconsin added a stipend to the offer of free tuition, I still turned them down. I needed to stay close to my parents. Exchanging warm California for cold Wisconsin didn't seem like a good move for me or for us.

Even though I'd declined grad school in Wisconsin, I still wished to begin studies for a master's degree in social work. The nearby University of California at Berkeley had yet to act on my application for the 1966 fall semester. If admitted, classes would begin four months from the baby's due date—not an ideal time. Nevertheless, when I received a rejection letter from UCB's school of social welfare, I was crushed. I wanted to know why I'd been refused entry, even if I might not attend in my pregnant condition.

I met with the school's dean. The fifty-something administrator sat ready for me in his Haviland Hall office on the UC campus in Berkeley. After introductions, I plowed straight ahead.

"Why was I denied entrance for this coming semester?" I asked, waving my rejection notice at his diminutive figure.

"The number of qualified applicants far surpassed the openings the school has for first-year students," he explained in a soft voice meant to calm me.

"But I don't understand," I said, trying to hold back tears, "My undergraduate grades qualify me, don't they?"

"Yes, and so does your Peace Corps experience," the balding man explained, looking almost as pained as I felt. "But you can reapply next year."

Disappointment and surging hormones overruled my usual strong composure. I broke down sobbing in the dean's office. He still didn't admit me.

I needed a vehicle to get to appointments and commute to my new job. Antonio's delay meant I'd have to overrule his request to participate in the decision of which car to purchase. I headed for the Volkswagen dealership to buy the latest model of the same car I'd owned and sold before I joined the Peace Corps. I felt confident I was making the best choice for our family and me.

Java-green, sea-blue, and ruby-red tops, like colorful round domes marching in from outer space, lined the lot at the VW dealership. Inside, the array of shiny compact cars reflected on the showroom's linoleum floor. For the past two years in Peru, I'd seen only rusty, dented, and pockmarked VWs chug up Avenida Sol in Cusco. Seeing so many brand-new cars made me marvel at my country's prosperity.

A dark-green VW called to me. It was the same color as the car I'd purchased to commute to college in 1963. The vinyl seat gave me a familiar hug as I slipped in behind the steering wheel. An enthusiastic salesman in an ill-fitting suit saw me and entered on the passenger side.

"This is just the car you should have," the middle-aged man offered.

"It looks a lot like the car I bought here three years ago," I said, longing for the economical auto that had transported me around the Bay area and California my senior year of college.

"Are there any features in particular you'd like me to demonstrate?" he said sweeping his hand in a grand gesture from the stick shift to the radio.

"Does the cigarette lighter work?" I asked, because Antonio smoked.

"Yes," the salesman said.

He pushed in a small knob on the dashboard. As soon as it popped out, he pressed the fiery-hot lighter to his thumb. The car filled with the smell of the salesman's burning flesh. I cringed. I couldn't believe the pain the salesman endured for a sale. I bought the car.

The hospital job gave me money for car payments and an apartment. I'd also have health insurance on July 19, a month after I began work. Before that, however, I'd have to pay for my first pregnancy checkup myself.

The only obstetrician I knew was Dr. Thelma Brown. She had been my mother's doctor when she was pregnant with my brother Randy six years before. I hesitated before I dialed her office. My family didn't need to know I'd be visiting Mom's obstetrician. But I'd promised the Highland Hospital intern I'd get a checkup, so I followed through. I drove my new green Volkswagen to the obstetrician's office.

"You and the baby are fine," Dr. Brown said with a smile after examining me. "Are your parents pleased?"

"They don't know," I said, my eyes downcast. "They wouldn't approve."

"Why is that?" the doctor asked, giving me a quizzical look.

"Because," I stammered, "I'm due sooner than nine months after my wedding. Please don't say anything to them. I'll pay for the appointment myself."

The doctor didn't ask more questions. She suggested I take vitamins and folic acid. I didn't make another appointment. Her $70 fee was too steep for my dwindling bank account. I shrugged my shoulders feeling relieved. I was grateful that health insurance from work would cover future wellness checks.

∿

My mother said we should have wedding announcements printed and sent out. That would conform to the US custom she believed in and legitimize my marriage in the eyes of her friends and our relatives. Mom offered to pay for the official notices, so I agreed. She might have had second thoughts about advertising my marriage had she known I was pregnant.

What a welcome surprise to receive wedding gifts after the announcements went out. Congratulations cards that contained money helped with my mounting expenses. Everything coming together so fast facilitated my adjustment to being back in the organized US. But then, I had to face my mother's intrusion.

One morning Mom heard me vomiting in the bathroom. When I left, she pulled me into her bedroom to explain how to avoid pregnancy using the rhythm method—the Catholic Church's only approved measure of birth control. I wanted to shout, *I could have used some information about birth control earlier in my life!* Instead, I chuckled to myself recognizing that having intercourse only during "infertile times" hadn't worked for my parents. They'd had six children using the method.

I longed to celebrate the new life that stirred within me. But there'd be no shouting about the joyous event here. My religious mother would judge me for my sin. I told myself that I'd just have to throw up more quietly from now on. I dreaded the day I'd have to tell her the truth. I'd wait until the baby came for that.

Mom and I looked for housing in Hayward, equidistant from my job in Oakland and my parents' home in Newark. After days of searching, we found an affordable place. The only drawback—it was in an "adults only" apartment complex. What could I do? If I told my mother that Antonio and I would have to leave the apartment in five months because of the baby, she'd reprimand me. So I paid the deposit and moved in the wedding gifts and my parents' discarded furniture.

I loved working in a hospital again. The year before, I'd trained in Abancay's regional hospital, hoping to provide basic medical aid to a nearby Peruvian indigenous community. There, I'd given injections and bandaged wounds. Now at Alameda County's public hospital, I worked on the women's burn ward answering the phone, requesting supplies, and transcribing doctors' written instructions. I also ordered medicines for patients in great pain, the result of accidents like falling asleep with a lit cigarette. From my desk in the hall, I could hear patients' moans and screams as the nurses scrubbed the scabs off charred skin. I vowed never to let fire touch my tender skin.

Hospital work was the perfect job for me as I assimilated back into American life. The care and work I'd had in hospitals gave me reverence for physicians and nurses. I admired how they calmed agitated patients with attention to their physical and mental suffering. And I found another bonus at Highland Hospital. I could relax in the medical setting feeling I'd be cared for if I went into premature labor. Unfortunately, Antonio wasn't experiencing the same contentment.

"You can't believe my disappointment," Antonio moaned on his

August 1 phone call. "I've been counting the days, hours, and minutes, dreaming of being with you and never being separated again."

"What's the problem?" I asked.

"My interview at the embassy progressed well," he said, anguish in his voice, "but the consul left out a required document. Now I can't leave until August 4."

On August 4, I received another call from Lima. Over the scratchy telephone line, I heard Antonio's exasperation.

"I've postponed my flight until Monday, August 8. I can't get a seat on a plane until then. I'll telegraph you at the stopover in Mexico City to let you know what time I'll arrive in San Francisco."

Antonio getting to me anytime soon seemed doomed. Monday's telegram read: "Arriving in San Francisco at 12:00 a.m." What else could go wrong?

I'd accepted my position at the hospital with the proviso I might need to leave work to pick up my husband at the airport when he arrived. On Monday, August 8, I entered the women's burn ward at four o'clock expecting to leave at ten, drive to the San Francisco International Airport, and retrieve Antonio at midnight. I imagined running to him—or waddling, my current gait—and throwing myself into his arms.

The phone on the ward rang at five o'clock. I answered, expecting a question from one of the patients' families. Instead, I heard a concerned woman's voice on the other end. She had a question for me.

"We have your husband with us here in Redwood City," the woman said. "Would you like to come and get him?"

"But Antonio is scheduled to arrive at midnight tonight," I sputtered and heard Antonio's voice respond.

"I arrived at noon, and you weren't at the airport," Antonio said. "I met this couple who spoke Spanish on the plane. When they saw no one was meeting me, they invited me to their home."

Embarrassed, but thankful for the couple's generosity, I explained the misunderstanding about the time to the woman, checked with my supervisor, and took off for Redwood City. The drive took forever. The traffic across the Bay Bridge and the freeway going south moved at a crawl. It was rush hour on the bridges. The shirt I wore dripped with perspiration. If I got to throw myself into Antonio's waiting arms as I'd imagined, I'd smell of sweat. This had been a comedy of errors that wasn't funny.

I arrived in front of the address I'd been given. The faces of Antonio and the couple lit up to see me as they approached my VW. I rolled down the window and thanked them for rescuing Antonio and opened the door for my long-lost husband. The pair hugged Antonio good-bye, then glared at one another.

The lost traveler greeted me with a quick peck on my cheek and whispered that the couple had been arguing since he'd met them. I heard them quarreling as we drove away. What a way to begin life in the US—being left at the airport, then caught in the middle of a fighting couple.

"Whose car is this?" Antonio asked once inside.

"Ours," I replied, aware of the surprised look that spread across his face.

Our marriage wasn't beginning much better than the Redwood City couple's. For starters, Antonio had given me the wrong time of his arrival in the telegram he'd sent from Mexico City, so I'd left him stranded. We were starting our married life together in my country, whose language my husband didn't speak, with a car I'd purchased, and in an apartment I'd selected—all supported by my earnings and without his participation. Could our marriage survive more communication trip-ups and power imbalances? It would have to.

New Life Begins

Antonio came bearing gifts. He brought my father an alpaca blanket and my mother a wooden jewelry box carved with Peruvian figures. At first, communication between Antonio and my family consisted of hand gestures mixed with my translations. His English was as limited as my family's Spanish. Despite the constraints, Antonio's warm smile and affectionate hugs won over my three sisters and two brothers—and even my usually emotionally undemonstrative parents. The family females remarked what a kind, handsome man I'd married. Everyone noticed his gentle and thoughtful ways. I let out a long exhale. My parents had succumbed to Antonio's charms much as I had.

Mary, a friend from high school and college, threw a wedding shower for me. She and Dave, to whom I'd introduced her, had married days after our graduation from Holy Names College. Good Catholics that they were, Mary and Dave now had a year-old son. My child's birth wouldn't meet their Catholic-approved timing. In six months, I, too, would be a parent—though no one at my wedding shower knew it.

Attendees included friends from high school and college. Most of the Amigos Anonymous group, with whom I'd performed volunteer work in Mexico the summer of 1963, came too. The gifts of colanders, mixing bowls, and towels, when added to my parents' cast-off furniture, were greatly appreciated and gave us the basics for our home.

Antonio and I reveled in being together again, cozy in our own apartment. For the first month, before Antonio began working, we stayed in bed until early afternoon. Mom called each morning to ask what I was doing. I was the first of her six children to marry, and she wanted to check in on me. Telling her the truth of the activity I'd been engaged in would have embarrassed us both.

I left for work at Oakland's Highland Hospital at three o'clock. From four to midnight, I fielded incoming phone calls from patients' concerned relatives, handed charts to the ward nurses, and transcribed doctors' orders. I worked, absorbed in the many tasks assigned me. Then, I drove home in our VW to my waiting husband.

Life revolved around helping Antonio learn to navigate his new culture and readying our lives for a new baby. I had little time to reflect on the country I'd returned to or how I'd changed. But I had changed. I now had to think of my new husband, home, and job instead of just myself.

One afternoon, flipping through the TV channels, *The Price is Right* appeared. Contestants jumped up and down, excited to guess the correct value of a refrigerator or washing machine. I watched, flabbergasted. I'd lived in countries where people couldn't afford food, let alone refrigerators and other major appliances. How could guessing the prices of expensive material possessions be a game? Households in the affluent US seemed to take these luxuries for granted. In my mind, lusting after such material wealth was obscene. I shook my head in disgust. People in the States seemed to assume they could own the vast array of goods they saw on TV. My friends in Mexico and Peru valued personal connection above high-priced washers, refrigerators, and TV sets, and I did too.

My chest tightened watching the many antiwar demonstrations and race riots that had become all too familiar in the media. I'd not experienced such deep hurt about the Vietnam war and racial inequality before leaving the country in 1964. Now the ache worsened each time I heard of violence at yet another demonstration or saw the multiplying numbers of young men dying in Vietnam. I wished the war and racial inequality would end. But they seemed to go on forever. I couldn't march with the demonstrators as I wished. My family responsibilities prohibited that. In Peru, Antonio had remarked that the rationale the US espoused for involvement in other countries often appeared suspect. US interests were often based on what we could gain, not on a concern for the other nation's wellbeing. I agreed but felt helpless to change US policies. I turned my attention to the immediate matters of getting us situated before the baby came. That had to be my focus.

Three weeks after Antonio's arrival, he enrolled in morning English as a second language (ESL) classes at the Hayward adult school. He was eager to begin the challenge of understanding the language and customs of the US. Mom suggested he apply for an afternoon job fixing bicycles at the St. Vincent de Paul facility in San Leandro. She said working with others would allow him to earn money and practice English. She may not have approved of my marrying someone who couldn't support me, but I could count on her to have ideas on how to succeed in life here.

Most people we knew in Peru didn't own cars, so Antonio had never learned to drive. Like workers in Cusco, he hopped on buses or taxis to get around. Antonio said he could take the bus to his job at St. Vincent de Paul. The trip to the second-hand store required two transfers and took ninety minutes. What he earned there amounted to little more than his bus fare. After a month his English had improved, but we decided the commute wasn't worth the hassle. He needed to find a higher-paying job, one that used more of his skills. And I needed to teach him to drive.

Sundays he practiced steering and grinding the gears of our stick-shift VW in any empty parking lot we could find. I sat on the passenger side and slammed my foot on an imaginary brake whenever we headed toward a stationary object. My teaching style alternated between shouting instructions and screaming to watch out for the lampposts.

"*Pisa el pedal izquerdo*—press the left pedal!" I shrieked in the language Antonio understood best.

Too often I became agitated with my instructions. Through gritted teeth I told him to depress the clutch, then let it out slowly while simultaneously pressing on the gas pedal and shifting into second gear. I didn't remember my dad shouting as much when he taught me to drive our Ford on Montana's dirt roads when I was fifteen. But there had been few lampposts to hit in little Ismay.

"I'm doing what you said," Antonio murmured in Spanish as the car jerked and died. "And you don't have to shout. It makes me nervous."

Following a driving session, we arrived home incommunicado. I concluded that a spouse teaching his or her mate to drive is danger-ous—for the marriage. Yet Antonio earned his license without either of us perpetrating any violence. But he didn't get to drive the VW often. Because I needed it to get to work, he continued taking the bus.

By late September, my stomach protruded as if I'd swallowed a water-melon whole. I stuck out so far in front that my hospital coworkers wondered if I was having twins. I smiled and assured them and my parents that my due date was in March, even though I knew our infant would arrive in January. I had a principled reason to mislead both. The county required that a pregnant woman quit her job two months before she gave birth. That meant leaving the county job the first part of November. I couldn't. My husband didn't earn enough for us to live on. And my parents would have been hurt to know that we'd had sex before marriage. I didn't want to feel guilty about having a baby seven months after marrying or about continuing work to support our family. So I fibbed.

Then too, simple things demanded our attention. We needed to use some of my limited income to buy clothes for Antonio. He had brought too many woolen garments with him, appropriate for Cusco's cold climate but not for California's warm weather. One Saturday in September we drove to the Sears store near our apartment to find him a pair of lightweight slacks.

"Where are you from?" the smiling salesman asked Antonio in Spanish after he heard us conferring in that language.

Antonio explained his origins and the conversation turned to his current job. The salesman, a Cuban, listened with interest. He had something to suggest.

"The manager of the nearby World's Faire Food Court is Peruvian," he said. "Why don't you apply there for a regular full-time job? I've heard they need busboys."

I loved the way immigrants looked out for one another. We thanked the man and bought pants we could afford. Because of the Cuban salesman, Antonio had a better work option. And he was excited to do more than repair bicycles.

The next day Antonio filled out an application at the buffet-style eatery. Soon after, the manager hired him as a busboy on the evening shift. To our surprise, the required union membership came with medical coverage.

Through his ESL classes and everyday conversations, Antonio soon learned enough English to resume his college education. He registered at nearby Chabot Community College. Mornings, he attended classes, then worked the two-to-ten shift at the restaurant. He was fully into the busy US way of life.

ॐ

I'd been fortunate to pass the physical exam when almost four months pregnant. Then my employer requested my obstetrician's written document stating our baby's birthdate. I faced a difficult decision. I couldn't tell the truth and be forced to leave my job early. My paycheck had to sustain us until Antonio's job could cover our expenses. I felt healthy enough to work up to my due date. I coped as I needed to—by forging ahead and trusting things to work out. So, when my obstetrician wrote on the required form that the baby would arrive around 1-9-67, I changed the birth month from "1" to "3." My forgery was successful, and I continued working until Christmas.

I also feared my parents' displeasure if they calculated fewer than nine months between my wedding and the baby's birth. If I could gain more months of my parents' approval before the baby came, I was sure our infant would win them over like his or her father had. I was counting on it.

In the meantime, Antonio was doing the best he could for us. By November 1966, the World's Faire restaurant had promoted him to be head of the busboys and in charge of dishwashing operations. His salary increased. I breathed easier. Using his intelligence and love of devising systems, my husband streamlined the dishwashing procedures at the restaurant. Maybe what he earned would be enough to sustain the three of us in the new year.

I looked forward to our child's birth, though some days I had misgivings. I looked at my protruding stomach and thought, *Too late to change your mind now, Evelyn. You got yourself into this, now deal with it.* How would we manage the expenses and responsibilities of caring for a newborn? We couldn't even afford a bed for the baby.

Then a small miracle occurred. The clerk at Highland Hospital, who worked the daytime shift before mine, had two school-aged children and a garage full of baby furniture. She looked at my swollen belly and said she wouldn't be having more children. Would I like her stored baby furniture? I accepted a crib, bassinet, bouncer, highchair, and walker. Her generosity saved me valuable money on baby necessities. Antonio liked the idea of not having to spend his hard-earned money on furniture that had only short-term use. We thanked the clerk most gratefully.

The time came to move from our current adults-only apartment into one that accepted children. I packed our hand-me-downs and wedding gifts in boxes that I couldn't lift with my abdomen full of our baby. Maybe I should have objected in August when Mom had recommended the adults-only place. But I wasn't used to opposing her. Antonio and I would make the difficult move together, only six months after I'd moved us in.

So, before Christmas 1966, we moved out of our adult apartment into a one-bedroom place where our child would be welcome. This less expensive dwelling stood on the west side of Hayward, still an equal distance between my work and my parents' home. I explained the move to Mom and Dad using the rationale that the more affordable place would allow us to live on Antonio's income alone.

The Christmas celebration at my folks' house introduced Antonio to the raucousness of my large family. We unwrapped scores of presents, sang carols, laughed endlessly, and ate turkey with all the trimmings. Everyone bought or made something for all eight family members plus my spouse and my sisters' significant others. After the unwrapping, scores of wanted and unwanted items filled my parents' family room. Antonio didn't embrace his new country's materialistic holiday scene. He bought a few presents at the last moment, so I compensated and bought his share of gifts to give to my family. I'd always enjoyed this holiday and wished he could too. His country celebrated the holidays in a different way.

His family attended midnight mass on Christmas Eve at the Cusco Cathedral and had a meal at a relative's house afterward. In his country, they celebrated the Feast of the Magi during six days in January more than December 25. Gifts were given to children, but not in the abundance produced by my family. Though not a devout Catholic, Antonio could never accept the commercial way we celebrated Christ's birth.

Our lives changed at six o'clock on the morning of January 12, 1967.

"Antonio, wake up," I said. "I feel some kind of cramp. I think it's contractions."

"You think I should take you to the hospital?" Antonio asked, yawning and looking tired. He had worked until late at the restaurant the night before. "It's too early in the morning."

"I'm not sure," I said. "I'll finish packing my bag. If the pains keep coming, you need to drive me to Kaiser Hospital."

I waited a bit, then called the hospital. The attending physician said to come within the next three hours—the baby must be on its way. The contractions seemed to come far apart and were only uncomfortable, not painful. Not knowing what to expect, I continued my duties.

After a light breakfast, I checked to see if I had everything ready. The bassinet with yellow sheets stood in the corner of our bedroom, ready for the new little occupant. A small, pink tub I'd found for a bargain price sat in the bathroom. I prepared breakfasts and lunches for Antonio to eat while I recuperated in the hospital for the customary three days. I knew he wouldn't go hungry. After all, he worked in a restaurant. But it comforted me to think I had everything under control.

At eight o'clock I crammed into our Volkswagen, my belly almost touching the dashboard. We sped the two miles to the hospital with Antonio behind the wheel. *Good thing I taught him how to drive.* Antonio parked the car, and we entered the reception area of the hospital. After a brief discussion with my obstetrician, the father-to-be turned to me.

"The baby won't come until ten," he announced. "I'll be back then." And he left.

My mouth dropped open in disbelief. My husband had deserted me. I completed the required paperwork holding back tears. A nurse put me and my travel case in a wheelchair and pushed me toward the delivery room. I didn't know which was worse—the increasing pain of contractions or my heartbreak over Antonio leaving. I knew one thing—Antonio should have stayed with me.

I remembered comforting a sixteen-year-old girl in labor at the Abancay hospital when I was a Peace Corps volunteer. Marie and I had taken turns holding her hand for the eight hours she moaned in pain before giving birth. The father of her child was nowhere about. Now my child's father had also disappeared.

Once again, I'd have to take on more responsibility than I thought fair. And this was a special event. But what could I do?

My heart raced in anticipation of bringing new life into the world. But I never counted on waiting for the delivery by myself. Antonio hadn't even seemed excited. My throat tightened. I'd married a guy who wouldn't stay by his wife's side during the birth of their first child. This wasn't the way it happened in the movies, and I wanted that. Maybe this marriage had been a mistake.

My situation reminded me of my mother's experience when my youngest sister, Teri Ann, was born in Miles City, Montana, an hour from where we lived. Dad didn't go to Holy Rosary Hospital to collect Mom and baby number five, so a kind neighbor brought them home. I was nine and believed Dad was angry with Mom. As a child, I didn't always know what my parents' actions meant. In later years, I realized that having another child must have depressed Dad. The baby was yet another mouth he'd have to feed. On his meager salary.

But why had Antonio left me on my own in the hospital? Maybe his native culture didn't dictate a need for male involvement in the birth process. He'd remarked more than once that the indigenous women in his country squatted, had their babies, and returned to work in the fields soon after. Or, perhaps he was like other men I'd observed. They saw themselves left out of the entire birth process. More likely, he needed to sleep after a strenuous night at work. His actions reminded me of my dad. The two were similar. I bit my tongue.

Bringing children into the world was not their idea. They took no effective precautions to prevent conception. Their kids just kind of happened. Once the child was on the way, they accepted their fate. Also, neither Dad nor Antonio wore wedding rings or showed enthusiasm for having children. Dad cared for his offspring by supporting them and planning for their educations. He even demonstrated occasional affection for them. I expected Antonio would too.

Men of Dad's era depended on their wives to raise the youngsters without them. Their idea of shaping little ones' behavior consisted of giving admonitions, threats, and lectures. I wanted Antonio to collaborate with me, but his initial actions echoed those of my father. Both were proud, stubborn, and uncommunicative.

The baby came regardless of Antonio or my actions. A boy. Though my husband seemed pleased, we started parenthood with a disagreement. We couldn't reach a decision on what to name our new bundle. I was eager to show compatibility between the Latino and Anglo cultures. I thought the name Adrian sounded good in both English and Spanish. After selecting the name, I saw a woman named Adrian on TV and changed my mind.

Antonio balked at every name I liked and didn't express a desire that his son's name be understandable in both Spanish and English. I wasn't sure what he wanted in a name, and all we did was disagree. So

our infant came home with "Baby Boy LaTorre" on his birth certificate. Soon after, I suggested we name our son after Antonio. At long
last, we agreed. We would call him Tony.

Parenthood and Problems

Our love child had come into the world at 9:42 a.m. on January 12, two days after my mother's forty-seventh birthday. I expected Mom to welcome her first grandchild with enthusiasm. She'd been a responsible mother to her own six children and seemed charmed by babies. I wanted to let my family know the wonderful news. I phoned Mom from the hospital with the announcement. She was silent. I could hear her doing the math. I'd married in 1966 and Tony was born in 1967 so I hoped subtracting the two different years might make a quick computation difficult. But my son arrived less than nine months after my wedding, a major sin in the eyes of my very Catholic mother.

"Was he premature?" Mom asked, when she found her voice. My call, two months before she'd anticipated, had caught her off-guard.

"No, Mom," I answered, "he arrived in perfect health."

A rush of relief surged through me. I could stop lying about my child's birthdate. But that didn't mean all would proceed well.

"You'll regret this the rest of your life," Mom said sounding disappointed.

My heart fell. Her religious beliefs denied her the joy of celebrating her first grandchild's birth. Out of respect for my mother, I didn't answer back. But Mom was dead wrong. If I hadn't been pregnant with Tony, Antonio wouldn't be in my life. He would have remained in Peru, and I'd never have seen him again. Now he was with me, and we had a son. My life, though full of responsibilities, was also full of love.

I was in love with little Tony from the first time I saw him. I gazed into the face of my beautiful dark-haired, dark-eyed baby boy as he gulped milk from my breast. I looked forward to him awakening me at night with his tiny cry signaling that he was hungry for another meal. My affection for my son overflowed like my lactating breasts.

His small eyes had a slight epithelial fold that reflected Antonio's Incan ancestors, who may have come from Asia. His long head resembled that of his father, and he had a cute button nose. I'd expected my child would have more of my features, but I saw little of me in him. Antonio said his fingers and legs looked like mine—plump.

Antonio proved to be an affectionate father, when not tired from working his evening shift at the restaurant. He gazed with love at his firstborn, uncertain that he had produced this squirming little human. I put a Peruvian hat on Tony and gave him a toy fluffy white alpaca I'd brought back from Peru. Antonio snapped photos. I sent the picture to his family in Peru to announce the birth of their first grandchild.

Our boy stood on two sturdy legs at two months and loved bouncing up and down on his father's knees. Antonio helped change Tony's diapers and fed him with a bottle after I no longer had breast milk. My supply ran dry when I began taking birth control pills for the first time. Antonio and I hadn't agreed how many children we'd have, so, even though the Catholic church prohibited it, I took "the pill" to prevent another birth too

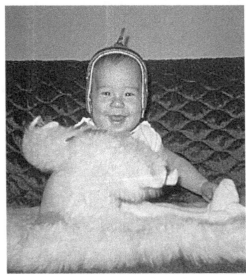

Tony in Inca hat with toy llama

soon. No one had warned me that my breast milk would dry up after taking the contraceptive. Maybe God was punishing me.

I also didn't know that my husband's inner Scrooge would return so soon. Money had been a bone of contention the previous September, just three months into our marriage. A door-to-door salesman had come by our first apartment and convinced me to buy several magazine subscriptions. He stated that the cost would be equal to the price of the pack of cigarettes Antonio smoked every few days. I committed to the magazines and suggested Antonio give up smoking to pay for them.

"Magazines in English," Antonio said glaring at me, "aren't something I want."

"Neither should cigarettes be," I retorted, thinking my need for reading material would indirectly benefit my husband's health.

Antonio's voice rose the more I asserted my right to spend money on items I desired. In Peru, he had never had to support himself, let alone a family. He sounded as if he believed he alone would rule the spending in our family. I had made decisions about the money I earned from the age of eleven. My opinions would count in my marriage.

I couldn't bear to hear more of his insistence that I'd been wrong to purchase the magazine subscriptions. I left the apartment, slamming the door on my way out. Then, I waddled over to a nearby vacant parking lot in my pregnant state, sat down on the curb, and sobbed alone until I was numb. For the first time I realized I might not always get my way. In marriage, I'd have to compromise.

The end of our argument wasn't satisfying. I received too many magazines to read, and Antonio didn't stop smoking. Our disagreements over money continued.

A few weeks after Tony's birth, I left to shop for household items that our new apartment needed. I returned with picture wire, a butcher knife, and a hammer and nails. Antonio hit the ceiling. I'd reignited a sore spot for him.

"You can't go spending money we don't have," he said, getting red in the face. "I make only enough for food and rent, not unneeded items like picture wire, knives, and hammers."

"I need to hang pictures on the walls to make our apartment look like a home," I said, crestfallen. "And if you want me to cut you a piece of ham, I need a good knife." My husband ranted on about how we'd have to learn to live on his income. His reaction made me think maybe he'd inherited the stinginess of his paternal grandparents in Lima. Perhaps his concern stemmed from being practical. But life on a shoestring budget didn't suit me. I didn't think any of my college-educated friends had to manage on such little income.

One of my magazines, *The Ladies Home Journal*, had a column that hit home. Each month when it arrived, I turned to the feature called "Can This Marriage Be Saved?" looking for advice. How could I stay in a marriage if I couldn't do or spend what I wanted? I sought solutions that would explain our differences. There were stories of unfaithful husbands, unruly children, and intrusive in-laws that created conflicts in marriages. The column didn't explain tensions between couples from differing cultures.

When Tony was two months old, I decided I'd solve our money problems by earning some income in a part-time job. My needs wouldn't be ignored. I wouldn't fade into the background just because I stayed home to raise our son. I wanted a voice in our expenditures.

Mom worked days for the Newark Police Department and said she could babysit Tony evenings. As I'd hoped, my mother didn't hold the too-soon birth of our son against him or me. Her religion didn't prohibit showing affection for her first grandchild. She seemed to enjoy Tony's development, and I valued how she helped me when needed.

Mom babysitting meant I could reactivate my name on county job lists. A nearby juvenile detention facility soon offered me the position as a substitute nighttime warden in the girls' unit. My job consisted of locking the delinquent girls in their cells at bedtime two or three nights a week. I read my magazines while the inmates slept.

Mom took care of Tony the nights I worked as keeper of the keys. Either Antonio or I picked up our son from Mom after our evening shifts, depending on which of us had the car. I liked the simple work but not the low pay. Employment as a part-time jailer didn't raise our income much above the poverty level. I had to earn more, which likely meant working full-time.

Back to Work

In spring 1967, Alameda County announced they would train new Aid to Families with Dependent Children (AFDC) social workers in June. The agency accepted my application. I hated to leave my five-month-old son, but besides more income, I yearned for more intellectual and social stimulation than I experienced at home or with the sleeping girls in the hall. I calmed my conflicted soul by finding a good babysitter.

I met Olga in the complex's shared laundry room soon after we'd moved into our family-friendly apartment. She had two older boys and a daughter, Anna, who was Tony's age. Her family had emigrated from Germany when the local Volkswagen dealership offered her husband a mechanic's job. We exchanged dinner invitations. Over Olga's tasty apple strudel, I found that we had similar views about the importance of stimulating children's minds by reading and talking to them. A month prior to beginning classes with the county, I asked Olga if she would provide care for Tony when I worked. She agreed. My guilt at leaving my baby lifted a little. In June 1967, I became a full-time-working mother.

Antonio needed our VW to drive to his work at the restaurant, so for three weeks I rode the bus to training classes in Oakland. My trip was an hour each way. I waved good-bye to Olga, Anna, and Tony. My babysitter waved back. I looked out the window of the bus as it pulled away from my A Street stop. A stream of tears trickled down the blush on my cheeks—the first makeup I'd applied in months. My heart broke to leave my son so soon. Despite my sadness, I smiled. I felt good about this new opportunity. And I wore a new dress—one not splattered with baby burp.

Most Anglo families in the 1960s, whom I knew or who were portrayed on TV, got along on one income. The mother stayed home to care for the children. But Antonio couldn't provide the income we needed working his busboy job. And I had the drive and the education to earn the middle-class income I wanted. With my college education, I could earn an adequate salary. So, unlike most US mothers of that decade, financial necessity drove me out of my home and to work. I benefitted and suffered.

Classes on the rules and regulations of the county's welfare system reactivated my brain. After training, the Hayward welfare office hired me as a full-time AFDC worker. I skipped to the bank with my first paycheck. Now I could buy what I needed and wanted. Antonio had never been the stereotypical Latino whose pride mandated that he be the family breadwinner. He had expressed greater pride in my education and employment capabilities than in his own. He applauded, not envied or resented, others' good fortunes. Our arguments went down as our income went up.

With more income, we could afford a larger apartment. Tony needed his own bedroom, so I asked the couple who managed our complex if there was a vacant two-bedroom apartment. The managers invited us to move to the only two-bedroom unit available—above their first-floor apartment. They usually kept that apartment empty so they wouldn't be bothered by noise above them. Our move proved embarrassing.

I didn't know the managers well and only occasionally encountered them. One morning, the landlady caught me as I left our second-story apartment headed for my office. She said she needed to speak with me.

"I'm happy you two enjoy one another so much," she said, a shy grin on her face. "But could you do something about that rhythmic bed squeaking every night?"

A warm flush crept across my cheeks. I assured the woman that we'd try to quiet our bed's squeaks, though I didn't know how. Then we discovered a way to tighten the screws of the bedframe, and the manager stopped complaining.

My social worker duties consisted of checking on a caseload of eighty families of women who couldn't support themselves. Most had absent husbands. I reviewed their histories, their needs, and their actual and potential income sources. More than once I recognized that their fate could be mine if I didn't take financial responsibility for my family.

Three family units stood out from my year as an AFDC worker: an overwhelmed mother, a mentally challenged young lady, and a helpful older citizen.

A mountain of wrinkled clothes greeted me whenever I visited the home of the divorced mother with four preteen and teenage sons. The family didn't lack clothing, just someone to take care of it. One day, the stressed mother complained about her ex-husband's lack of financial support. I said I'd look into her concern and called the woman's former husband.

"For the last four years I've given that woman every one of my IRS refund checks," he said, perplexed. "And they were big ones."

"That's very interesting," I said, pondering the discrepancy.

Fathers, if we could find them, had to provide support for their children. The state required welfare recipients to report all the money they received. Their income streams offset the amount the county paid them. This father's ex-wife had never reported the IRS money, a legal requirement. I had no recourse but to turn her case over to the fraud unit. They prosecuted her for having undisclosed income. I recognized that she'd needed the added money and felt sad about her situation. But she had also lied and used monies provided by honest taxpayers. She and her kids could have taken better care of their garments.

An adult woman with Down syndrome needed a refrigerator. A colleague showed me how to find the extra funds to help her and still stay within welfare regulations. The young woman hugged me with delight when her new refrigerator arrived. She was ecstatic that I had also found the money to purchase the washer and dryer she needed. I left her with the kinds of appliances I didn't own. I was pleased I could help someone less able to help herself.

"I'd like to donate my old set of pots and pans," an older woman client on my caseload said. "I bought new ones. Can you find someone who could use these? They're still functional."

"I know of such a household," I said with a smile.

I didn't tell her that the household was mine. She could afford new cooking implements when I had only discards. That would have to do for now.

I had empathy for these clients whose homes were better equipped than mine. Most of our furnishings were secondhand goods from others. I didn't mind the hand-me-downs. I'd lived in poorer worlds in Montana, Mexico, and Peru. Most of the people in those areas lived contented lives without the new acquisitions that my welfare clients possessed.

Our household was happy too. Tony was developing. He walked on his own at thirteen months. He danced, steady on his feet, to music or even the tick-tock of a clock. He sang "Happy Birthday" and blew out any candles he came across after celebrating his first birthday, hoping for another party. The Beatles songs we

Tony reading a book
on our bed

played on our phonograph inspired him to sing along. Our son could also be quiet and reflective. He appeared to be deep in thought when placed in the middle of our bed with a book. Antonio too savored sitting and reading his books. The time had arrived to consider continuing our educations at the university level.

Off to the University

By the spring of 1968, Antonio spoke reasonable English and had completed the required basic courses at Chabot Community College in Hayward that made him eligible to enroll at a four-year university. He had earned good grades by applying himself to his studies while holding down a demanding full-time busboy job and helping care for our son. We enjoyed spending as much time together as our obligations allowed.

I'd recognized Antonio's intelligence in the discourses we had when we first met. He'd learned how to work, study, and drive in my country in less than two years. If I hadn't been working so hard myself, I might have complimented him on his rapid mastery of a foreign language and adaptation to a new culture. He'd also had an influence on me.

My sisters noted that the frenetic pace I'd kept before my marriage now had slowed. In my undergrad days, I'd been regional vice president of an organization for Catholic college students and driven to their meetings throughout the Bay Area a couple evenings a month. On weekends, my little green VW had transported me to Fresno's Central Valley, 168 miles south, to work for migrant labor causes. Between work, classes, and my activities, I was constantly on the move.

My grades had suffered from tensions at home and my many pursuits. I almost lost the scholarship that allowed me to attend a private Catholic college. Now, having a husband who didn't leap at every opportunity like I did had a calming influence on me. Or maybe it was because I was a new mother. Nevertheless, in September 1968, we both jumped at the chance to complete academic degrees at the university level.

Antonio had wanted to earn a bachelor's degree ever since his college schooling was interrupted in Cusco when he moved to the US to be with me. My last months in the Peace Corps, he'd watched me complete scores of applications to colleges where I could earn a master's degree in social work. Many of my Holy Names sociology-major colleagues had already graduated with that higher degree. My father had moved his family from Montana to California in 1959 so his children could attend college. Most of us had. My husband, like me, would shoot for the highest level of education he could attain. We made our plan. Both of us applied for entrance to the best university in the area, the University of California at Berkeley.

I could earn a master's degree in social work in two years as a full-time student. He would finish his BA degree. I resubmitted the same application to UCB's School of Social Welfare that I'd sent them in 1966. This time I didn't cry in the dean's office and beg for admission, as I had done two years before, when pregnant with Tony. My hormones were more in check now.

Antonio submitted his application along with his translated transcripts from Peru. To accomplish what he wanted, he'd need to be a full-time student. He thought he could graduate in a couple of years if the university credited most of his three years of studies from the university in Cusco. With both of us studying full-time, however, we couldn't work. We'd need an income from somewhere.

The state of California had a scholarship that offered tuition plus a $300-a-month living allowance. To qualify, an applicant had to have worked for the county welfare department for at least a year. The thirteen months I'd been an AFDC worker for the Alameda County Welfare Department, qualified me, and I applied. Getting the award meant we'd have an income. With our numerous applications completed and submitted, we spent sleepless nights while we waited for a notice from UCB.

We thanked the heavens when letters arrived granting us both admission to the university and giving me the tuition and stipend award. However, there was a catch. I would have to work for a state welfare agency upon my graduation. I didn't have to think twice. Social work was my chosen profession. I signed the contract. Now to find affordable housing.

I'd be studying for a master's degree, so we qualified to live in married graduate student housing. UCB reserved five hundred one-, two-, and three-bedroom apartments for graduate students and their families, two miles from the Berkeley campus in Albany Village. The residences were grouped on seventy-seven acres in the flatlands near the 880 freeway in Albany. The original barracks had housed military and shipyard workers during WWII. These one-story flats rented for $69 a month. Antonio and I wouldn't build ships, but with our college degrees, we hoped to sail on to more satisfying jobs.

Students who lived in the former barracks said they often shared their apartments with rats and mice. I'd had my fill of the little rodents in my Peace Corps converted storeroom house in Peru. So I chose an apartment in the newer, two-story section built in 1962. The two-bedroom, 635-square-foot units rented for $100 a month. The higher rent was worth not having to deal with rat infestations.

In September 1968, Antonio said good-bye to his busboy manager's job at the World's Faire Restaurant. I bid farewell to my fellow social workers at the Alameda County Welfare Department in Hayward. Both of us were twenty-six and our son, Tony, a year old. We loaded up my dad's pickup with our belongings and moved twenty miles north to the student housing compound in Albany.

The four separate apartment buildings in our complex circled around a friendly patio and an outdoor clothesline. Our clothes seldom dried on the lines, however. Fog from the San Francisco Bay usually hung around until ten in the morning, receded for four hours, then rolled back in around two in the afternoon. I didn't mind. I brought the clothes inside to finish drying. I had time to dry clothes—and enjoy my toddler son and student husband.

The liberal political atmosphere of Berkeley suited us. I'd been able to view my country through different eyes when abroad with the Peace Corps. Absent the usual media filters in Peru, and with Antonio's more extensive knowledge of history, I'd come to new realizations about my country's government. I'd seen how ruthless US policies could be when they disagreed with other countries. In the Peruvian press, I'd read about violent police actions against domestic disturbances at home. These events shook me more upon my return to my homeland.

Race riots and demonstrations against racial injustice and the Vietnam War had occurred regularly in most major US cities since I'd returned from Peru. I agreed the US should get our troops out of Vietnam and enforce integration of schools in the South. But I didn't join the protests. Instead, I registered voters whenever I could steal the time from housework and studying.

Antonio loved that he could devote all his energies to his chosen fields of physics and math. At the university in Cusco, he had majored in economics, a course of study picked for him by his stepfather. He loved the language of physics more than his required ESL courses. Each semester that he continued to study English, his communication skills improved. We could now argue in my native tongue instead of his.

In our first years of marriage, I had thought it fairer to Antonio for our occasional arguments to be in Spanish. I had better verbal skills in Spanish than he had in English. I would complain in his native language about how he never proposed taking me out for a movie or a meal. In the same language, Antonio defended himself saying that he had neither time nor money to plan entertainment that included me.

But which language we argued in became an issue for me when Tony began talking.

At eighteen months, our son's first words were in Spanish. He said, "beera," an attempt at the Spanish word, "mira," or "look." I wanted my son to speak Spanish and be proud of his Latino heritage, but I didn't want him to learn the angry Spanish words Antonio and I spoke during disagreements. Tony might think Spanish was the language for arguing. So I shifted to communicating with Antonio in English. Because of the language change, Tony wouldn't become fluent in Spanish, something I regretted.

I loved using my mental abilities to explore my chosen field of social work. I learned about family dynamics, Carl Jung's theories of psychoanalysis, and counseling techniques. For my required fieldwork placement, I'd chosen to specialize in group work, which involved managing social, educational, and work groups. But after two sessions with a disorganized group leader, I'd not learned anything new. So I requested a change to casework, guiding individuals' welfare. The school's administration moved me to the Alameda County Welfare Department in Oakland. This proved fortuitous.

I was assigned to an experimental program where a cadre of first- and second-year students were to write a group master's thesis instead of individual ones. The second-year students, motivated to graduate on time, chose the topic, assigned the research, and assembled the final text. They made certain we first-year students submitted our papers on time, so the required treatise could be completed before their graduation date. As a result, I entered my second year of studies without the pressure of having to write my own master's thesis. However, I still needed to plow through the books on my reading lists.

In the Spanish version of *The Reader's Digest,* Antonio had read about a speed-reading program that President John F. Kennedy had had his assistants take. The thirty-fifth president needed several people to quickly read over reams of important information and summarize it for him. When Antonio learned of the Evelyn Wood Reading Dynamics course being given in Berkeley, he said I should take it. He believed it would allow me to quickly finish the required reading for my classes. Antonio said he read English too slowly for the course to benefit him. Financing the course was a stretch, but Antonio agreed to watch Tony the evenings I attended the classes. The payoff would be more time spent with my son and husband than with my books.

One assignment was to read books in an unfamiliar subject. I chose to read those in Antonio's field of physics. I learned that physics was filled with formulas and mathematical equations, a very foreign language to me. I could understand its attraction to Antonio. He didn't have to wrestle with the inconsistencies of English words. Formulas were consistent and interpreted the same way. As for me, my reading speed increased, but my understanding of my husband's field of study did not improve. It was good that he enjoyed it. Physics was a language of its own. I'd stick to sociology and psychology.

Albany Village's apartments for married graduate students offered more than housing at a bargain price. Living and studying at UCB provided us the quality of life that we couldn't have afforded elsewhere. I had more time to devote to the intellectual development that fulfilled me. Our new home had another important amenity, quality day care on a sliding income scale.

The first day I dropped our twenty-month-old son off at the Albany Village Child Care Center, he didn't cry. But, out of his sight, I did. My heart broke to see him bow his head and pout as I left for my classes.

I hoped his early language development in English would serve him well when interacting with the other children. At twenty months he spoke in phrases saying, "I said no," and "I mean it!" He picked up many expressions from television such as, "How could that be?" "You have housatosis" (from a room freshener commercial), and "Appreciate it!" He said his friend Richard was "simply delightful."

When I came to pick him up from the childcare center, I saw that his new friends all wore the red superman capes I'd made for the school. I no longer worried about his adjustment to being away from me.

"Now, you sit here," Tony said, pointing a miniature superman to a small chair. "No, you go here," he ordered another.

When he spied me, he slid the cape's elastic, cut from Antonio's worn-out underwear, over his head. He placed the red rectangle in the costume box and hugged two of his little friends. Then he waved good-bye, smiling. Both of us had adjusted.

Antonio and I saved on childcare costs if we coordinated our class schedules. So we developed a child-exchange routine. I brought our toddler to campus and handed him over to Antonio in front of Haviland Hall, where I had my classes. Antonio took Tony home and fed him. Then, he brought him back to me when my classes ended. This arrangement allowed our son more time with us than at the childcare center. The only time our routine didn't work occurred if Tony were ill.

Tony's illnesses, like colds, were minor—until November 1968, two months before he turned two. I'd just begun my fieldwork placement at the Alameda County Welfare Department and was examining clients' records at the county office. Tony had a cold and I didn't want to spread it at the daycare center. I'd asked the neighbor who lived below our apartment to care for my twenty-two-month-old the four hours I had to be away. Two hours after I left him, I received an urgent call.

"Come quick," my neighbor said, sounding desperate. "Tony went into convulsions and turned blue."

"I'll be right there," I said, chills of fear running down my spine.

I jumped into our VW, my knees shaking. I recalled watching two of my younger siblings lose consciousness with high fevers when I was young. The incidents had given me nightmares afterward, even though Mom had taken care of the situations, and my sisters had regained consciousness. I clenched my jaw now. Convulsions could be so dangerous. My neighbor was a nurse, a minor comfort for me. But I'd heard panic in her voice. Maybe this episode was more than she could handle. My adrenaline spiked. I imagined my son dying.

Half an hour later I knelt by Tony's side. My little son was limp and perspiring, but alive. The neighbor had been unable to reach me when Tony's convulsions began. So she'd bathed him with rubbing alcohol and cold compresses until he regained consciousness. His convulsions had stopped, and his fever declined. Still, his skin was clammy, though no longer blue. My gratitude went out to my neighbor.

Our pediatrician said that Tony had minor pneumonia but would recover just fine with no brain damage. I swallowed hard and felt guilty that I hadn't been there when my son had become ill. There had been no way to reach Antonio at his classes, and I always took care of our son's medical needs anyway. I pledged to be easier to find whether at school or in the sprawling welfare building.

Another welfare building also caused me anxiety. I had to go there to continue our eligibility for food stamps. I felt awkward entering the Alameda County welfare satellite office as the petitioner instead of the eligibility monitor for welfare clients. Instead of my checking clients' incomes, a compliance worker now verified mine. Showing proof of our low income so we could receive food stamps embarrassed me. But I could endure the uncomfortable feelings of humiliation if it helped us afford food.

I shopped for staples at a local grocery store on Gilman Street in

Albany, a few blocks from our apartment. One day at the beginning of December, I handed the cashier enough food stamps from my envelope to cover my purchases and then departed with my groceries. Days later, when I needed to buy more food, I couldn't find my envelope with nearly a month's worth of stamps. I mentally retraced my steps and realized I must have left it on the counter at the store on my previous visit. My stomach churned. Those stamps were a lifeline between hunger and enough to eat. I knew what I must do. I returned to the store and asked for the manager.

"I left a business-sized white envelope full of food stamps at your store a few days ago," I said to the black-haired man towering over me. "Without the stamps," I continued, my voice rising higher, "I can't buy food for Christmas, or anything more this month."

"I'll check lost and found," he said, walking away.

I waited, hoping against hope that he'd come back with my familiar envelope. But he returned a few minutes later with his hand empty. My heart sank.

"I'm sorry," he said. "I couldn't find what you describe. How much were they worth?"

"Almost an entire month's worth of food," I said, fighting to maintain my composure. "I set them down on the counter when I paid and gathered up my grocery bags. Then I forgot to pick them up before I left."

"Tell you what," the manager said, "I'll give you a store voucher for what you lost."

I couldn't believe what the kind man said. Perhaps he'd once been hungry and knew how crucial my food stamps were. I could have danced in the aisle with relief as he wrote out the voucher.

"Thank you so much," I said.

My words seemed paltry compared to the manager's generosity. Because of him, my family would be fed during the holidays. And I could still afford to buy a few presents.

The grocer's kindness paralleled what small-town businesses did where I grew up in Montana and where I'd lived in Peru. Merchants and neighbors looked out for those in their communities. The grocer in Ismay had given my parents blemished fruit and me a wristwatch. The friendly, personalized treatment, on a grander scale, was what I liked about living in the Berkeley–Albany area.

Our housing unit had a co-op group that traded babysitting hours and enabled Antonio and me to go to an occasional movie or out to an inexpensive restaurant—if I planned and paid for the excursions. At the nearby Berkeley Co-op grocery store, I learned to read labels and cook low-cost, nutritious food. Antonio also valued our environs and focus on learning.

Tony enjoyed being read to, and Antonio thought his two-year-old son intelligent enough to learn to read on his own. He encouraged me to teach Tony to read. Wanting to please my husband and my ego, I read Glenn Doman's book, *How to Teach Your Baby to Read*. I would prove that Tony was advanced for his age. I spent hours creating two-foot-long flashcards with six-inch high red letters that spelled out "Mommy," "Daddy," and the names of objects in Tony's world. Doman's book said the flashcard game should be fun and free from pressure. The smile on my little one's face during our sessions told me he enjoyed the game. But I didn't like how much work it took to make the blasted cards.

Antonio viewed us with approval when he waltzed out the door for a "men's night out" with his best friend and fellow student, Romualdo, a Chilean PhD candidate in physics. The two men enjoyed going out for a beer or to play table tennis together after a week of classes. After they left, I spent twenty minutes sitting on the floor across from Tony coaxing him in clear, even tones, to "read" what I pronounced on the cards. After I put him down for the night, I made more flash cards.

With each card I completed, I gritted my teeth. An imbalance existed in our family obligations. I, too, wanted to be free from responsibility and be out having fun like Antonio and Romualdo. Instead, I sat home performing a task Antonio had requested. Though I agreed with teaching our son to read, the work it required had fallen to me. Not fair.

Antonio returned four hours after he'd left with tales of how Romualdo drove them over the hills of San Francisco trying to imitate Steve McQueen's driving scene in the movie *Bullitt*. With his male friend, Antonio had apparently rediscovered the freedom he'd had prior to our marriage. He and Romualdo had escapades while I labored away at home. So much for not having the time or funds for our entertainment. I pursed my lips, boiling inside. Why didn't Antonio take me out for a pleasurable time once in a while? To keep the peace, I remained silent. My mother had suffered in silence when my father ignored her wishes. I did that too—until I couldn't.

One Friday night, Antonio bounced in the door close to midnight. Tony lay in bed asleep and I lay in wait. My husband had enjoyed another evening out having fun while I'd been at home cooking, cleaning, caring for our son, and making the Doman reading cards.

"Why do you get to leave the house and have fun?" I said as Antonio entered.

I reached down and grabbed one of my black flats. I took aim and hurled it.

It flew through the air straight toward his head. Glaring, I continued.

"You leave me at home alone, working!"

"What are you so angry about?" Antonio said. He ducked as the shoe grazed his head. "I just wanted to relax a bit after studying all week."

"I take care of everything around here and study too," I shouted, removing the first shoe's mate from my foot.

I didn't fling the second shoe. Antonio stood there, a bewildered look on his face. I headed to our bedroom and slammed the door behind me. It took us two days to make up and become our usual affectionate selves.

My idyllic life had begun to match some of the marriages I'd observed in Peru. During our courtship there, I'd once remarked to Antonio that after Peruvian men married, they often continued their bachelor ways, even after their children were born. I didn't want a marriage that ignored my needs. Antonio should take me out once in a while for all my efforts, not enjoy freedoms I didn't have. Despite my temper tantrum, Antonio took no action until, a month later, Romualdo's working wife complained.

She also resented her husband's wife-free Friday nights and some-how got our men to curtail the jaunts. In their place, the guys arranged for our families to go camping together and limit their carousing around on their own. I still studied hard during the week, then enjoyed a few weekends lounging and cooking at Standish-Hickey State Park, 187 miles north of Berkeley. We all watched the kids, and the men fished and built the campfires. Nature and the slower pace of life rejuvenated my spirits. Not so, my reading classes for Tony.

After several months of the Doman method for early reading, the novelty of the colorful cards wore off. When I threw them into the trash, Antonio chose not to notice. The university culture promoted raising educationally advanced children, and Antonio had wanted his child to be a genius. But I didn't want to spend what little free time I had forcing early literacy on my cherub. Tony didn't need to be an infant reader or a little genius for us to love him.

At age three, Tony could rattle off the names of every dinosaur from allosaurus to triceratops. Then he made up names for novel kinds of dinosaurs and drew pictures of them. When gas stations gave away toy dinosaurs with each fill-up, Tony insisted we collect all fifteen. He entertained himself by putting them in order by size. When we made cupcakes to celebrate his fourth birthday, he delighted in decorating each one with an animal cracker and a lifesaver. My son's creativity enchanted me.

Tony had a vivid imagination, so I gave him hats I bought at flea markets that he could pretend with. I braided him an assortment of tails of the animals he imitated, from my discarded pantyhose. One minute he was a fireman, the next a pointer dog. With a tail tucked into the back of his pants, Tony could change into a monkey, a water buffalo, a lion, a mouse, or a cat. His preferred books were *Golden Nature Guides* with pictures and explanations of fish, birds, and insects. Maybe he would grow up to be a zookeeper, a veterinarian, or a farmer.

One spring day we visited my parents forty miles south of us in Fremont. Tony pushed his favorite brown tail into the back of his pants and got down on all fours. He crawled around meowing like a cat, then he meandered over to the cat's dish—and ate its food. Mom jumped up with surprise. She said I should stop him, but I didn't. It was fine that my child loved animals and could imagine being one. I wouldn't squelch his imaginative mind.

We enjoyed our little Tony—except when he had temper tantrums from not getting his way. Then he'd kick and scream, hold his breath, and writhe on the floor. He'd protest at the top of his lungs when he awakened upon arriving home after a trip in the car. I feared neighbors would accuse us of child abuse. They didn't. So we weathered Tony's illnesses and tantrums during our first year at UC together—until summer. Then we had another dilemma, not caused by our child.

The stipend for my first year of graduate school paid me during the nine months school was in session. Neither Antonio nor I had thought ahead about how we would support ourselves from June to August, during summer vacation. In May, we were startled to realize that, if we didn't take some action, we'd soon be without an income. Time to search for employment.

A friend in Antonio's ESL class told him about a busboy job at a twenty-four-hour restaurant. Antonio had no desire to return to his former line of work, but I insisted. As the man of the family, I believed he should take the lead to support us. Antonio applied and was hired for the four-to-midnight shift. We'd have the money for rent.

I received two offers of summer employment through UCB. One required me to commute to a secondary school where I would work five days a week, with mentally handicapped teens. The professor in charge hired me on the spot after my interview. But before the position began, a research assistant job opened up at the same pay that allowed me to work from home. The professor in charge of the school program was angry when I backed out of his job to accept the research position. He didn't empathize with my desire to have more time with my son. I stood my ground to do what I wanted and not what he demanded.

My desired position put me at 558 Clayton Street in San Francisco, meeting with Dr. David Smith, the founder of the Haight-Ashbury Free Clinic. For two years, without judgment or fees, he had treated thousands of patients for hallucinations from bad trips, gastrointestinal disorders from eating rotten food, and septicemia from botched abortions. Benefit concerts, organized by Bill Graham, provided much of the funding to support the treatment center. In 1969, the clinic opened the first drug detox unit. Young people looking for drugs and love had little money, so they lived in San Francisco's parks, streets, and crowded apartments. The multitudes who came from all over the country thought San Francisco's summers were sunny and warm. Instead, they found chilly weather, and the health center treated their colds and pneumonia.

I came from a protective background and had taken only doctor prescribed drugs. Newspaper accounts told of those who'd had bad trips caused by tainted drugs, but I didn't know anyone who'd "tripped out." I hoped I wouldn't have to interact with any druggies. I relaxed when Dr. Smith directed me to search for studies of free clinics in the Cal library and not at his clinic.

I scoured the university's libraries and found a few articles, which I read at home next to my son. At the end of August, I wrote a report based on the little information I had found. Dr. Smith's health center was a precursor to free clinics throughout the US. Soon there would be twelve hundred free or low-cost clinics nationwide, modeled after San Francisco's. The social change brewing in the Bay Area confronted me again when we returned for classes in the fall of 1969. UCB was the center of mounting civic unrest.

Students throughout the States had been protesting the Vietnam War since 1964. I hadn't experienced the turmoil at Holy Names College or as a Peace Corps volunteer in far-off Peru in the early '60s. But antiwar sentiment and civil unrest escalated from a squall to a storm during the years we studied at Berkeley.

In April 1969, the underground newspaper, *The Berkeley Barb*, put out a call for volunteers to convert a downtown dirt lot off Telegraph Avenue into a "People's Park," a place to give antiwar speeches, open to everyone. When the university announced they would turn that parcel into athletic fields, students and locals decided it should be a park. Hundreds responded to the newspaper's call to plant the con-tested area with trees, sod, and flowers.

Then Governor Reagan saw UCB as a haven for communist sym-pathizers, protesters, and sex deviants. He convinced Berkeley's mayor to send in officers to destroy most of the plantings and construct a fence around the park. The demonstrations escalated. Some four thousand protesters marched in Berkeley's streets shouting that they wanted to keep the park. Between the free speech, anti-Vietnam War, and People's Park rallies, the areas on and around the UCB campus were in constant turmoil and became unsafe places. The worst hap-pened on May 15.

One of the hundreds of police, highway patrolmen, and National Guard members sent in by the governor shot and killed a student who'd been observing a march on the Southside of UCB, around Telegraph Avenue. Pellets from the police blinded a local carpenter. Nobody expected this. The scene made me sick to read about.

To make matters worse, the governor ordered tear gas dropped on the protesters from helicopters. The noxious vapors drifted into elementary school playgrounds and neighborhoods, sending hundreds of residents of all ages to local hospitals. Antonio and I could smell remnants of the gas when we went onto the Cal campus.

I sympathized with the reasons for the protests but chose not to march. As a mother with a small child, I didn't want to put him or myself in harm's way. Also, Antonio and I lived in Albany, the community next door to Berkeley, so were spared most of the violence but not the disruptions. At one point, the school administration canceled classes. Faculty members said they were unwilling to teach until peace was restored and troops were removed from campus. Instead, we met in our professors' homes to continue our courses. Eventually, there was a temporary truce, and we returned to our classrooms. But minor disruptions continued around the university into 1970.

The evening of Thursday, April 16, 1970, I had a function to attend on campus. I had organized a joint meeting of some forty students from the School of Education and the School of Social Welfare. I entered the UCB campus with caution, skirting around the barbed wire that ringed parts of the grounds. Authorities had placed it there to keep advocates of People's Park from coming on campus. I made my way to the UC School of Education in Tolman Hall on the southeast edge of campus. Thankfully, I heard no shouts of "We want the park!" that signaled a crowd.

Organizing the seminar in the middle of continual civil disobedience hadn't been easy. One of my key speakers had backed out saying the violence on campus made it too dangerous to participate. The invited students, who would work in schools, attended in spite of the danger. I had to be present on campus regardless of barbed-wire barricades and tear gas. Attendees would listen to a panel of practicing school professionals—a social worker, a counselor, a school psychologist, and two administrators—answering the question, "How do we work together, or should we even try?"

Once I saw the panel seated and attendees safely inside, I requested the doors be locked. As we concluded, the discussion turned to how professionals in the schools could teach peaceful ways of resolving differences before violence occurred. The interaction between professionals and students made my struggle to hold the meeting worthwhile. Pride filled me as I observed the thoughtful group I'd convened. I planned to join the ranks of school professionals like those on the panel.

The university had given almost no credit for Antonio's previous classes in Cusco, so he had at least another year before he would earn his BA. His studies meant I'd need to put my new master's degree in social welfare to the test. So, upon my graduation in May 1970, I began a search for good-paying and satisfying work with a California State Department of Welfare agency, in accordance with my scholarship contract. I was ready to fulfill my state obligation, but the state was not.

Inching toward Employment

I'd spent two years earning top grades in graduate school, all while trying to be a good wife and mother. The stipend from the state of California had supported us while I earned a master's degree, so I would now work for a county or state welfare department. I didn't want to have to return the $3,000 stipend money to the government. Days after graduation, I began searching for a social work position that would fulfill my obligation to the state. I hoped to find just the right place for me.

The head of the foster care division entered the conference room at the Alameda County welfare office in Hayward, smiling—a good sign. My interview for the social worker position in her department had gone well. Maybe I'd soon be checking on children removed from situations of abuse and neglect and putting them into approved foster homes. I needed the fulltime, well-paying job.

"I'd really like to hire you," the director said, her smile fading. "With your knowledge of Spanish, you'd be the perfect person for the opening. But you know, there's a hiring freeze. I can't place anyone in a job until Governor Reagan rescinds his no-hiring order."

"How soon will you be able to employ someone?" I asked, wanting a positive answer.

"They're trying to work things out in Sacramento, I hear," she said. "But no one knows when the state will allow new hires."

The supervisor at Fairmont Hospital, in the nearby town of San Leandro, chose me to fill an open medical social worker position. I'd worked in medical settings before—at Highland Hospital in Oakland and in the hospital in Abancay, Peru. My social work education had taught me how to design plans for discharged patients. I liked hospital work. The supervisor and I both sighed together when she reported that she couldn't hire me because of the employment freeze. I kept searching.

Antonio took the initiative and found a summer office position at the Social Security agency in San Francisco. He rode the bus and left the car for me to carry out my job search. Day after day I put on my powder blue knit tube "interview" dress, slipped into pantyhose, and squeezed my feet into my good shoes. I left Tony at the day care center and drove our green Volkswagen to appointments around the San Francisco Bay Area. The car carried me up and down Highway 101, from Marin County to San Jose. I interviewed with scores of government agencies that had open social work positions. But none were being filled during the ongoing hiring freeze.

I could only assume that the personnel departments of the welfare agencies scheduled meetings with potential candidates to have workers ready to start whenever Governor Reagan lifted the employment freeze. But I couldn't wait for that. Antonio's job would end in August when he'd return to his studies. I needed to provide my family an income by September.

During June and July, I interviewed for every state and county social work opening for miles around. Time after time I heard the same lament: "You can't be placed on our payroll until the hiring freeze is over." I became desperate. I called personnel at the state social services department to inform them of my dilemma and get a financial reprieve. They were not sympathetic.

"To meet the requirement of your stipend," they said, "you'll have to move to any place in California where you can be hired in a county or state job."

A move out of the Bay Area wasn't possible with Antonio still in school. He hadn't finished in two years like he'd wanted. I didn't understand the California department's reasoning. If no welfare departments in the state were allowed to fill their positions, how would I get a job anywhere in California? The governor had thwarted my efforts to work.

The hiring freeze continued into August with no signs of thawing. Our family's fate rested on me. At my most despondent, I received a ray of hope—a phone call from Dr. Wasserman, chair of the School of Social Work department at UCB.

"San Francisco Unified called me today," the department head said. "They need a Spanish-speaking school social worker for the coming year to fill in for a woman on leave. I thought you might be interested."

"I'm not sure I could consider it," I said, swallowing hard. "I'm obligated to work for a county or state agency, but no one is hiring."

"Well, you might want to check it out anyway," my considerate mentor said.

After a brief interview, the San Francisco Unified School District offered me a school social worker position in a Mission District elementary school. Ironically, I'd replace the woman who had backed out of my invitation to be on the panel of school personnel I'd organized at UCB the previous April. Now she had requested a leave of absence from her SFUSD position to have her second child.

I explained my county welfare obligation to the woman who would be my supervisor. She said I could work during summer school to earn extra money, if that would help. Social workers always thought of humane solutions. I felt proud to be one of them.

I had a day to consider whether to accept the district's offer. That evening Antonio and I sat at our kitchen table, paper and pencil in hand. At $12,000 a year, the salary would be more than enough to live on and enable Antonio to finish his undergraduate studies. If demanded, I could repay the $3,000 the county had spent on my graduate school education by working during the district's two-month summer session. No other offers came my way, so I signed a contract with the school district for the 1970–71 school year.

I'd received glowing reports during my student placement in the Oakland Schools in my last year at UCB. Nevertheless, I wasn't certain I was suited to work in schools. I felt less secure about performing social work duties in the schools than I did about working in the county jobs for which I'd interviewed. Perhaps I'd been too eager for a paycheck. But I couldn't have waited for a welfare agency job. I began my new job with misgivings.

Dealing with teachers felt like walking on eggshells compared to performing mental health work elsewhere. In agencies that valued counseling, I might have a greater positive impact on clients' mental health. In a welfare department, I could be more forthright in examining the basis for client problems. That system felt more welcoming to mental health professionals than school districts. But I needed a job—and having a young child, working ten months of the year was an attractive option. I had two requests.

I asked to be assigned to a single school instead of the usual three or four and to receive regular supervision from an experienced school social worker. To my delight, the head of the district's social work department arranged for both. I was assigned full-time to Hawthorne Elementary School, and Mrs. Hines, a licensed clinical social worker with many years of experience, became my mentor. She met with me for an hour each week. Years later, her supervision qualified me for a clinical social worker license. I'd hit the employment jackpot.

The school's principal valued personnel with counseling skills, so he used special federal money to pay for me to be in his school five days a week. I warmed to the staff and held weekly teacher support meetings. We exchanged ideas on how to improve student performance and handle challenging pupil behaviors. One of my challenges included a fifth-grade teacher whose put-downs of her students made them cower in their seats. Together, she and I set up a reward system for positive behaviors. Her students' creativity increased as her loud scolding diminished.

When the patriarch of a Spanish-speaking family was incarcerated, leaving his wife helpless, I stepped in. I steered the mother to where she could apply for financial assistance and taught her teenage son how to balance a checkbook. Success fed my confidence.

Several Saturdays, I gathered my three-year-old son, dressed in the superman cape I'd made for him, and drove to Hawthorne School. There I met with a group of the school's troubled boys. Five years before in the Peace Corps, I'd taught PE to groups of unruly boys whose language I didn't speak. Now I used my group work skills with the willful boys who attended Hawthorne Elementary School. A morning of organized sports activities, followed by food I brought, rewarded them for their improved school behavior.

Tony pouted at having to share me with these older boys. I already spent so many weekdays at work away from him. I promised that just the two of us would go for donuts after my morning's activities. Until then, he moped. But I'd made a commitment to these students and would fulfill my promise, even if I didn't get paid extra for my efforts. Playing games Saturdays improved the school behavior of these inner-city youth during the week. I could help improve the attitude of the school's adults too.

Hawthorne Elementary had an older, grouchy vice-principal in charge of discipline who had no use for social workers. Conferring with him hadn't resulted in a more positive tone or decreased his threats to students. I had an idea. On Valentine's Day, I secretly placed

Tony in his Superman cape
at Hawthorne School

a two-by-three-foot greeting card on his office chair signed, "From a secret admirer." I don't think he guessed who had given him the card, but he bellowed a bit less after that.

An agitated instructional assistant complained that her husband mistreated her and never responded to her needs. I took note of her problems, then told her to get a good night's sleep and return the next day ready to discuss options. The following day she thanked me. A good night's sleep had made her more confidant to speak to her husband in a rational way about her needs and concerns. Their relationship began to mend.

A teacher friend, recently married to a Latin American, said her husband hurt her physically and emotionally when he bent back her fingers during an argument. I wasn't sure how to help her. The professors at UCB hadn't discussed what to do about spousal abuse. I'd had my own experience with an aunt's mistreatment.

When we were in elementary school, my two younger sisters and I used to visit our favorite Aunt Sue for a couple weeks every summer. We lived with her so we could attend religion classes at the Catholic school in Sue's North Dakota town. Sue treated us girls special because she had three older boys. The last time we got to stay with her, I awakened in the middle of the night in terror. My uncle had come home drunk and I heard him threaten Sue with a broken beer bottle, then beat her. I'd been paralyzed with fear and couldn't move to help her. Big bruises appeared on her arms the next morning. I told another aunt what had happened, but no one took any action to stop the beatings. Years later, at Hawthorne School, I also didn't know how to handle spousal abuse.

I asked the teacher who'd come to me what she had done to make her husband so angry. Later in life, I knew that wasn't the best approach. Her husband had no right to abuse her. Both my aunt and the teacher should have removed themselves from their abusive households and called the authorities. I would never allow myself to be physically mistreated. I cringed in the face of these women's maltreatment and continued with the challenges I could handle.

My Heart's Desire

By the fall of 1970, I had a good-paying job and Tony was three-and-a-half-years-old. I didn't want him to be an only child or more than five years older than a sibling. I'd come from a family of six children. The first five had all arrived within nine years. My mother had had little rest between births. I couldn't imagine settling for only one offspring.

Antonio said he didn't want to add to an already overpopulated world. Besides, if we had a second child, he wanted it to be born in Peru. He hoped we'd live there someday. I hadn't agreed to live in Peru but said nothing. Antonio hadn't made any plans that I knew of that would return us there. Knowing my husband as I did, I felt he wouldn't reject his own child if we had another one. So I took a risk.

I informed Antonio that I would go off birth control pills. I predicted that he would take no contraception precautions, since he had never done so. I wanted our second baby to be a girl, so we'd have a child of each sex. An article in *Life* magazine explained how to conceive a girl. Antonio enjoyed the frenetic effort it recommended. As I expected, he didn't take any measures to prevent conception. Mere weeks after I took my last birth control pill, I could feel that I was pregnant.

Two months later, my doctor verified my suspicion. After informing Antonio, I told my parents. They were happier about the upcoming birth of their second grandchild than they'd been about the first. I had conceived this baby during marriage, not before. I shared the happy news with everyone from the beginning—a joy I'd been denied with my first pregnancy.

Antonio didn't share my elation. He didn't want more responsibilities while still in college. I understood his hesitance, but I had confidence that a second child wouldn't make our lives as difficult as he feared. As my stomach grew, my usually loving husband remarked how unattractive I looked. My eyes watered with his rejection. I hadn't expected my decision to put our marriage in jeopardy. I promised to take full responsibility for our second child. But how could I?

I looked at the envelope with the return address of the state of California. Chills of worry went through me. I recognized the official-looking missive. I tore open the envelope and read the neatly typed letter. In stern language it said that I needed to send evidence I was currently employed by a state or county welfare agency. My pulse raced. I had no such proof. I knew when granted the graduate school scholarship, I was legally bound to work in a state welfare department or repay the $3,000 stipend. But I'd hoped the authorities might forgive my debt when the hiring freeze prevented me from getting a job that fulfilled their requirement. This third official notice proved they hadn't. And I didn't have the money to repay them. Once again, I ignored the state's request.

I couldn't repay California their money by working the summer session because our second child was due the first week of July. My summer would be filled with caring for the new family member. I mentioned my dilemma to fellow school social worker Jill, also pregnant. She had been hired at the same time as me.

"I don't know what I'm going to do," I said to Jill at our social workers' meeting in December 1970. "With the baby due the beginning of July, I won't be able to work during summer school. And the state keeps sending me letters demanding I repay them $3,000."

"My husband is a lawyer," Jill said. "Why don't you make an appointment with him? He might be able to help."

The next week, I explained my situation to Jill's husband. He sympathized with my catch-22 predicament caused by the state's hiring freeze. He had a proposal.

"We'll send a letter," he said, sounding annoyed with the officials in Sacramento, "to the state welfare department from your lawyer. I'll confirm that you were willing to work but weren't allowed to through no fault of your own."

He sent the letter before the holidays. I waited to hear from the state, hoping for a Christmas gift in the form of a forgiving letter. I began to set aside as much savings as we could afford in case the state officials didn't agree with the rationale for my noncompliance.

I received the Christmas gift I wished for, but by default. I never again heard from the state. I paid Jill's lawyer husband $30—one of my best expenditures ever.

And Baby Makes Four

I unwrapped pink diaper bags, pink onesies, and frilly pink dresses at the April 1971 baby showers thrown by the Hawthorne school faculty and the women in our student housing unit. Those who doubted that I could choose the sex of my baby, thought impossible in 1970, gave me yellow blankets, sweaters, and booties.

Our family of three took a trip to Southern California during spring vacation. I knew such adventures would be more difficult with two small children. At Disneyland, four-year-old Tony beamed to see Mickey Mouse, Goofy, and the cartoon figures he recognized from TV. At six months pregnant, I looked like a fat dwarf myself as I whirled around on the spinning cups and saucers ride with my son. Tony squealed with glee when the performing dolphins splashed us with water at Sea World. He clenched and unclenched his little fists and rocked back and forth on his tiptoes to show his delight at the sight of the animals he loved at the San Diego Zoo. Antonio had never seen such amusements either and reacted with as much enthusiasm as his son.

Though enjoyable, our vacation had cost money. To save on food expenses we took up farming. Student families in our housing compound grew a variety of vegetables in the Village's community garden. That summer, we requested one of the eight-by-twelve-foot plots. On our patch of Albany soil, we raised tomatoes, corn, cucumbers, potatoes, and lettuce. Antonio was comfortable cultivating produce

Evelyn and Tony at Disneyland

because he'd farmed on his grandparents' hacienda below Machu Picchu. My four siblings and I had hoed weeds and watered an acre of vegetables in rural Montana. Living in Albany Village was like returning to small-town living in Montana.

We couldn't afford to eat out, so I made home-cooked meals from some of our home-grown vegetables. Instead of Montana steak and potatoes, I tried to recreate the tasty Peruvian dishes Antonio and I liked, with mixed success.

I borrowed my mother's sturdy thick stainless steel oval pot to cook *chicharrones*. I covered two pounds of one-inch pork pieces with salted water and boiled them until the water was absorbed, then browned the meat chunks in their fat. After waiting the three hours it took, we were hungry enough to gobble up the meat and the potatoes fried with it, even if I hadn't found all the spices the dish required.

Ceviche was easier because the fish "cooked" in lime juice. The onion and chile peppers supplied the spices. This specialty was often my contribution at Village potlucks. International students loved it.

I had to find a fireplace to cook the *anticuchos* over charcoal like I'd seen in Cusco. The rub of chile peppers, oregano, cumin, annatto, and garlic gave the beef heart the flavor I remembered. Finding the main ingredient, however, was as time consuming as the four-to-five-hour wait while everything marinated. In Peru *anticuchos* were served with yucca. We had never eaten yucca in Montana, so I served it with potatoes.

Work and children eventually prohibited my spending hours making the cuisine that reminded us of Peru. Antonio never said he missed Peruvian food, or that he appreciated my culinary efforts. I continued to make my favorite, *lomo saltado,* but I ceased making the other Peruvian dishes, save *ceviche* for special occasions.

Our lives overflowed with fertile activities—producing a second child and growing vegetables in the garden. At eight months pregnant, I tended our garden, ready for this baby to be born.

Evelyn in the community garden

The school year ended mid-June and I enrolled in a two-week summer class on behaviorism at the Berkeley UC campus. Fellow students took bets on which of us two very pregnant women in class would leave for the hospital before the course concluded. We both lasted to the class's July 4 conclusion.

When birthing Tony, I'd been caught off guard by the pain. Then my obstetrician had quickly administered a saddle block anesthetic. The painkiller deadened me to all feeling in my lower extremities. For days afterward, I had excruciating headaches every time I lifted my head. I didn't want a pain-deadener with this second birth. I wanted to experience the pleasure of a natural birth, like so many women did in the '70s. I enrolled in weekly evening Lamaze classes the month before my due date and hoped for a painless, enjoyable childbirth.

I arrived unaccompanied at the Albany Adult School at seven in the evening on July 6 for the third Lamaze class entitled, "Labor Pains." Antonio hadn't come with me to any of the classes. Childbirth wasn't a major medical event where he came from. He said women in Peru delivered their babies without their spouses involved in classes. Antonio hadn't been present when Tony was born, so I wasn't surprised by his lack of involvement with our second child's delivery. It had been my decision to have this baby, and I would attend Lamaze classes by myself. I gritted my teeth and went alone.

"Your abdomen will become hard," the perky, young Lamaze instructor said describing a labor pain, "and you'll feel pressure on your pelvis."

I looked around at the circle of women leaning against their husbands. The couples resembled wheelbarrows holding various sized pumpkins. Most appeared more relaxed than me, even though most were first-time parents. I was a single pumpkin reclining against a pillow with no wheelbarrow to hold me.

A sharp movement around my abdomen startled me. I couldn't recall having felt this tightening before Tony's birth. Alarmed, I sat upright and raised my hand.

"The contractions move in a wave-like motion from the top to the bottom of the uterus like a cramp," the teacher continued, then looked over at me.

"Yes, Evelyn?" she said, swishing her blond ponytail.

"I'm feeling something," I said, concerned. "Could it be a contraction?"

"Can you wait another fifteen minutes until the eight o'clock break?" she asked, looking at the clock above the blackboard.

A warm glow went through my body. I felt so mellow I could have agreed to anything. I nodded and rested against my big pillow. After all, I was having my second child. I should know how a contraction felt. Maybe my daughter was just changing her position.

At the break, Miss Perky felt my belly, timing what she now agreed were contractions. I waddled behind the instructor to the office of the night school principal, Mr. Hughes. The principal looked at me with unsmiling concern. Then, without warning, my water broke and sprinkled over his office floor.

"I think," the instructor said, now less cheerful, "you need to get to a hospital right away, and I need to get back to my class."

Principal Hughes's eyes opened wide with bewilderment. I looked at him amused, still in a euphoric state. I'd driven to class in our little VW. Mr. Hughes said he'd come to work on his motorcycle. With my contractions now seven minutes apart, I needed to get home so Antonio could take me to Kaiser Hospital in Oakland. I called Antonio on the office phone and told him to get Tony ready to stay with a neighbor. Antonio sounded surprised but calm. I hung up and got back to Mr. Hughes.

"I need to get home. This baby feels like she's about to slide right out of me."

"I can't just put you on the back of my Harley," the hip principal said.

"If you can drive a stick shift," I said, "you can drive me in my car."

"I don't," the principal said, "but you shouldn't go alone."

"Okay," I said, "I'll drive. You can sit in the passenger seat."

I got behind the wheel of the VW with Mr. Hughes beside me. Each contraction felt stronger than the last. The car and I reacted together, halting with each spasm. I stepped on the gas. I cringed each time we hit a bump. The principal and I drove the two miles to our apartment avoiding conversation. I had no time to be concerned about how Mr. Hughes would get back to his office. We certainly couldn't drop him off on our way to the hospital.

As soon as I arrived home, I called the woman in the complex who'd agreed to watch Tony. The neighbor arrived. I grabbed my bag. We raced to the hospital. My contractions were now coming so close together and so strong I was certain Antonio would have to stop driving and deliver our daughter in the car somewhere along Interstate 80.

The attendants at the emergency entrance rushed me into a delivery room. This time Antonio stayed around to complete the admission papers, unlike when Tony was born. I was in no condition to do so. The nurses had no time to prep me or ask about painkillers—the baby was too eager to come out. I endured the natural childbirth I'd planned for, but with pain and tearing. I waited to hear my baby girl's cries.

At 9:23 p.m., the doctor said, "You have a beautiful baby boy."

"Are you sure?" I said, surprised, but grateful to have the birth over with. "I was supposed to have a girl."

"Well, you have a healthy boy," the doctor repeated.

I hadn't felt the physical pleasure of this natural childbirth like I'd expected but was happy to have a healthy baby boy. The physician placed my infant on my stomach. Any disappointment at birthing a second son evaporated. I gave thanks for my precious boy. Except now all those pink baby gifts would have to go back.

We named our boy Timothy Alexis, another of my attempts at a name that sounded good in both English and Spanish, for when we returned to visit Peru. I remembered listening to a radio program in seventh grade called *One Man's Family*. A woman on it counseled that a boy's name should sound like that of a baseball player. Timothy LaTorre sounded like that. Tony had choice comments about his new baby brother.

"Oh, he's so cute," my first-born said. "He gots little hairs and a little mouth. Did the baby come out of your tummy? Mommy, I think I have a kitty in my leg to come out."

We laughed at his remarks. At Timothy's baby clinic appointment, Tony had seen an African American baby and remarked, "But Mommy, I wanted a little Black baby."

Timmy had delicate features—blond curly hair and big, dark eyes with long eyelashes. Like with his brother, I couldn't see much of me in him, save the lighter hair color. From the beginning, he demanded greater social interaction than his more reserved sibling. He wouldn't sit still with a book for long periods like Tony unless he sat in someone's lap. He rolled over ready to take off whenever Antonio or I changed his diaper. My little extrovert was always on the move, usually looking for a play pal.

My two boys couldn't have had more different personalities and physical appearances. The rapid pace of their physical and linguistic developments, however, were nearly identical. Timmy, being very social, had different expressions than his brother, whom he called, "Toty." At age two he spoke in phrases he'd heard like, "All righty," "Come here," and "Hello, howareya." He walked at eleven months and never slowed down.

I continued to use my sewing skills to save money, much as I'd done in the Peace Corps when I'd made sixty marching uniforms for my group of impoverished students. It disappointed me not to be sewing frilly dresses for a daughter. Still, I made them for myself. Often, I had enough yardage left from sewing my dress to make matching pants for the boys and a shirt for Antonio. I put four-inch hems in the boys' pants so they wouldn't grow out of them for years. My sewing results didn't please Antonio.

My husband refused to wear his matching shirt at the same time the rest of us dressed in our coordinated outfits. He said he didn't want to wear "the LaTorre uniform." When he suggested I discontinue making the boys' pants, I had to agree. Our sons looked a bit ridiculous in the baggy pants with the enormous hems. My mother began passing along my youngest brother's outgrown pants to Tony, so I stopped sewing for all my guys.

The summer of 1971, I enjoyed my sons, grateful I didn't have to work to repay $3,000 to the state. I liked being the mother of two but found working full time didn't allow me time to be the attentive mother I wanted to be. Antonio's studies for his BA from UCB seemed never ending, so I couldn't quit my job and stay home. Someone had to bring in an income. That's why, in the fall of 1971, I did the next best thing.

Less Salary, More Rent

My coworker Jill, whose lawyer husband had helped me mollify the state's demand, had just given birth to her first child. She wanted to spend more time with her new daughter. I wanted to spend more time with my sons. We conferred with one another prior to beginning the 1971 school year and came up with a plan. We'd split a school social worker position. We approached Miss Callow, our San Francisco Unified supervisor with our request.

"As you know," I said, when seated in our boss's office, "Jill and I both have newborns. We have an idea for the coming school year."

"And what would that be?" Miss Callow asked.

"I don't want to totally leave my social work position," Jill said, her eyes wide with anticipation. "So, I'd like to work one day a week during the 1971–72 school year."

"And I could work the other four days," I said, crossing my fingers. "That way we would fill one position."

Miss Callow looked down at the roster of school social workers. I knew our appeal must be unusual. If I could, I, too, would ask to work fewer than four days so I could spend more time with the new baby. But I needed to continue as our family's primary breadwinner while Antonio studied. Four days a week would pay $9,000 a year. We could get by on that.

"Hmm," the white-haired lady in front of us said. "I see where that might work."

"That way, when I'm ready, I would still have some seniority," Jill said. "I might want to work half- or even full-time again someday."

"I really like my work," I said, "and don't want to inconvenience anyone."

"The district is here to accommodate your needs," Miss Callow said, "not for you to sacrifice your families for the district."

Jill and I looked at one another with surprise, then rested back in our chairs. We thanked our supervisor and went home to give the good news to our spouses. Our initiative had paid off.

I pondered Miss Callow's unusual statement. I'd never met an employer with so generous a work philosophy—and most likely never would again. I loved the humane attitude of the social work profession and vowed to be a dedicated, loyal worker for this benevolent school district. My family and I, and maybe the world, would be better off because of Miss Callow's family-centered guiding principle.

I'd taken a chance that Antonio wouldn't reject his new son, and I'd been correct. He organized his fall classes so he could care for Timothy during the hours I worked. I wondered what the men in his home country would think of him taking on the childcare role. I'd seen very few men in either the US or Peru care for their infants all day. Timothy gazed into his father's eyes whenever Antonio fed him a bottle of formula. But I longed to continue breast feeding my infant. Still, seeing father and son bond together pleased me.

The arrangement with Antonio lasted six months. When Timmy no longer slept most of the day, Antonio couldn't study. I took a deep breath and found a babysitter in Albany Village. Tony continued to attend preschool at the Village's daycare center.

Working four days felt like I had a holiday every week. I used it to bond with my youngest son. Timmy and I attended exercise classes together—he in kinder gym and me in aerobics in the next room.

He loved somersaulting, bouncing on the trampoline, and all kinds of physical activity. He kept me on the move.

Timmy also loved the water, so I enrolled him in baby swim classes. He wanted to take baths several times a day. His delight in water play continued at meals where he dumped his milk on his highchair tray and with great vigor splashed the liquid with both hands.

Timothy splashing in his milk

Despite my contentment with job and family, the problem of our future housing had been hanging over us ever since I'd graduated in May 1970. Five months after my master's degree ceremony, the University of California sent a notice requesting that we vacate our Albany Village apartment reserved for graduate students. By then, however, I was pregnant with Timmy, and the UCB housing office granted us a reprieve until the baby came in July. I uttered a soft thank you to them. When Antonio's graduation was delayed yet again, I requested a second postponement. To my delight and relief, that too was granted until December 1971. We'd pushed our luck as far as we could and been granted permission to stay much longer than the rules permitted. The low rent for the past year and a half had allowed us to save a good portion of my salary. We got ready to move.

I checked the ads for rental units available in Albany. We needed to remain near the university until Antonio graduated. Who knew when that would be?

I couldn't believe my eyes when I saw a two-bedroom house to rent for $150 a month. I didn't want to be turned down because we had two children. So Antonio and I went alone to view it. The landlady asked about children. I admitted to having a four-year-old, which she said was fine. She said we'd be responsible for maintaining the yard. I hesitated. Antonio didn't know how to mow a lawn or trim roses and blackberry bushes. Cusco didn't have lawns or blackberry bushes. He had been raised on his grandparents' hacienda, so knew about growing sugar cane, but little about the kinds of greenery we had in California.

Antonio didn't indicate that caring for the yard would be an obstacle. I determined that this house with a yard to maintain would be a trial run for when we bought our own home. We signed the contract. On December 1, 1971, the four of us moved into the house—appropriately, on Evelyn Avenue.

A Modern Woman

My father had been proud to support his large family on his wages alone, until he needed additional funds to send his children to college. To afford our post-secondary education, my mother had to earn a salary. No full-time jobs for her or nearby colleges for us children existed in Southeastern Montana in 1959, so we moved to Northern California where Dad had been hired by the Federal Aviation Administration. Mom found a position in the Sears customer service office right away. But unplanned child number six, Randy, arrived eleven months into our California lives and she had to quit. However, the new baby wouldn't derail Dad's plans for his children to attend college. Dad encouraged Mom to find another job so his offspring would have the opportunity for a college degree that he'd not had.

Mom returned to work a few months after Randy's arrival. She seemed pleased to use her skills outside the home. We four girls became substitute mothers to our colicky baby brother. Nights, we walked the floor with him. Days, we continued to make family meals and clean the house. Everyone pitched in. By collaborating, we enabled Mom to pursue her career. We understood her work would pay for our college educations.

Mom's example wasn't what we saw on TV. Mothers like June Cleaver, Harriet Nelson, and Donna Reed fed their TV husbands' egos and kept spotless homes—all while wearing dresses, pearls, and heels.

The commercials on TV extolled the virtues of specialized cleaning products to produce sparkling bathrooms and clean kitchens. I hated cleaning bathrooms and kitchens.

Only Lucy of *I Love Lucy* tried to have a job outside her home, and she failed, though with humor. The girls in my family didn't mind. We sensed the difference between Lucy, our Mom, and those other TV moms and wives.

American society and Mom said the man headed the family and the wife should comply with her husband's wishes. That's not the type of wife I wanted to be. A major gas company had told me I was inferior to my husband when it denied me a credit card in my name. The company said my husband could get one—even when I earned most of our family's income. Their chauvinism set my pulse speeding. I swore I'd never purchase gasoline from that company. Then I had to face my own unequal situation.

Antonio graduated from UC Berkeley in May 1972 with a BA in physics, four years after he'd begun. His three years in college in Peru plus a year at Chabot and four in Berkeley meant he'd spent a total of eight years earning a BA degree. When he said he needed a master's degree to be employable and could finish in two years if he went full-time, I gave him a skeptical look. Maybe I should be grateful that he had the ability to study physics and math and was happiest when doing so. But would he be a perennial student?

I assumed he knew better than I what degrees might culminate in a job. He applied to San Francisco State College. But his decision meant I'd have to continue as the family's main wage earner—a position I hadn't planned to stay in forever, or at least not this long. My insides quivered. When would his education end so he could support us?

He gave me a big hug when the letter arrived from SFSC's physics department, accepting him into their fall graduate program. My heart ached with a desire to spend more time with my two young boys. But breadwinner was the role I'd filled for most of the past six years. I swallowed my resentment. My mother sympathized with my plight.

"A good husband supports his family," she said in her usual serious tone. "You should be staying home caring for your children."

She hadn't done that after her sixth child. It looked to me that she much preferred using her mind and communication skills as a clerk for the local police department. We had all been proud of her when she was chosen over scores of other applicants for the choice position. But my situation was different from my mother's. She hadn't been forced to be the sole breadwinner like me.

I was caught in a quandary. My parents had sacrificed so I could gain a college education, but for what? Mom discouraged me from using my master's degree in social welfare for a job because I had young children. And the dilemma was my fault. I'd accidentally become pregnant with the first child and made the decision to have a second one before my husband could support them or me. I could hear my Mother thinking, *You made your bed, now lie in it.*

Similarly educated women with children in the '70s didn't hold full-time jobs. Their husbands supported them like the women on TV. I knew there existed populations of married women who worked for a few years to put their husbands through medical, law, or other professional schools. They'd reap their rewards later with a move to an upper income level. And of course, I recalled the husbandless moms who had been on my AFDC caseload at the county welfare department. But I didn't fall into either the striver or the welfare mother category. Neither Antonio nor I had been raised to live for money or prestigious positions. We weren't intentionally upwardly mobile, and I wasn't a single mother—yet.

Still, like it or not, I was part of a new wave of able women with children who held down jobs to support our families. I had mixed feelings about full-time work vs. full-time mothering. My heart ached with a desire to spend full days with my two young boys. But I'd continue as long as I had to. Work provided me intellectual challenges, feelings of competence, and a bigger say in our family's spending. I'd opted for higher education to make me a capable earner.

I saw no models of married women with young children who worked to support their families. Articles in magazines reported that working full-time, while raising children, required a superhuman effort. A woman reporter had said that combining an engrossing occupation and a happy, productive marriage was impossible. She bet that only one woman in a thousand could do it—and then only if she were a genius. I wondered if she were a full-time reporter with children.

Not everyone believed the "Children equals no career" motto. I had read a book that contradicted it. My sociology professor had assigned us to read Betty Friedan's *The Feminine Mystique,* when I was a senior at Holy Names College. The popular 1963 book illustrated many cases of unhappy college-educated women who filled their days with homemaking duties. Cleaning, cooking, childcare, and tending to their husbands left these wives and mothers without identities outside their well-kept homes. Though women had comprised 50 percent of the professional workforce in 1930, Ms. Friedan wrote, in 1960 the percentage had dropped to only 35 percent. This, although the number of women college graduates had tripled. I'd witnessed the accuracy of that statistic.

One-third of the women who'd entered Holy Names College with me as freshmen in 1960 married before or right after our graduation in 1964. Many had not completed their college educations. A few classmates admitted to attending college to get an "MRS" degree. I recalled a Rhodes Scholar awardee a couple grades ahead of me. She'd had to choose between marriage and graduate school abroad. She elected to marry and declined the prestigious honor and the opportunity to grow her mind. Her decision disappointed her professors—and me. I would have opted for education at Oxford University in England in a minute.

Ms. Friedan's conclusion, controversial in 1963, was that many women with educations were happier using their minds to fulfill their intellectual and creative needs than they were living through the lives of their husbands and children. I agreed. I never wanted my tombstone to read, "She kept her husband happy in a tidy home."

I'd earned money and paved my way through life when I worked as a hired girl on ranches six days a week each summer from ages eleven to fourteen. I overcame homesickness, fear, and the grind of hard physical labor then to earn more money for clothes than my parents could supply. My mother's strong work ethic, combined with my desire, resulted in my working to purchase such items as a pair of sandals, a stylish dress, or a bicycle. I learned to translate my labor into what I wanted.

The nuns who taught my classes at College of the Holy Names, an all-women's college, were models of wise, scholarly females. I respected these women with PhDs who, though they adhered to strict religious rules, encouraged us students to use our minds. They exposed us to the latest research of leading scholars. However, the messages I received from the professors of my two majors, psychology and sociology, contradicted one another.

Sister Paulina Mary, chairman of the Psychology Department and a popular public speaker, urged us future mothers to remain at home to raise our children. Everyone loved this lively teacher whose black veil swished and whose brown eyes sparkled as she wrote a new list of references on the blackboard. The latest research supported her belief that children are better off with full-time mothers.

"There is no substitute," my mentor said, "for a mother's presence in the life of her child. You can't work outside the home and also adequately care for your child."

She delivered her message and down-to-earth opinions with a keen sense of humor and an engaging style. PTA members and women's groups asked Sister to speak at their meetings. The popularity of this intelligent and caring nun with the bubbly personality didn't surprise me. Her generous attention had included me. She'd awarded me a full tuition scholarship to the college and listened with empathy to my woes when my grades plummeted and I almost lost my award because tensions had increased at home. Her lectures exhorted me to practice what she preached.

Sister's words followed me when I became a mother and couldn't be with my children twenty-four hours a day. I paid some other mother to care for my boys because I worked. The guilt I felt then bordered on self-loathing. Would my decision stunt my children's emotional growth? I had received a contrary message from my college advisor.

Sister Antonia Marie, head of Holy Names' Sociology Department, stood tall with perfect posture. She didn't exhibit humor or tolerance for deviating from the words in the books she assigned us. Her lectures, rarely spontaneous, followed a predictable outline from the textbook. Her classes, however, gave me an understanding of how different societies adapt to their environments. I learned that income and gender equality was an important value for Danish men. They helped with the housework. Among the Incas, both men and women worked in the fields, and the grandparents took care of the children. Many forward-thinking countries provided quality childcare when both parents worked. I, too, would adapt to the financial situation of my family.

Antonio helped wash the dishes, vacuum, and care for our children, though he never did the laundry or cooked. Household drudgery was more fulfilling when we put our heads together to figure out efficient routines. We found we could accomplish most cleaning between study and worktime. We trained the boys to return their toys to their bottom dresser drawer, and we rarely made the beds.

Contrary to my husband's male models in Peru, he liked that I had a career. He didn't want me to squander my eighteen years of education on household duties alone. He advocated for my career more than his. And, if I worked, he could study.

As I prepared to return to work after the birth of our second child, a tightness gripped my chest. Would my boys suffer because I worked outside the home? I didn't know. I only knew that life was more fulfilling with an interesting job. And I had more control over family finances when I worked.

Back in School

The 1972 school year began with an extra challenge. My social worker predecessor had discovered that numbers of Hispanic children had been placed in classes for the mentally delayed simply because they didn't speak English. Then lawsuits led the state to pass laws requiring credentialed school psychologists to administer their tests in a student's native language. San Francisco Unified determined that in place of social workers like me, the district needed more psychologists to perform the required tests.

Someone at the top decreed that the district's school social workers would have to become school psychologists. To fill that role, they'd need to return to college and obtain the required credential. This new mandate resulted in a few of my colleagues retiring early. They were too old, they claimed, to pursue a credential they'd use for only a few years. Some transferred to school programs that needed full-time social workers, such as classes for behavior-disordered students. Still others with teaching credentials decided to return to the classroom. The rest signed up for two years of evening and summer classes at San Francisco State College.

A day of work followed by classes each evening at SFSC was out of the question for me. Evening courses would require me to be absent from my boys more than my job already demanded. And I didn't like the late-night drive in the dark after classes across the Bay Bridge back home to Albany. I had to find another way to meet the district's requirement.

I contacted Dr. Wasserman, director of the school social work program at UCB, where I'd graduated in 1970. The kind mentor came to my rescue again, as he'd done when recommending me for the job with SFUSD two years before. Now he counseled me to check out the school psych program at Cal State Hayward. That college had day classes and was on my side of the Bay. He said the chairman of the program, Dr. Mitchell, was a caring professional.

I called Cal State's admissions office and was told that the school year had begun. But hope welled in my breast. I'd have to develop a strategy if I wanted this new credential. I called the school psychology department. My stomach quivered. I needed to be convincing.

"The fall quarter," the secretary said, "will begin in just a few days. To be allowed in at this late date, you'll have to apply directly to the head of the department."

My heart sank. I had to be admitted to this program or I'd be out of a job the next year. I hoped Dr. Mitchell's secretary would let me schedule an appointment with him.

"It's very late to apply," Dr. Mitchell's secretary said.

"But could you please book me for an appointment with Dr. Mitchell anyway?" I asked, my body tightening. "Dr. Wasserman at UC Berkeley suggested I speak with him."

"You'll have to come in tomorrow," she said, "and wait in line. Maybe he'll see you."

On a sunny September morning, I stood third in line to see the head of the school psychology department. Besides official transcripts, I carried letters of recommendation from two of my former UCB instructors who knew Dr. Mitchell. The department's catalog listed course requirements that included many I'd taken at Berkeley a few years before. I thought I shouldn't have to repeat classes such as "Family Dynamics" and "Human Behavior." But I'd need to persuade Dr. Mitchell of that—if he admitted me to his program.

Two women waited in line ahead of me. Each of them entered

Dr. Mitchell's office separately to request admittance to the school psychology program. From the hallway outside his office, I heard the professor's pronouncement each time.

"I'm sorry," I heard him say from the open door to his office, "but our first-year class openings are full."

I watched both women leave in tears. My lips pressed tight. My preplanning and powers of persuasion had to work.

"Dr. Mitchell," I said with confidence when my turn came, "I believe I could complete your program in a year. I finished a master's degree at the school of social welfare at UC Berkeley two years ago."

"Well, there's no time to determine that," the gray-haired professor said in a tired voice. "Today is the last day to admit students to the program, and I'd need to see your transcripts."

"I have them right here," I said handing him the sealed envelope containing my official transcripts. "I also have two letters of recommendation from instructors whom I believe you know."

The fifty-something instructor opened the first envelope and surveyed my grades, all A's. Expressionless, he looked me over, then turned back to read the letters. I couldn't tell what he was thinking as he shuffled my documents. I held my breath. My hands perspired. My future lay in his.

"It looks," he said at last, glancing up from the transcripts, "like you've already had many of the required courses. You could probably complete our program in a year if you arrange your schedule to take the classes you'll need."

I exhaled and smiled. The caring department head had made my day, my year, my life. But he had a major condition.

"We'll accept you into the school psychology program," Dr. Mitchell said. "But I don't want everyone from San Francisco Unified who needs a psychology credential to think they can enter my program."

And with that, I became a student again. Now to figure out how to attend school, continue working, and care for my family. That night Antonio and I sat down at the kitchen table to discuss the situation.

We determined the only way I could attend day classes at Cal State would be to reduce my workweek further—from four days a week to three. With both of us in school, we'd spend more on childcare. We calculated our expenditures. Rent for our two-bedroom house on Evelyn Avenue was $150. Gas to commute to San Francisco cost forty cents a gallon. The babysitter for one-year-old Timothy cost fifty cents an hour. Five-year-old Tony was an afternoon kindergartener who could spend mornings at the Albany Village Child Care Center. Thank heavens they charged on a sliding scale. If we continued our frugal lifestyle, we could manage. Antonio and I would drive to San Francisco together in our VW. He could take the bus home. In addition, Antonio planned to apply for a teaching assistantship at San Francisco State. We could survive on our combined income of $800 per month.

My understanding supervisors figured out a way for me to work three days a week. I'd serve several schools instead of one. I scheduled my work around my classes and attended two required courses after my workday. Like my husband, I enjoyed learning, but, unlike him, my work and classroom schedule left me few intervals to write papers and study for tests. I also had to attend to the educational needs of Tony, who had just begun kindergarten.

I accompanied Tony to the first day of his afternoon kindergarten class at MacGregor Elementary School in Albany, in fall 1972. Team teachers, Mrs. Halpern and Miss O'Neal, both commented on what a handsome son I had. I thought so, too—with his shiny, thick black hair and dark eyes. Like his dad, I thought, except Tony's hair was as straight as Antonio's was wavy.

When Timmy and I picked up Tony at the end of his first school day, he oozed excitement about all the new activities. His teachers had let him play with the animal puppets and picked him to erase the blackboard. He squeezed his hands open and closed and rocked back and forth on his tiptoes—the way he showed happiness. I welcomed the teachers' involvement in expanding my son's world and promoting his learning.

After a few weeks, the teachers informed me that my left-hander insisted on writing several alphabet letters backward. They suggested I work with him at home. Of course, I would. Our son should excel, or at least not fall behind others in his class. Before long, Tony printed his letters correctly—except for *e*. Nothing I said convinced him to turn the letter around.

"Tony," I said, after weeks of gentle reasoning, "most people write the *e* heading forward, but you can write it the way you want."

He persisted for a few more weeks, then changed the *e*'s direction. Writing became one of his favorite activities. And, like Antonio and me, he loved going to school.

From the beginning, Tony's schoolwork seemed adequate. So I was surprised when in October, his teachers called us in for an impromptu conference. In my school social worker role, I often requested parent meetings to discuss a teacher's concerns. Now I cringed at the thought that our son might have school problems. Antonio accompanied me to the school. Mrs. Halpern motioned us to two tiny kindergarten chairs.

"Tony is having frequent outbursts in class," the older of the two teachers said. "He gets along with the other children but often takes a completed assignment and, without letting us see his work, wads it up and throws it into the wastebasket."

When he'd first enrolled, Mrs. Halpern had said what a well-mannered boy he was. Apparently, that had changed. Maybe my son wasn't the well-adjusted, almost six-year-old I believed him to be. Even as his parent with social work training, I didn't know why Tony would throw away work the teachers said he'd completed correctly.

Now I sat in the hot seat. I knew from experience that teachers couldn't always understand the roots of children's behavioral difficulties. They sometimes needed those of us in the social work and psychology professions, combined with insight from parents, to help unravel the mysteries of what motivated a child's conduct. Tony's earlier temper tantrums, when he didn't get what he wanted, had subsided. He had many friends and seemed happy. I squirmed in the tiny chair searching for an answer.

"Do you see similar frustrations at home?" Miss O'Neal asked.

"No," I said, "he plays fine with his younger brother. He loves being read to, recognizes many words, and enjoys imitating animals he's seen or read about. He seems fine at home."

"Hmm," Mrs. Halpern said, her face lighting up. "I think maybe his status in the family has changed since his brother came along. Maybe he's reacting to being displaced."

Tony had begged for a sibling and seemed delighted when I brought Timothy home from the hospital. When he began to interact with his brother, he loved to tell him about animals he'd looked up in the set of discarded encyclopedias I'd brought home. However, Timmy wasn't mature enough to engage in many of his brother's imaginary games. Tony gave complicated instructions too difficult for his one-and-a-half-year-old brother to comprehend.

So Tony settled for hugging and kissing Timmy instead. He more than tolerated his sibling—unless Timmy snatched Tony's favorite truck or dinosaur. Then, he'd grab it back, even if his younger brother protested. In all, the boys seemed happy together. I didn't think the birth of his baby brother had affected Tony. With four and a half years between the two boys, I didn't see how Tony would feel displaced.

"I suppose that's possible," I said.

Antonio said nothing. I considered darting into the hall to escape the teacher's judgment. My mind raced to rationalize my child's behavior in the eyes of his teachers.

Tony didn't appear to mind sharing us with his brother. Still, he had protested that my parents were *his* grandparents, not his brother's. And he disliked being interrupted until he finished whatever playing or writing project he'd started. On many mornings he fussed that he had to feed the animals that lived up the hill from us at the public farm in Tilden Park. When I said he'd have to wait until after school, he objected. So, if I had time, I drove the few miles to the farm and watched him feed stale bread to the goats and chickens before he went off to school.

Now I clutched my purse to my chest in front of his teachers. Maybe they had a right to be concerned about my son's behavior. Then a light bulb went on in my head.

Tony was already reading and writing, so maybe my bright little boy had mastered much of what kindergarten could teach him and had become bored. I didn't want to challenge the kindergarten teachers' observations or teaching methods, so I proceeded with caution.

"Perhaps," I said, "Tony thinks his work isn't up to his standards,"

"Yes," Antonio said, awakening. "He likes what he does to turn out a certain way."

"Maybe he's a perfectionist," Mrs. Halpern said. "I think maybe we should refer him to our school psychologist."

We'd always thought our boy to be clever and bright. Testing him might prove that and provide his kindergarten teachers a path to better comprehend his behavior. Then maybe they wouldn't blame Tony's behavior on Timothy's existence. Antonio and I looked at one another, relieved.

Work, Raffles, and Tests

I guided our little green bug up and down the hills of San Francisco after I dropped Antonio off at his college classes. Then, I continued on to my schools to help teachers understand their pupils' emotional challenges. I loved feeling needed and important when I shared my child development and family dynamics expertise with school personnel. Some of my knowledge I'd acquired in graduate school. But much had also come from the two families I'd lived in—my parents' sometimes tense pairing and my own unequal one.

I gunned the motor of the Volkswagen and charged up California Street into Chinatown to check on the young Chinese woman whose son hit others in his preschool class. The boy's grandparents, with whom the mother lived, had pleaded for help. I didn't speak Mandarin, and the grandparents and mother knew only a few words in English. I communicated through gestures and smiles while the boy's mother looked at the floor. Her parents indicated that their daughter said little to them or her son and rarely left the apartment. I determined she must be depressed.

Back in my office, I found the phone number of a Mandarin-speaking psychotherapist she could see and gave it to the family. On future visits, the woman glanced at me but refused to leave the apartment to seek help. My unproductive efforts reminded me of my less than earthshaking attempts in the Peace Corps to impact another culture whose language and customs I had known for only two years. In the case at hand, surprisingly, the preschooler's outbursts diminished. The added attention from the school and his family helped improve his behavior, despite his mother's problems. I had better success in the African American community.

I'd been assigned to work with San Francisco Unified's preschool program. One of my schools was located in the predominantly African American community of Hunter's Point, near Candlestick Park, the baseball stadium at that time. The area contained mostly families with low incomes. The Anglo preschool teachers often accompanied me on visits to the homes of their African American students. We found that the conferences proved more productive when school personnel went to students' homes rather than insist that the parents always come to the school. The families received us graciously, even when we needed to discuss their child's acting out behavior or need for immunizations.

In April 1971, the US Supreme Court had upheld busing as the way to achieve racial desegregation in schools. So, in September 1972, San Francisco devised a plan for racial integration that involved busing students between Anglo and African American neighborhoods. Hunter's Point was paired with predominantly Anglo, working-class Visitation Valley. I organized evening meetings between the preschool parents from both city sections. Though awkward at first, the two groups soon discovered little to fear in one another's parts of the city. Both had similar interests—the wellbeing of their children. After a couple of gatherings, anxieties about busing small children to unfamiliar parts of town lessened, and my afterschool time and weekends again became my own.

One Saturday, just after New Year's 1973, the boys and I accompanied Antonio and his best friend, Romualdo, to several car dealerships on Shattuck Avenue in Berkeley. Neither college student could afford to replace his vehicle, but both guys liked to dream about what they'd buy "someday." That January day they went to where they could dream together.

Tony slipped around a sleek copper-colored Jaguar in the dealership's showroom. He extended his hands like lion paws, and his dark brown eyes widened. He roared and pounced at his eighteen-month-old brother squirming in my arms.

"I'm going to eat you," my oldest son said, loud enough for everyone in the showroom to hear.

Timothy giggled with delight and buried his face in my shoulder. His brother's roar could only startle, not frighten him. Tony didn't look like a shaggy lion—I'd trimmed his jet-black mane that morning, and he wasn't wearing one of his tails.

My two sons had as little interest as I did in the shiny, expensive autos. But, like me, they enjoyed getting out of our cramped two-bedroom house. I also loved the smell of new tires. I'd loved the rubber-like fragrance since childhood when I'd visited my favorite aunt at her John Deere Tractor and Tire dealership in North Dakota. For the boys, the showroom was a fresh place to play their hide-and-seek game.

I set Timothy down. He stood, confident on strong little legs that had supported him since he was three months old. He'd learned to walk at the age of eleven months, and now scampered away. He ran to hide behind a nearby black convertible, his blond curls bouncing like springs.

A raffle box in the center of the sales area called to me. My hands free, I headed toward it. If I entered, I could win an assortment of prizes. I paid little attention to the awards. To win anything lifted my spirits and reinforced my belief that I was lucky. I'd already won a clock radio, a frozen turkey, and an Indian-head penny in contests advertised on the radio, in magazines, and in newspapers. Why not enter here as well? Maybe I'd reap an unexpected reward later when I needed a lift.

Nothing in the competition rules on the raffle box limited how many times I could enter. My kind of contest—the faster I wrote, the more entries I could submit to improve my chance of winning. With my sons playing, I wrote my name and phone number on scores of entry slips. When the guys announced it was time to move on to the next dealership, I stuffed the last of my submissions into the box, gathered up my sons, and followed the men out the door.

A month after Tony turned six on January 12, 1973, we heard from Albany School District's school psychologist, Miss Nichols. She invited us to review the results of the tests she'd given Tony. The notice surprised me. I hadn't known that Tony had been tested. The psychologist said she'd meet us in Tony's kindergarten classroom after school. We had no one to watch the boys, so Antonio stayed with them. I drove the several blocks to MacGregor Elementary and sat down in the small chair across from the psychologist. What began with cordial greetings soon had me squirming in my seat.

"He's obviously been coached," the young psychologist said. "When I had him complete a drawing, he said, 'Oh, my mom had me do that.'"

The psychologist didn't wait for me to reply. I felt my face flush with embarrassment. I opened my mouth to explain. But Miss Nichols continued.

"And when I asked him questions from the Stanford-Binet IQ test, he remarked, 'Oh, my mom asked me that.'"

A new law mandated that parents give written permission prior to a school psychologist testing their child. Albany school district had neither told me when they would test my son nor obtained my written permission to do so. If they had, I could have told them that I'd practiced administering IQ tests on my son as part of the school psychology program at Cal State. The rules on psychological testing in schools had changed, but the district's policies apparently had not.

I sat stiff in my child-sized chair, trying to appear adult-like. My discomfort turned to upset. My jaw tightened. I had to defend myself. Miss Nichols was out of compliance, not me.

"It doesn't matter," Miss Nichols said, without letting me speak. "His performance measures his abilities, not your input. He is gifted. His above-average intelligence might explain Tony's perfectionist attitude and lead him to destroy writing and artwork he thinks is inferior to his standards."

My defenses dropped. The psychologist changed her tone. I rested against the back of the chair.

"I agree," I said.

My practice tests had shown the same results. My oldest son scored above average on the intelligence tests I'd administered to him. My classes in test administration taught me to react impartially to a child's responses and never correct or provide even a hint of the probable answers. So Tony's responses had been his own, not mine. Perhaps he'd been more relaxed when taking the tests because he was familiar with them. He enjoyed being challenged. I had violated no ethical guidelines.

"I'm recommending he receive more stimulation," the psychologist said.

"That would be great," I said, letting out a deep, gratifying sigh. "Maybe someone could teach him more about animals."

With more challenging assignments and greater responsibilities, Tony's kindergarten teachers had no further complaints about his behavior. However, I wished they would take him to the Tilden Park farm, so I didn't have to.

Then, in an instant, we were forced to turn our attention to our youngest son.

Child and Car Crises

We sat in the living room on a cold and gloomy February 1973 weekend keeping watch over Timothy who lay moaning in my lap. His body burned with fever. He had the flu. The thermometer registered a temperature of 102 degrees. I removed most of his clothes and applied cold compresses. Nothing cooled his little nineteen-month-old body. Then he'd gone limp and turned blue. I thought he'd stopped breathing.

"Oh God, he's dead!" I screamed at Antonio. "My poor little boy!"

Amid our panic we arranged for a neighbor to watch Tony. Then we jumped in our VW and raced to the Kaiser Hospital emergency room down the same freeway we'd driven on my way to give birth to the toddler who now lay lifeless on my lap. My hands shook. I prayed and tried to breathe life into my son's limp body. Antonio drove as fast as the four-piston engine would go. I couldn't believe my toddler, so full of life the day before, might now lie dead in my arms.

Somehow the Kaiser Hospital emergency staff revived our son. Later, his pediatrician said there appeared to be no brain damage and it would be best to keep Timothy hospitalized for three days of observation. They said the fever had caused the unconsciousness. The doctor prescribed him daily doses of phenobarbital to prevent future convulsions.

I remained by my youngest son's side day and night, missing work and several classes. My professors at Cal State were sympathetic and allowed me to make up the assignments I'd missed. I hoped I'd never again have to experience the near-death experience of someone I loved.

༄

One spring evening a month later, I was driving my trusty VW along Highway 580 on my way home from a late afternoon class at Cal State in Hayward. Near the turnoff to the Oakland Zoo, I heard a horrible grinding noise come from the engine in the rear. The motor stopped. I coasted into the lit-up gas station—a godsend on the side of the road. All the attendants were pumping gas into other vehicles, too busy to check my car.

My mind didn't believe my trusty VW would fail me. I took for granted that my car would always get me where I needed to go. I kept it filled with regular gas and changed its oil myself every three thousand miles—even when I was eight months pregnant and could hardly fit under the car to loosen the oil tank knob. My car kept going like I did.

I had to get back home to Albany and collect Timothy from the babysitter. Maybe the car had just overheated and would run now that it had cooled. I held my breath and tried to restart the engine. The motor purred alive, and I breathed again. I drove back onto the freeway, determined to make it home. Antonio would help figure out the problem there. I had no time to waste.

No sooner was I back on the busy thoroughfare than I heard a loud thump. The motor stopped again. Dusk had turned to darkness as I coasted onto the shoulder of the road and came to a stop. The VW refused to switch on again. Cars zoomed by in the dark at top speeds. A six-foot high wire fence, with no opening, ran along the

Evelyn Changing the VW's Oil

roadside next to me. I was trying to decide whether to walk toward the faraway off-ramp or back to the filling station to seek help, when a vehicle stopped behind me.

I watched from my rearview mirror as the headlights of passing cars revealed a young man getting out of a modern sportscar. He walked toward me in my stranded VW. I could hear my mother's admonitions about not talking to strangers or accepting rides from them. The man tapped on my car window. I cracked it open an inch.

"Do you need help?" the young potential rapist said.

"My car just stopped," I said, casually hitting my wedding ring against the window to let him know I was married. "I need to get home to pick up my son."

"Hop in my car," he said. "I can drop you off on my way home to Antioch."

I needed help but didn't think I should accept a ride from a male stranger. Then again, what else could I do? Hiking down the freeway would be just as dangerous as accepting this man's assistance. I had no choice.

I got into the man's comfortable car and we drove toward Albany in the night. The gentleman offered to haul my broken-down VW to his uncle's auto repair shop the next morning. I thanked him and said my father would pull it in to our mechanic. The good Samaritan drove me to collect Timothy, then dropped us off at my house. I thanked him again and took his uncle's information in case I needed it. Relieved that the kind man had helped, not hurt me, I vowed to never again take a vehicle for granted. And I needed to learn more about automotive mechanics than changing a car's oil.

My trusty VW had thrown a piston, a serious problem that necessitated a new engine. The price of a motor at the Volkswagen dealership was exorbitant—an expense we couldn't afford on my part-time income. My father recommended we find a rebuilt motor that cost much less. He found one at an automotive junkyard and we bought it. Our mechanic installed the rebuilt motor at a quarter of the price of a new one, though not a good deal in the end. The rebuilt motor resulted in a car with failing engine power.

∽

A couple of months later, on my way to SF school district's central offices, my ailing car could barely make it over a small hill on Van Ness Avenue. That was the last straw. I wouldn't be marooned again. I spied a bright blue hatchback in the window of a nearby Mazda dealership and drifted in. My brother-in-law had just purchased a Mazda with the new rotary engine and gave it high marks.

I had no way to reach Antonio at college. Within an hour, the salesman took the VW as a trade-in and arranged for payments we could afford for the Mazda. I signed on the dotted line and drove away with the shiny new car from the window. My purchase was both impulsive and necessary.

"Whose car is that?" Antonio asked when he arrived home from school that evening and saw the bright blue Mazda in our carport.

"It's our new car," I said, hoping he'd understand. "I know we should have picked out one together, but the VW lost power. I didn't want to get stranded again."

My husband said little. He didn't appear as enthusiastic as I'd hoped. This was the second time I'd purchased a car without Antonio's input. He realized we needed a dependable auto but said I should consult him on major purchases. I rationalized that my income had qualified us for the purchase—probably why the salesman didn't insist on obtaining my husband's okay.

Maybe I was too independent for any husband and should have taken my mother's advice. She'd suggested I act more helpless. But my culture emphasized independence—though mostly for men. In the breadwinner's role, I'd become a modern woman and the dominant decision-maker in our marriage. However, Antonio and I worked in partnership on our next major purchase.

Stretched Thin

By spring 1973, our four-room rented house had become too small for our family. Years earlier, in Peru, I had introduced Antonio to the game of Monopoly. At that time, we laughed when one of us paid dearly for not buying property early in the game. Now we played a real-life property game and realized we couldn't build up equity by continuing to pay rent. If we wanted to win at the real estate game, we would need to buy a house of our own.

In three years of employment with San Francisco Unified, I'd saved $3,000 in case the state came after the money I'd received for their stipend. No threatening letter had come from state authorities after December 1970, when the lawyer had written to them explaining my reasons for not complying with my contract. We could now use our savings for a down payment on a house.

Unfortunately, Antonio had at least another year left before he'd earn his master's degree, so there'd be no income from him for a while. But when my credential studies ended in June, I could seek work as a school psychologist. We agreed that it wouldn't hurt to look for a house.

We loved the North Berkeley area with its co-op grocery store, the Mr. Mopps toy store, and the activities on the UC campus. The liberal political atmosphere matched our values. But we couldn't afford the high prices of the older homes in the Berkeley area. Every place we looked at needed repairs and remodeling. By comparison, the new tract homes in the southeastern corner of the Bay Area looked more affordable and modern. We toured one or two developments whenever we visited my parents in Fremont. Friends with two full-time incomes had purchased a modern ranch-style home there. But we didn't have two full-time incomes.

Antonio earned $100 a month as a teaching assistant at SF State. My three-day-a-week salary from the school district was $700 a month. Our present earnings allowed us to survive but wouldn't qualify us for a home loan. Yet, we still talked and dreamed of a home of our own.

As often happened for me, an opportunity arose when most needed. The director of San Francisco Unified's preschool program said she needed to increase her social work staff by two days. I enjoyed collaborating with the young teachers and parents in the preschool program. Together, we encouraged the mothers and fathers of the three-to-five-year-olds to read more and spank less. Timothy occasionally came to work with me when we accompanied a classroom on a field trip. The two of us fit right in with the preschool parents and their children. The teachers said I modeled good parenting for the other mothers. The preschool director smiled and accommodated my wishes when I said I'd like to add the two days to the three days I already worked in her program. I began working full-time on April 2.

I wasn't certain how to juggle my school, work, and home commitments. I still needed to complete the psychology credential program, a top priority. But we could now qualify for a home loan.

A problem popped up as I registered for my final quarter at Cal State. Two required classes, "Personality Assessment" and "Learning Disabilities," usually taken in different years, met at the exact same time. I couldn't attend both classes. I requested permission to take the course covering personality tests as an independent study. The arrangement saved me time in class. Another dilemma solved in a way that suited me just fine. Life would be hectic; however, I'd have my psych credential by June.

More jobs were available for school psychologists than for school social workers when I checked employment notices from school districts. So in April I began applying for school psychology positions in Bay Area suburban cities. I didn't want to commute to San Francisco if we found an affordable home in the South Bay. I hoped my three years' experience in San Francisco's schools would make me an attractive candidate. Armed with lists of school districts within commuting distance of Fremont, I sent out inquiries offering my services as a Spanish-speaking psychologist. The few localities to respond said they had yet to set their budgets, so they couldn't offer me a position. Alum Rock School District's director of psychological services said he'd need a bilingual psychologist for fall 1973 but couldn't make an offer until the San Jose district's budget was final. I crossed my fingers and continued to send out my placement file.

Meanwhile, many of my fellow school psychology students accepted internships for the 1973–74 school year. Hayward Unified hired fellow student Peter for less than half the salary of a regular psychologist. That was okay for him. He was single. A year-long internship would provide me additional experience and boost my confidence to administer the Wechsler Intelligence Scale for Children, the Stanford-Binet, and other IQ tests. But the $6,000 annual intern pay wouldn't allow us to buy a house until after Antonio completed his master's degree and found work. Who knew when that would be? In between writing term papers, I wrote to more districts suggesting they hire me.

I now worked five days a week, was enrolled full-time in a graduate program, and had two young children. My youngest son had almost died, and my car *had* died. Pressures mounted. Final exams loomed at the same time we searched for a house. With the end-of-the-year strains at work, my plate was full—too full. Life became super stressful. I told others and myself that I could do it all—work, study, look for a house and a job, and still be the calm mother my sons needed.

My mantra became, "Nothing is worth losing my mind over." But I wondered how long I'd stay sane.

Just when I thought I couldn't manage juggling the demands anymore, I got lucky.

Lucky Me

On a Saturday in early March 1973, I was busy in the kitchen of our Evelyn Avenue home mixing a quart of powdered milk with a quart of regular milk. The kids could tell when I'd altered their milk and didn't like it. We hadn't qualified for food stamps since I'd graduated from UC Berkeley. My frugality saved us grocery money. The phone rang. I sprinted into the living room to answer.

"Congratulations," a voice said, "You're a winner."

Thinking the call was another offer about "a fabulous time share opportunity in Puerto Vallarta," I almost hung up. But the "winner" reference intrigued me. I stayed on the line.

"You've won a three-day Princess Cruise to Mexico," the man said. "We selected your entry from the contest box at the Jaguar dealership."

I searched my memory and recalled the January Saturday when I'd stuffed the raffle box with entries while Antonio and Romualdo looked at cars they couldn't afford. Elated that Lady Luck had again graced me, I whispered the wonderful news to Antonio who'd stopped watching basketball on TV to listen in on the call.

"Ask if we can get the money instead," my husband whispered in my ear.

My joy turned to chagrin. I knew we could use the money for our car or eventual house payments, but I needed this trip. Everything I'd been through recently—Timothy's three-day hospital stay, my return to full-time work, and the pressure to complete the last twelve credits for my psychology credential—had me near the breaking point. Add to those strains the responsibility of maintaining a functioning

household with two young children. No. I deserved a childfree weekend away on a ship. Nevertheless, I saw Antonio's point.

"Can I forego the cruise," I said, in a flat, monotone voice, "and
receive the money?"

"No substitutions," the man said. "We'll send you the details by
mail. Congratulations again."

Weightlessness entered my body. I did a little dance. This was the
respite I needed from my current life strains just when I needed it
most. I deserved this reward.

The award letter said the three-day cruise, over a weekend in
April, would sail from a port near Los Angeles. The prize included
free airfare to Long Beach, four hundred miles south of Albany. We'd
be whisked from Long Beach to the port of San Pedro where *The
Spirit of London* cruise ship was docked. In three days, the ship would
sail around the islands of Santa Catalina and San Clemente, dock in
Ensenada, Mexico, and return to its US port. Perfect. We both spoke
Spanish, so time in Mexico suited us. I began preparations.

My mother agreed to take the boys for the three days. The Jaguar
company would pay for everything. I couldn't wait. But Antonio
balked. He said he had schoolwork, classes, and teaching assistant
duties to consider. I swallowed hard and felt heavy again.

My husband didn't care that we'd never taken a vacation away from
our children since Timmy had been born. True, we'd taken Tony to
Disneyland and traveled to several state parks with both boys. But
most of our excursions the past few years had involved camping in
the woods along Northern California's Eel River with Antonio's good
friend, Romualdo, and his family. Preparing beans and hot dogs over
a smoky fire and sleeping in bags on the hard ground couldn't com-
pare with delicious meals and soft bunks on a swaying ocean liner. I
wanted us to take this mini vacation cruise. I needed time away from
mothering and work. I'd earned it.

"I think Peter in my classes at Cal State would accompany me," I
said, trying to make Antonio jealous.

But he wasn't the jealous type. He remained steadfast in his decision not to go. No one ever spent money on cruises where he'd been raised. I was heartbroken that my husband would deny me time with him away from all our daily hassles. Then, I thought of a bargain he might agree to that would also please me.

"If I can get my weight down to a hundred twenty pounds, would you go?" I said, knowing how hard it would be to reduce my post-baby body down to my wedding weight.

Antonio had never commented on the twenty-five pounds I'd gained since bearing his children. My excess girth bothered me more than it did my thin husband. But I aspired to fit into my pre-pregnancy size ten clothes. Three months after Timothy's birth, I'd already dropped twelve of the twenty-five pounds I'd gained. I had confidence I could lose the last thirteen. Antonio looked skeptical.

A new program called Weight Watchers met at a nearby shopping center. I joined. The plan required eating liver once a week, drinking nonfat milk, and making my own catsup. Sacrificing the confections I loved showed on the scale at the Saturday morning meetings. Now, though, I'd have to lose the weight even faster.

"You can't lose another thirteen pounds," Antonio said, "in the six weeks before the April trip. But if you can, I'll go."

He underestimated my resolve and my cunning. Between my work, school, and home duties, I had little time to eat. As long as I didn't succumb to the ever-present tasty pastries in the school faculty lounges, I would see success on my scale prior to the cruise. A stress eater who went for sweets, this time I had an important deadline to meet.

The week before we were to leave on our trip, I got on my scale in the privacy of our bathroom. My mouth dropped open—the dial registered 122 pounds, two over the agreed-upon goal. Unbelievable. I'd tried so hard. Now Antonio might not accompany me. I jiggled the scale's adjustment dial. Like magic, my weight registered at 120 pounds. The number impressed Antonio when we did the official weigh-in later. I felt light again.

༄

I had a marvelous trip lounging on the ship's deck wearing one of the three new form-fitting outfits I'd sewn for the occasion. I'd been near exhaustion trying to manage a multitude of responsibilities. Now I unwound. Antonio was more relaxed than I'd seen him in months. He took photos of the seals on San Clemente Island and gobbled up the plentiful food on the ship. After months of starving myself, I too ate whatever I wanted. I enjoyed all of it—especially the desserts. This trip had come at the right time.

We spoke Spanish when we arrived in Mexico. It was almost like being back where we'd met in Peru. We acted like the two honeymooners we'd been seven years before. A shoeshine boy polished our shoes in Ensenada for a few pesos. Antonio insisted on giving him a big tip. I think he saw himself in the boy. We bought a piñata for Tony's next birthday. We watched movies in the ship's theater and took romantic strolls along the deck in the moonlight.

Neither of us drank alcohol or took part in the gambling happening in the lounge. Our eyes bulged to see fellow cruisers lose hundreds of dollars on a single bet over a fake frog race. We splurged on a photo of us—two slim thirty-one-year-olds in front of a huge ocean liner.

Antonio never said he regretted going on the cruise. I think he felt at home in the Spanish-speaking country on our southern border. The time away rejuvenated me enough to face the challenge of finding a new job and buying a house.

Evelyn on the Deck of
The Spirit of London

A Home of Our Own

On a warm summer Sunday afternoon in June 1973, Antonio backed our Mazda down our friends' driveway and onto Darwin Drive in Fremont. We waved good-bye to our friends Monica, Federico, and their two youngsters. I could still taste the smoke from the barbequed hamburgers we'd eaten.

We often visited our friends after they purchased their Fremont home in 1970. Tall, thin, blond Monica and I had volunteered weekends to take a census of migrant workers in the Central Valley near Fresno with Cesar Chavez, when we both attended Holy Names College. That's where I first became enamored with the warmth of the Latino culture. Monica had joined the Peace Corps in 1965, a year after me. During her two-year commitment, she taught math in Costa Rica in the same high school where Federico taught Latin, Spanish, and French.

Unlike me, Monica had returned to California unmarried. Brown-haired Federico, slim and several inches shorter than Monica, followed her back to the US and asked her to marry him. They wed in January 1967. Monica and I renewed our friendship soon after. We now had the Peace Corps, Latino husbands, and young children in common.

What we didn't have in common was working husbands. Federico had come to California with a college degree and teaching experience. Nevertheless, he first worked the night shift in a cookie factory while he attended classes to earn his California teacher's certificate. He went to college in the daytime, earned his teaching certificate, and soon was teaching Spanish full-time in Bay Area middle and high schools. I never heard him say he wanted to return to his home country someday, like Antonio did.

Federico and Monica both taught fulltime while commuting (she, thirty-eight miles to Richmond and he, twenty miles to San Jose). Together, they earned enough to buy their house in Fremont. The couple had two cars and more money than Antonio and I had accrued. I too wanted a house like theirs.

"Monica says there's a new housing development at the end of Darwin Drive," I said as we drove down the street, "Let's stop by and see the models."

"We've already looked at lots of homes," Antonio said, sounding weary from standing over a smoking barbeque. "I have thirty miles to drive to get us back home."

"We need to find a house soon," I said, "so I can find a job in a nearby school district. I can't keep commuting across the Bay Bridge to San Francisco every day. If we move south of the Albany–Berkeley area, we might find a place we can afford and a job nearby for me."

Antonio had a change of heart and drove the ten blocks to the end of Darwin Drive and parked the car. We each grabbed a boy and went into the garage that served as the office for the Creekside Homes models. A rectangular table displayed diagrams of one-story ranch style houses with two, three, and four bedrooms.

"We're interested in looking at the biggest house you have," Antonio said taking charge of the hunt.

Whenever we looked at houses, Antonio said we should buy a large one. Over the past seven years we'd lived in one- and two-bedroom places, most without a yard or garage. I, too, wanted to spread out in an abode of our own, but thought a three-bedroom home adequate. I'd lived in a thirteen-room house growing up in Ismay.

My mother, three sisters, and I spent all day Saturdays cleaning it. A four-bedroom domicile would just mean more area for me to dust and vacuum.

"You're in luck," the balding salesman said, "we just had a four-bedroom house come back on the market for thirty-one thousand. The couple couldn't qualify."

All sixty-four residences in the Creekside development were new. Most had families already living in them. The salesman showed us the four-bedroom, partly finished model that measured 1,544 square feet. It had a living room, four reasonably sized bedrooms, two bathrooms, and a large room whose purpose wasn't clear to me. At one end of the twelve-by-eighteen-foot room were kitchen appliances—a dishwasher, built-in avocado-color double ovens, and an electric stove. At the other end was a large open space. I wondered what kind of furnishings I should put there.

The original buyers had selected the avocado-colored linoleum floor and a gold-and-mint mix shag carpet. I didn't care what colors they'd chosen. This place was palatial compared to the homes I'd lived in since leaving Montana. The boys ran through the home to pick out their bedrooms as if the house already belonged to us. Antonio examined a handful of soil from the back yard and said he could plant trees there. I began imagining how to fill the six rooms with the hand-me-down furniture from our present seven-hundred-square-foot rental home. We said we'd take the house.

We completed the Creekside Homes' purchase application and attached a check for the required $150 deposit. Our friends lived at the other end of the same street and my parents were seven miles south. We could afford this house if a bank would qualify us for a home loan. This was the right place for us.

The $12,000 a year I earned working full-time for the San Francisco Unified School District proved that we had a steady income. We cashed in our only savings, a $3,000 annuity, for the required 10 percent down payment. I was confident that the state must have forgiven my debt for their stipend, though I had no official letter from them.

San Francisco State took forever to verify Antonio's $920-a-year income as a teaching assistant. We had a hug fest with the boys when we received word that our combined incomes satisfied the bank. Now, because I didn't want to commute to San Francisco from Fremont, I needed to lock in childcare and a job closer to our new home. I approached my mother in the kitchen of her house in the Mission San Jose area of Fremont.

"Mom," I said the month before our scheduled move, "you know I have to work to make our house payments. Could you help with babysitting? I could drop Timothy off on my way to work and put Tony in first grade at Chadbourne Elementary near you. He could come to your house after school."

"You know," Mom said, washing a couple breakfast dishes and parsing her words, "I plan to retire soon and want to spend my time practicing the piano, gardening, and doing the things I've missed out on the past fifteen years when I worked."

"I know," I said in my most empathetic tone, "but Antonio has to go to San Francisco State daily for his classes. So he can't take care of the boys. I need someone dependable who can."

"I raised six children," Mom said, drying a bowl without looking at me, "and I don't plan to raise my grandchildren."

Mom loved my boys, even though I sensed she preferred girls. She had loved teaching her four female children the domestic skills she believed we'd need to be good housewives. She'd help her six children with whatever they needed, except regular childcare. Mom had earned a rest, but I felt her rejection in the pit of my stomach.

"I'll check with Carolyn across the street," Mom said. "She has a girl Timmy's age and might be interested in babysitting."

The next day Carolyn agreed to provide child care for me, and my stomach unknotted. My two-year-old would have a kind babysitter and a companion his age. My mother had come through for me. Now I needed a school district to do the same and employ me.

I'd applied to the Alum Rock Elementary School District, located in a predominantly Hispanic area of East San Jose. Each time I'd called during the past three months, Mr. Leonard of psychological services had said the school district might hire a Spanish-speaking school psychologist for the coming year. I called him for the fourth time in early July to find out if his district had approved the position in their 1973–74 budget. He invited me to come to San Jose for an interview. My heart leapt. If hired, I'd only have to commute twenty-two miles and not over a bridge. My interview went well.

The third week of July, Mr. Leonard offered me a full-time position with Alum Rock. I almost danced a jig while signing the San Jose district's contract. I submitted my resignation to San Francisco Unified. I'd miss my coworkers but not the commute. Everything was on schedule—except for the house.

I'd given notice to our Evelyn Avenue landlady that we'd be out by the end of August. The Creekside salesman called the week before we planned to move. The news was not good.

"You can stop packing," he said, "the builder finished the house and it's ready, but there's a delay with the city inspectors. We're likely looking at another month before you can move in."

"But we have to move now," I said, sashaying between packed boxes pulling the long cord of the phone behind me. I couldn't believe what I was hearing. "My job in San Jose starts on September fourth."

I pleaded, but the man didn't say much. Nevertheless, he must have sympathized with my plight. The week before school began, we received the keys to our new house. Someone at the Creekside office must have broken a few rules.

Dad, with Antonio's help, filled his truck with our bed, TV, dressers, and desk. Tony packed his books, toy dinosaurs, and animal puppets. Timmy helped by throwing his teddy bear and toy xylophone in a box. Then he came to help me pack his sippy cup with the dishes in the kitchen. Excitement mixed with chaos on moving day.

"I'll put the clothes from the closets in the Mazda," I said, opening the hatchback and filling it so full I couldn't see out the back window.

I said good-bye to the Berkeley–Albany area where we'd lived for the past five years. I wouldn't miss the foggy mornings and my commute to work across the Bay Bridge. But I would miss the ambiance of the college town.

A handful of soil in our new front yard sifted between Antonio's fingers. He lifted the dirt to his nose and breathed in the earthy smell. Then he got busy digging the trenches for an underground sprinkler system before the fall rains began. He studied the best time and type of seed for a lawn in our climate. He planted a peach and an apple tree in the backyard. His life on the hacienda below Machu Picchu made him a natural farmer. My doubts about his ability to maintain a home and yard vanished.

My sister Patti and her husband were about to sell a wood frame sofa and chair with removable cushions they didn't want. I bought it for our living room. Mom sewed eight new slipcovers for it, and we had a place to sit while we warmed by the fireplace.

The kitchen–family room was bigger than the converted storeroom where I'd lived during my Peace Corps years in Abancay, Peru. Nine years before, Marie and I had felt fortunate to find living quarters there with a concrete floor and nearby running water and toilets. Windows and a cooking shed had been bonuses. Now I was planning how to use the twelve-by-eighteen-foot room that comprised just our kitchen and eating areas. This one room was almost a quarter of our entire house space. And we had two indoor bathrooms and indoor running water. How my fortunes had changed!

We installed a decorative divider, castoff from my parents, to make a visual separation between the kitchen and the rest of the big combo room. The realtor said this new "open concept" design was in vogue and called a family room. I furnished the large extended space as our eating area. At a used furniture store, I found a rectangular oak table that expanded to nine feet, big enough for the fifteen members of my extended family and a few more. The table and its six heavy chairs helped fill the cavernous combo room.

Inexpensive drapes went across the sliding glass door that led to the patio near the kitchen sink. I sewed curtains for all four bedrooms. We bought the latest fad, a waterbed, for Tony. I wallpapered his room with a sports theme of balls—football, basketball, soccer, and tennis. Timothy imitated his airplane wallpaper by zooming toy planes around in it. Our room and master bath I painted blue. The boys now had their own bathroom where they bathed every night in the tub.

We converted the large fourth bedroom into a place to watch TV. Scores of Peruvian decorations I'd brought back in my trunks seven years before now found places on our walls, floors, and dressers. A large alpaca rug covered a wall near the long family room table and made that portion of the open room feel more inviting. A small round alpaca rug graced the TV room. An Inca-design cloth covered a bureau. The blue *montera* hat decorated a passageway wall. We had it all—even a double garage for our single car. Our place was coming together within our tight budget. We were living the American dream.

The neighborhood contained friendly working-class and semipro-fessional people. On one side of us lived newlyweds. He worked as a technical illustrator for Ford Aerospace, and she was a stay-at-home wife and cake-decorator who sometimes took a substitute teaching job. On the other side, we became good friends with an African American couple and their son, Jason, two years older than Timmy.

Teddy, the father, was a baggage handler for United Airlines, and Thelma, the mother, a receptionist for a local spice company. Teddy and Thelma installed a swimming pool in their backyard before the fences went up. They invited our kids to frequent their pool, with or without Jason in it.

One weekend in October, the men of the neighborhood finished building the fences around our homes. After the neighborhood pot-luck dinner, I gathered the remains of my sausage casserole from the makeshift table in my next-door neighbor's garage. I looked at the woman who collected the remnants of the salad she'd brought and knew she lived on the other side of my back fence. About then, I heard the men pound the final boards of our mutual enclosure into place.

"I guess I won't be seeing you again," I said, half-joking.

She smiled. For the seven years we lived on Darwin Drive, I never again interacted with my fenced-off backyard neighbor. That was the way in suburban California.

New Jobs

O ur lives settled into a routine after the rush of moving into our new home in Fremont. Most mornings, Antonio caught a bus to the closest Bay Area Rapid Transit (BART) station, took the train to San Francisco, then jumped on a bus again to arrive at his graduate school classes at San Francisco State College. When I'd lived in Peru, most everyone I knew, including Antonio, depended on public transportation. Living in the Bay Area suburbs, I used our only car, while buses and trains again had to be Antonio's main mode of transportation.

I drove the Mazda to southern Fremont where I dropped Tony and Timothy at Carolyn's. This tall, friendly mother of two greeted the boys as I ushered them out of the car. She would see Tony off to his first-grade class five blocks away, then engage Timmy and her youngest daughter in reading storybooks, playing with Legos, or watching *Sesame Street.*

I waved to my mother who watered baskets of magenta-colored fuchsias hanging from her front porch across the street. Mom smiled and waved back. She had found an attentive caregiver for my boys, which I appreciated. I couldn't blame her if she didn't want to babysit her grandsons. Mom enjoyed tending her plants more than caring for two active grandkids. She could pop over to Carolyn's if she wanted to see my boys. Mom had raised six children. Soon to retire as a police clerk, she wanted to spend her remaining years doing what she loved—gardening, practicing the piano, and attending daily Catholic mass.

Mom had been raised a Protestant and converted to Catholicism before her wedding. Her devotion to her new religion was more fervent than Dad's. When each of her six children were born, she made certain we completed all the church's milestones—baptism at one month, first communion at seven, and confirmation around twelve. She wished for all her children to continue with the traditional Catholic rituals and marry a Catholic partner in a Catholic church in a Catholic wedding ceremony.

To supplement her religious teaching in our youth, each summer Mom arranged for young men, who were studying to become priests, to teach religion in our small Montana town. These seminarians instructed us on how to be model Catholics. For two weeks Ismay's twelve Catholic children sweltered in a classroom learning about sin, and sometimes sex.

We memorized the approved prayers, learned the appropriate Catholic rituals, and listened to records explaining male and female differences. After learning about venial and mortal sins, we recited an Act of Contrition so the priest could forgive us in confession for having committed one or the other.

I'd won rosaries when I raised my hand to say I'd never committed a mortal sin or that I wanted to become a nun. Because of the classes and Mom's supplemental teachings, I was well versed in the seven deadly sins, the eight beatitudes, and the Ten Commandments.

Mom believed a family that prays together stays together, so we said our prayers every evening and recited the rosary together every Saturday. Threats of going to hell or purgatory helped our parents keep our unacceptable behaviors in check. We sacrificed eating candy for the seemingly endless six weeks of Lent. The promise of heaven kept us praying and seeking to become holier every day.

Dad did his part to impart his religion by driving us to Sunday mass. When the time came for me to go to high school, he arranged that I attend the Catholic Sacred Heart High School in Miles City. There, sixty miles away from home, I lived in apartments with a different roommate every year. From ages thirteen to sixteen, I endured rain and snow to attend daily mass. When I was sixteen and we moved to California, I lived at home and attended public high school. I resumed immersion in Catholicism when I attended College of the Holy Names.

I had attended mass on Sundays and sometimes during the week when I lived in Abancay, Peru. I sought solace and guidance in Abancay's confessionals as I was falling in love with Antonio. When I wrote to Mom about Antonio, her first question was, "Is he Catholic?" I wrote back that he was a kind, good person—and a Catholic. I think she cared more about his religion than his character.

Antonio had been raised a Catholic but seemed less dedicated than I was about his faith. His mother was as devout as mine, so she made certain he completed the same Catholic milestones I had. However, he once confessed that he went to Sunday mass to be with me, not because it was required. One of his best friends was Padre Gálvez, who officiated at our wedding.

The announcement I sent to Mom—that I would be marrying in Peru before returning to California—upset her. Too bad Mom couldn't have been present in the ancient Spanish chapel in Cusco, Peru, for my wedding mass. I was the only one of her six children who was married by a priest, inside a Catholic church in a traditional religious ceremony. Still, she said I'd set a bad example for my siblings by breaking the cardinal rule of no sex before marriage. Once married, I followed my husband's lead in religion more than my mother's.

Antonio had stopped attending mass with Tony and me when he began his busboy job and had to work late on Saturday nights. On Sundays, he slept in while Tony and I walked to nearby St. Joachim's

Church in Hayward. But as my toddler grew, he became increasingly restless during the service. He refused to sit still and climbed all over the pews. When I could no longer keep Tony quiet, I ceased Sunday church attendance. I didn't wish to waste Sunday mornings wrestling with my son while looking at the back of a priest who spouted Latin from the far-away altar. Too many sermons asked me to contribute more money to the church. I stopped attending mass around 1968 and didn't look back.

I'd begun complying with the Catholic milestones Mom held dear and had Tony baptized. She didn't approve when I stopped attending Sunday mass. To please her, I continued going on Christmas and Easter, but not every Sunday.

Pope John VI eventually instructed priests to face the congregation and speak in a language we could comprehend. Over the years, religion became less important for most of my Catholic-raised siblings and me than for our devout parents. I didn't argue with Mom about the importance of religion any more than I debated her belief in men as primary breadwinners. I did what I needed and wanted to do. For her part, Mom let me know that she prayed daily that I'd return to the church.

After dropping off the boys at Carolyn's, I continued twenty miles down the freeway to Alum Rock Elementary School District. There I consulted with teachers and administered achievement and IQ tests to elementary-school-age students exhibiting learning difficulties. I exchanged my sense of sadness at leaving my sons for the excitement of beginning a new profession as a school psychologist.

At lunchtime, I ate in the faculty lounge and consulted with teachers about their students. In the half hour we had, we sometimes touched on the role women were expected to play in education.

"I've yet to run into a female administrator in this district," I said to the teacher sitting next to me at the lunch table.

"Oh," the teacher said unwrapping her sandwich, "I could never work for a woman."

"At San Francisco Unified," I said, "we had women principals and females in administrative positions at the central office. Besides running schools, they were in charge of programs for behavior-disordered students, preschool, and pupil services."

"With a male principal I know someone experienced is in charge," the respected educator said.

I was about to point out that if women were never hired for administrative positions, they'd never accrue administrative experience. But the bell rang for class, and we left. She went off to collect her thirty fourth-graders from the playground. I departed to administer the Spanish version of the Wechsler IQ test to a third-grade, Spanish-speaking student unable to read in either Spanish or English.

Unlike the teacher, my fellow school psychologists were a forward-thinking group who welcomed me, a newly minted psychologist, into their ranks. They joked around, invited me to their parties, and shared their wisdom. And, since I had the most recent education in state laws affecting our profession, my colleagues designated me to be the psychologist to explain the new Education for All Handicapped Act to the district's school principals at their monthly meeting. I could do this.

I'd spoken in front of sizeable groups of parents in San Francisco. However, I'd never presented to school officials. The assignment to speak to the administrators in my new district gave me sleepless nights. For days I prepared what I'd say. Dennis, a veteran psychologist, agreed to accompany me to the meeting for moral support.

I tried to look official in my navy-blue suit and white blouse. My heart pounded, and my palms turned sweaty. I hoped I didn't look as uneasy as my churning stomach suggested. The cacophony of twenty males talking sounded like a bunch of magpies arguing over a plum. I entered the walnut-paneled meeting room eager to get my part over with.

"Good afternoon," I began. "I'm on your agenda for a few minutes to inform you about important changes you need to know that will keep your school in compliance with new legislation."

The talking didn't subside. They hadn't heard me. It was important that these school leaders be familiar with their new responsibilities. I increased my volume.

"The recent law," I said in an authoritative voice, "says each student with a disability is entitled to a free and appropriate education. What that means for you administrators . . ."

The men continued their own lively discussions. I even heard laughter. My face became warm and moisture gathered in my armpits. Frustrated, I turned to Dennis and handed him my notes. This experience had been humiliating.

"Here," I said, "maybe they'll listen to you."

Dennis began, using the same words I'd used. The room quieted. Why hadn't they stopped to listen to me? I saw the veteran teacher's point. People took men more seriously than their female counterparts, even if the women were better prepared and informed. The same phenomenon had been true in Peru where competent women, even ones who'd sacrificed children and marriage to further their careers in education, weren't awarded the administrative jobs for which they were qualified. But I had to live with the workplace inequities a few more years until more of us protested.

∾

The friendly veteran Alum Rock psychologists taught me what I needed to know about assessing students' qualifications for special education classes and writing psychological reports. I learned to observe the strategies students used in arranging the red and white blocks or completing the mazes portion of the WISC IQ tests I administered. In conferences with parents and staff, I followed my colleagues' examples and supported my conclusions with test data.

School personnel and administrators found my recommendations more believable when I backed them up with achievement and IQ test scores, as opposed to behavioral observations alone. Before, when I'd worked as a school social worker, I'd provided similar explanations for students' behaviors as now. But my insights had more credibility as a psychologist because I provided test data. For example, if I told a teacher that I'd seen how confused a student was in viewing a complex drawing on the blackboard, she'd look doubtful. If I showed her the student's below average score on the blocks subtest of the Wechsler Intelligence Scale, she could see my point. She then simplified her drawing and added a clearer verbal explanation to help the pupil understand the concept. I believed in observations as much as test scores, but now I was competent to offer both types of analyses.

Alum Rock's administration instituted programs that had the potential to enhance students' classroom behavior and participation. The superintendent of schools arranged for support staff, head teachers, and administrators to be trained in a new program called "The Magic Circle." At all-day in-service trainings, we learned techniques for conducting class meetings in ways that encouraged every student's participation. The informal, friendly atmosphere of the practice sessions allowed me to connect with many personnel in the district. During one of the conversation circles, I got to know a teacher married to a Latin American partner. Our friendship continued for decades after this first introduction.

The benevolent workplace provided me the confidence I needed as a fledgling first-year school psychologist. And there were additional monetary benefits. During the summer hiatus, the district hired me to test and identify students for their mentally gifted classes. I used the money to further my own and my children's music education.

The extra money I earned administering the Stanford-Binet IQ tests, enabled us to purchase the piano I longed for. Mom had arranged for lessons when I was seven, and I continued them until age fourteen. I was given top billing in Ismay's piano recitals. When I'd lived in Peru, Antonio loved hearing me play *Nola, Anitra's Dance,* and *Clair de Lune,* on a piano at a mutual friend's home. I worked extra in 1974 to afford my own piano.

Antonio's college classes were on hiatus, so he watched the boys on the summer mornings I did the gifted testing. We picked out the piano together. He said the spinet model had to be sturdy enough to survive being shipped to Peru when we moved there. I went along with his opinion still wondering when and how our move to Peru would take place. In Montana, performing at piano recitals had caused me anxiety. In Peru, it was a way to feel Antonio's love and admiration. Now it was a way to relax after a hard day's work.

Antonio graduated with a master's degree in physics from San Francisco State in June 1974, eight years after he'd begun his college studies in the US. He never shared his grades with me, so I didn't know how he did. Good grades or bad, we both expected he'd soon have a full-time job. In anticipation of his earnings, I asked Alum Rock to decrease my workweek for the 1974–75 school year. I longed to spend more time at home with my children, now ages seven and three.

My being home for our sons was less important to Antonio than to me. I'd have resented my husband's attitude more if I had wanted to be a full-time mom. But I didn't. I wanted both a career and more time with my sons. The only way to accomplish that was if Antonio worked full-time and I worked part-time. I asked to work three days a week.

Alum Rock granted my request. But I had been too optimistic. Antonio had difficulty getting hired. He applied to the Lawrence Livermore Laboratory, which advertised many jobs for physics majors. No luck. The lab couldn't consider him. US citizenship was required for a security clearance. He had never applied for US citizenship because he didn't want to give up his Peruvian citizenship. He said we would return to live there some day. I wasn't surprised. I knew Antonio missed his homeland but I questioned how we'd survive in Peru.

Antonio obtained a community college teaching credential and applied to teach math and physics at many Bay Area community colleges. His numerous interviews didn't yield a job. From his reports, I knew he didn't know how to emphasize his talents. Americans expected self-promotion. He believed in facts, so he wouldn't embellish or exaggerate his resume in any way. I admired his insistence on honesty, but it wasn't getting him work. His slight Spanish accent might also have been a deterrent to being hired. Whatever the reason, he must not have impressed those who conducted the hiring. A week after each interview, he received the same response: "Thank you but we chose someone else."

I admired Antonio's truthfulness, but his failure to advocate for himself meant he had less chance than his competition for the available jobs. When no place had employed my self-effacing husband by the end of the summer, I knew I'd have to return to full-time work.

I learned that Fremont Unified School District was hiring psychologists. I thought I would add two days' there to my three days at Alum Rock. Working near home meant two days I wouldn't need to commute. Less driving meant more time at home with my sons. I called the district.

"Yes, I'll hold for Mrs. McGee," I said, eager to discover a new possibility.

Mrs. McGee, director of student services for Fremont, was in charge of hiring psychologists for the FUSD schools. Antonio stood next to me at our kitchen wall phone. I waited with bated breath.

"Yes, Fremont Unified has openings for a psychologist," Mrs. McGee said when she came on the line. "Tell me a bit about your background."

"I've completed a year as a bilingual school psychologist in San Jose and three as a school social worker in San Francisco," I said letting my breath flow easier. "I am currently scheduled to work three days a week for Alum Rock District. But I'd like to work closer to home."

Antonio could hear the positive interaction. As always, he appeared more interested in my employment opportunities than his. He had an idea.

"Why don't you ask if Fremont has a full-time position?" he whispered. "That way you don't have to commute at all."

Great idea. I did. They did. No longer would I need to drive twenty miles each way to work. As with San Francisco Unified, I hated to leave the close friendships I'd formed. But it was more important to work near my sons. And the 1974–75 school year found me working full time as a bilingual school psychologist in the city where I lived.

Mrs. McGee assigned me to the school in my neighborhood plus three others. However, working and living in the same community had disadvantages. If I took a "mental health day," I'd run into school personnel when shopping at local businesses. And I encountered a parent problem.

The third-grade girl who lived across the street from us had difficulties learning math. Her teacher referred her for testing. I requested permission from the girl's mother to administer the required psychological and academic tests. Her mother refused. She didn't want me, her neighbor, to investigate her daughter's problem. I was an acquaintance, not the girl's shrink. Chastened, I asked another psychologist to test the girl and returned to my role as neighbor.

∾

Colleges turned Antonio down in interview after interview. Then, Gavilan Community College in Gilroy, a city south of San Jose, hired him as a part-time math teacher for women returning to school. Finally, someone recognized my husband's capabilities. I whispered a soft prayer of thanks to an unknown power.

Taking a bus for the fifty-mile commute wasn't practical, and I needed the Mazda for my work. We'd have to buy a second car. This time, Antonio selected it—a new, bright red Fiat coupe with reasonable gas mileage. We finally had use for our two-car garage. But driving an hour each way three days a week to teach a total of three math courses paid for little more than the gas the car used. Then one Monday in November, I received an unexpected phone call.

"Your husband is on the line," Edwina, the school secretary of Fremont Elementary School, said. "He sounds agitated."

"I've been in an accident," Antonio said, sounding frazzled. "A car behind me didn't stop and hit the rear of my Fiat."

"Oh, no!" I said, "Are you all right?"

"I think so," my newly employed spouse said, "but the guy dented the back of the car pretty bad."

"Will it run? Or should I come and get you?"

"The car is pretty dented in back but still runs. When I called the college to say I'd be late, they canceled my classes for the day. I'm coming home."

Antonio said he was all right. But he hadn't escaped injury. For months afterward he had headaches from the whiplash he'd suffered. The car was repaired sooner than he was.

The following quarter he found teaching jobs at community colleges closer to home, but he continued to earn little from the part-time employment. My work allowed us to make our house and car payments.

I wanted more help from my husband with cooking and other household chores. But he interpreted my requests for assistance as nagging, became sullen, and stopped communicating. Something was changing in my caring husband. Antonio continued to do the yard work and search for more teaching hours. Despite the years spent in higher education, we'd achieved the reverse of what we'd gone to school for: Antonio worked part time and I held down a full-time job. Fortunately, we were soon in for a pleasant surprise.

Revisiting Peru

The phone rang on Saturday morning on May 31, 1975. The static on the line alerted me that it must be a call from overseas. When I heard the familiar voice, I motioned for Antonio to pick up our other phone.

"I'll be coming to the United States next week," Adolfo Eguiluz, Antonio's stepfather said on the other end. "The US State Department awarded me a scholarship to attend a four-day seminar in New York City for newspaper editors from Latin American countries. I'll come visit you afterward."

"That's nice," Antonio said, "but you know we live on the other side of the United States."

"That's no problem," Adolfo said. "I've arranged to fly to San Francisco after the seminar and stay for a week."

We'd heard from Antonio's family a few times a year since we'd left Peru in 1966. I'd sent birth announcements when each of our sons arrived and occasional letters with photos of our family enclosed. The Eguiluzes responded with letters filled with greetings and congratulations. Every Christmas I mailed gifts to whichever Peruvian city Antonio's parents had moved to. A change in cities meant Adolfo had changed jobs again. Adolfo, Livia, and their three children, ages ten to nineteen, now lived in the southern Peruvian city of Arequipa where Adolfo was editor of the major newspaper.

❧

Adolfo arrived bearing gifts for everyone. My parents welcomed him with hospitality, even though they could communicate only through my translations. My mother remarked that Adolfo looked dashing in his snappy sports coat and stylish ascot scarf.

Antonio and I had to work the week of his visit, so for a couple days, Adolfo accompanied me to some of the Spanish bilingual classes I served. A first-grade teacher lowered a map to show the location of Peru to her class. The country wasn't there—or on any map she pulled down. She could find Central American countries and pointed below them to where Peru would be. Geographical education in my local schools fell short. Embarrassed, the teacher apologized. Adolfo was offended that his country wasn't represented on any school maps.

One workday, when my father-in-law stayed home, he rearranged the thirty cans of food in my bottom cupboard. He said he'd never seen such an array of stored food and thought we had too many. In Peru, the hired help or Antonio's mother went to the market daily to buy fresh food. I'd done much the same when I lived there. I had purchased hot dogs in cans before I knew how to buy meat at Abancay's open market. My neighbor had used the emptied cans for a new roof on his house. Peruvians rarely used canned foods.

Adolfo hugging Timmy

My father-in-law had brought his caring culture with him. Evenings, Adolfo cuddled with his two grandsons. Timmy loved Adolfo's affection without hesitation. Tony stood back at first to evaluate his brother's reaction before he too succumbed to this new grandfather's affections. Adolfo reminded me of the warmth of Latinos—and how cold Antonio had become with the pressures of his job search and the fast pace of life in the US.

On the weekend, we showed Adolfo around the San Francisco Bay Area. We basked in the light of his genuine feelings of fondness. Antonio became more animated than I'd seen him in years when they discussed political happenings in Peru. He relished news of the cousins he'd grown up with. When Adolfo flew home after the week, he took the ardor of the Peruvian culture with him.

An emotional void filled our home. I suggested to Antonio that we visit his family during our upcoming summer vacation since neither of us had work obligations. He said we couldn't afford the trip, which was true. Besides, he preferred to visit his homeland after achieving some success in the US. He'd never planned to return to Peru jobless. But he had to agree with me that his mother would love to see her only grandchildren.

After a week discussing our options, I convinced my husband we could take out a loan from our credit union for the trip. Antonio had a current Peruvian passport and a green card. The boys and I obtained one passport for all three of us. I purchased tickets on Braniff Airlines and mailed a letter to Arequipa the third week of June to tell the family that we'd arrive there the morning of July 11. We landed in Arequipa to a surprise.

No one was at the airport to greet us. Three weeks before, I'd written to tell the Eguiluzes the day and time our plane would land in Arequipa. Mail between the US and Peru took a minimum of three weeks to arrive, the same amount of time it had taken when I'd lived there nine years before.

"You're where?" my father-in-law shouted through the receiver of the pay phone at the Arequipa airport.

Antonio held the phone away from his ear. I cursed under my breath, tired from the twelve-hour flight. Not a great beginning to our first trip back to Antonio's homeland.

"We're at the Arequipa airport," my husband said over the noise in the bustling facility. "We'll get a taxi and find you if you give me your address."

The Eguiluzes had moved many times and didn't always tell us where. When we'd married, Adolfo and Livia Eguiluz had lived with their three children in Abancay, near Cusco. Two years later, Adolfo moved the family to Arequipa, where his political party had appointed him editor of the city newspaper. They'd moved from one rented home to another. This time we knew the correct city, just not the street.

I could understand why the family would move from the cold, mountainous Cusco area to warm, level Arequipa. The two major cities of Peru were opposites in many ways. Cusco was freezing in the June and July months of the South American winter. I'd never seen snow on its cobblestone streets, but the thin air at twelve thousand feet made me shiver and gasp for breath. Cusco's local population stood at 143,000 and had increased less than 50 percent since Antonio had last lived there in 1966. Tourists filled the city year-round on their way to see the market at Pisaq or the Incan ruins of Machu Picchu or Sacsayhuamán. The latter site, outside Cusco, consisted of multi-ton granite boulders stacked on top of one another like a rock fence belonging to giants. The Incan stone walls were impressive—but gray, cold, and gloomy when dark clouds and rain rolled in.

Arequipa, at 7,660 feet, bustled with manufacturing and commerce. Since I'd first visited in 1965, the city's population had doubled to over 300,000, due to work in its wool, food, and construction industries. An old convent and a few archeological sites were the only places for its few tourists to visit. *La Ciudad Blanca*, the white city, as Arequipa was called, had many downtown buildings constructed of the white lava stone mined from the symmetrical mountain, El Misti, that towered over it. And Arequipa was sunny three hundred days a year. I felt comfortable in this warm, architecturally diverse, modern city.

∾

The cab dropped us off near the city center at the street number Adolfo had given us. My father-in-law flew downstairs to greet us with fervent embraces. Livia, my mother-in-law, and her children followed in quick succession. Their warm welcome conveyed better than their few letters, that we had been missed. Their affection went straight to my heart. I'd forgotten how loved Antonio's family and culture made me feel.

"I mailed you a letter to say we were coming," I said to Adolfo, tearing myself out of his too-tight squeeze, "over three weeks ago. Right after you left California. Didn't you get it?"

"No," Adolfo said unconcerned, "but I'm sure it will arrive any day now."

Much had changed since Antonio and I had left Peru. His black-haired, brown-eyed younger brothers had been little boys in 1966. Adolfito had grown from a plump six-year-old child into a slim, handsome, long-haired fifteen-year-old adolescent. Ricardo, a year old when we left, was now ten—two years older than our Tony.

Adolfito and Ricardo hauled our four suitcases up to their second story flat. Adolfo left to go borrow enough beds to accommodate his four unexpected visiting relatives. Livia instructed Brigida, the same kitchen helper they'd employed in Abancay, to put the tea kettle on. I gave Brigida a big hug.

Patricia, Antonio's half-sister, grasped my boys' hands and ushered them up the stairs. Patricia, now nineteen, had been ten when I'd last seen her. Still stick thin, she was now an attractive, budding woman with the wavy black hair and the brown eyes of her mother. Patricia, Livia, and Brigida smothered the boys with Peruvian affection. Livia, overcome with emotion, shed tears of joy and held onto her only grandchildren until they protested.

Love enveloped us and made up for the long lapses in communication over the past years. Contentment flowed through me like a warm bath. I needed this infusion of caring. Maybe we all did. The family's attention made up for my husband's coolness toward me over the many past months when he'd unsuccessfully looked for a full-time job.

As each job possibility back in California had faded, the emotional chasm between us had deepened. His inability to support our family had made us both discontented. Letters stating, "Thank you for applying but . . ." could have filled an entire wall. Each rejection notice had lowered Antonio's self-confidence. My suggestions of where he might search for work and how to approach interviews didn't help. He interpreted my advice as further evidence of his incompetence. Our economic struggles in the US over the past years had diminished our expressions of passion. I wasn't certain our marriage would endure the strain. This return to his home country began to replenish the love we'd both lost. For at least the next month, we didn't need to think about jobs.

I embraced Arequipa and the affection shown us by Antonio's family and friendly culture. My husband laughed and joked with his siblings. He put his arm around me, like he'd done often in our ten years together. I bubbled with lightness as I relaxed in the country where we'd first fallen in love. Time with his caring family revitalized us both.

Invitations poured in. We had lunches and dinners at the impressive, modern homes of Adolfo's three brothers and three sisters. Unlike Adolfo, his siblings had worked in steady jobs for years and owned their own homes. Two older unmarried sisters had worked for decades in government jobs. All had fared well financially—except my father-in-law.

Adolfo's upper-middle-class parents had given early inheritances to all their children. They'd advised them to build secure futures with the money. Instead of buying a business or studying at a university like his siblings, Adolfo used his money to travel and explore the country. As a result, he had no occupation and depended upon politically awarded jobs, like head of the Food for Peace program in Abancay and the editorship of the Arequipa newspaper. He preferred jumping from job to job and having fun rather than being stuck in the same rut year after year. He said he'd enjoyed more freedom than his siblings. But depending on political handouts had a major disadvantage. Adolfo was out of work whenever his political party was out of office. Optimistic, he was certain sufficient income would roll in from any number of his latest money-making schemes.

Adolfo worried less about having enough funds for food and rent than did his wife. Yet he was too proud to allow Livia to work outside the home. The month we visited, Adolfo had a salary, so the family had a place to live. Several times before, however, they'd been forced to move when he couldn't pay their rent.

Between socializing and eating, I set about arranging our temporary lives in Antonio's country. I enrolled Timmy in a local preschool, thinking the morning classes would be an excellent opportunity for him to learn Spanish during our month-long stay. But on the first day, my heart broke at the sight of his tear-stained face looking out the window of the minibus that transported him to school. I decided against sending him. I had to be away from my sons for work during the school year. I didn't want any separation from them during the summer. Tony and Timmy would have to pick up Spanish by interacting with their young uncles. So I kept them with me—until Tony had a meltdown.

Tony, at age eight, was as headstrong as he'd ever been. He knew what he wanted and often fussed until he got it. As a preschooler he'd insisted on collecting all the different dinosaurs gas stations gave away. At age five, he'd persisted in his demands that I take him to see the animals at the Tilden Public Farm in Berkeley before he left for school.

His kindergarten teachers had been concerned when he'd thrown his finished projects in the garbage instead of turning them in. His latest obsession was Disney films.

"Mommy, I have to go back to California," my film aficionado son said halfway through our stay. "I have to see the movie, *One of Our Dinosaurs is Missing*."

The movie wasn't playing in Arequipa. I didn't keep up on the latest Disney film so didn't know when and where it had been released. I was incredulous that somehow my son knew this movie was out and insisted on seeing it.

"But we still have another two weeks here," I said. "You can see the movie when we return."

Tony remained his usual demanding self. Once he decided something, no one dissuaded him from his goal. Much like me. He whined endlessly wherever we went. No trips to parks or playgrounds substituted for the movie he wanted to see. His fussing interrupted my conversations with family. His demands were ruining my enjoyment of the trip. I was certain Antonio's relatives saw my son as spoiled. To have peace, I gave in.

Braniff Airlines could change Tony's return ticket and put him on a flight from Lima to San Francisco in two days. My sister Patti had offered to keep him whenever we needed her to. The Braniff ticket agent in Lima said they'd notify my sister of Tony's arrival. The flight attendants would look after him during the twelve-hour flight. I gave them Patti's phone number and I didn't call her on the expensive, undependable Peru-US phone lines.

A few days earlier, Antonio had flown alone to his hometown of Cusco to see colleagues and professors he'd known when he'd attended college there. As I prepared to take Tony to Lima to return to the US, I received a phone call from Cusco.

"The university here wants to hire me as a full-time physics teacher," Antonio said. He sounded uncertain and hopeful.

"I suppose it would give you some full-time teaching experience," I said, "and look good on your resume."

"One drawback," my job-seeking husband said. "Peru doesn't allow money to be sent outside the country."

Thoughts raced through my mind. We'd depended on my wages to pay most of our living expenses for much of our nine-year marriage. Antonio's earnings wouldn't be missed. Maybe teaching for a year in Peru would help him obtain employment in the States when he returned. His job in Peru wouldn't add to our income, but it might lift Antonio's spirits. Better yet—perhaps the boys and I could come live with him for a couple of years while he taught in his home country. And the kids would become fluent in Spanish.

"Maybe I could get a leave of absence from my job," I said. "The boys and I could come be with you after you find us a place to live."

"Then it's settled," Antonio said, sounding as though a burden had been lifted from his broad shoulders. "I'll tell them I can start as soon as I see you off to the States."

I loved Peru and the Latin value of a close-knit family. The boys were the ideal ages to learn a second language. I might get a part-time job teaching English at a school in Cusco, and Antonio could be the main breadwinner I'd always wanted him to be. Living in Peru now would be like being back in the Peace Corps, but this time with kids.

In Lima, I obtained a separate passport for Tony. But getting him through passport control at the International Airport turned out to be a nightmare. The authorities insisted that, since his father was a Peruvian citizen, Tony couldn't leave the country without some official papers that I didn't have. Adolfo came to my rescue and, after some fast talking and arm twisting, the authorities finally let Tony board his plane. I was relieved that my English-speaking, movie-seeking son wouldn't be detained in a country he felt no desire to stay in.

On August 9, 1975, my sister Patti and her husband Mark drove from their Berkeley home to meet Timmy and me at the San Francisco Airport. Antonio had seen us two off in Lima and then flown back to Cusco to begin his teaching job. I'd not seen Tony since we'd waved good-bye at the Lima airport when he'd flown to the US alone to see his movie. I hoped my eldest son was as excited to see us as I was to see him after our two-week separation.

"Where's Tony?" I asked Patti, not seeing him in the back seat of their Mazda.

"Where is Antonio?" Patti asked me, not seeing him with us.

"He stayed in Peru to teach at the university in Cusco," I said. "So, where are you hiding my son?"

"After taking him to see his movie," Patti said as we got into the car. "He wanted to stay with Mom and Dad in Fremont. But he almost didn't get to us at all."

"What do you mean?" I asked, disbelieving.

"An hour before he arrived, we received a call from someone at Braniff Airlines informing us that Tony's plane would arrive late. This baffled us because we hadn't known he was coming. We were surprised to hear the airline spokesman say that Tony was by himself and we'd need to pick him up at the airport."

"What?" I didn't believe my sister's words. "The personnel at Braniff in Lima promised to phone you from Peru that he was coming."

"They did—but I don't think it was from Lima. I think they called from San Francisco just before he arrived. It's good that we were home."

I was mortified to realize that not only had I sent my eight-year-old alone on a twelve-hour international flight, but I hadn't double-checked to make certain they'd told my sister he'd be coming like they'd promised.

I hadn't called Patti because I believed the airlines could get through on Peru's phone lines easier than I. Apparently, that hadn't been the case. I shook my head in dismay.

The disappointment over this undependable and irresponsible aspect of Peruvians rekindled my memories of the many times in the Peace Corps I'd been promised a ride that came hours after the appointed time. Or not at all. But this current fiasco had endangered my son. In a flash I imagined what harm might have come to my first-born. Chills cascaded down my spine. My breath caught in my throat. How careless and impulsive I'd been. I hoped Tony hadn't suffered.

When Timmy and I picked up Tony from my parents, he didn't look traumatized by his experience. Patti had taken him to a double feature showing two films he wanted to see—*One of Our Dinosaurs is Missing* and *The Apple Dumpling Gang*. He had spent a week being pampered by my childless sister, then another week playing with children his age in my parents' neighborhood.

However, he wouldn't be pleased with my latest news. Now I'd have to tell him that we'd soon return to Peru. This time for a year or more.

Parenting Alone

In August 1975, Antonio began teaching physics at the Universidad Antonio Abad in Cusco. The boys and I waited in Fremont for word that he'd found a place for our family to live together in his hometown. If we couldn't join him to live in Cusco, I feared our union might not survive. We'd grown apart over his past year of unsuccessful job hunting. His ardor and mine had only recently been rekindled while visiting Peru.

I missed my husband's affection and yearned for someone who could help raise our boys and maintain the house. The hasty decision to uproot our lives made me worry.

What would our lives be like living in the third world country? Could Tony and Timmy learn enough Spanish to succeed in school in Cusco? Would the quality of education in Peruvian schools help or hurt our gifted sons?

Feelings of loss and trepidation overwhelmed me. I needed all the fortitude I could gather to carry on in the face of our uncertain future. A sense of duty guided my emotional bearings and furnished the strength I needed to provide for and nurture our sons on my own. I leaned on the support of my parents now more than ever.

Another of my mother's neighbors, Jan, requested to babysit Timothy. She had a son, Brian, the same age. Jan had enrolled her four-year-old in Mrs. Greig's preschool and she could take both boys to the morning session and care for them in the afternoon. Timmy liked Brian. He'd taught him how to tie his shoes. Mrs. K had taken excellent care of Timmy, but Jan's offer of school and a male playmate seemed like the best arrangement for my youngest son.

I proceeded to coordinate my boys' childcare and school attendance, like I'd always done. I kept Tony, now in third grade, in our neighborhood school where he'd gone the previous year. I hung a key around his neck so he could let himself into the house after the school bus dropped him off at the corner of Darwin Drive. My oldest son was bright and responsible. He'd be fine alone for a couple hours before I returned home with his brother. After all, he'd flown from Lima to San Francisco by himself.

While studying at UC Berkeley in 1968, Antonio and I had become fast friends with an Italian couple, Michele and Angela Bruni. The day after I returned home from our visit to Peru, Michele called to say he'd arrived in Berkeley from Italy and would spend the fall semester at UCB conducting research and writing his doctoral dissertation. He'd been working to complete his PhD in economics since he and Angela had returned to Bologna in 1974. He was disappointed to miss Antonio but delighted to see Tony and Timothy. We renewed our friendship.

Michele had no means of transportation in Berkeley, and I didn't need two cars. So I offered him the use of Antonio's Fiat during his stay. In exchange, Michele offered to help me pass the new math course I needed for my lifetime K–9 Standard Teaching Credential. I enrolled at the UC Berkeley extension and asked Mom to watch the boys the evenings I had class. Michele tutored me each week. His friendship and assistance were a comfort and helped me pass the course.

⌒⌒

My boss, Mrs. McGee, assigned me to four elementary schools for the 1975–76 school year. In October, I requested a leave of absence from January to June of 1976 from my school position stating that I planned to join my husband in Peru. The school board approved my leave, and I began to make plans to rent out our Darwin Drive house. I believed Antonio would soon have a place for us to live in Cusco. I waited, anxious to hear what arrangements he had made.

I received few letters from Peru that fall. In the two he sent, Antonio sounded like he had settled into his new position as a physics professor. With his master's degree, he had more education in his field than any of the other instructors. His students had no textbooks, so everything they learned came from Antonio's spoken lectures and notations on the blackboard. They copied his words into notebooks. My husband appeared satisfied to be teaching a subject he loved in his native language. However, he encountered problems.

Students didn't prepare for their exams and Antonio often caught them cheating. They smuggled tiny books of information into the exam room, which they consulted during tests. He confiscated the books. Others wrote information they should have learned on their arms. Despite the challenges, my husband seemed to enjoy teaching. He had found his calling.

Antonio said he lived comfortably in his Aunt Lastenia's home. Both she and her adult son were excellent cooks and made many of the delicious Peruvian dishes like *ceviche, chicharrones,* and *anticuchos* that I'd ceased preparing when my life in the US became too hectic. I was disappointed that Antonio didn't say he'd found a home for us, or that he'd even searched for one. I wondered, *would we soon move to Peru or stay in California? Which country should I plan to live in?* In the meantime, I performed duties that Antonio should have been doing.

I bought and installed a swing set for the boys—which they rarely used. They preferred the more stable ones at the local playground, not ones that tipped when they swung back and forth. How to brace playground equipment eluded me.

With the boys' help, I mowed the front and back lawns instead of paying a gardener. I planted a climbing rose below the chimney in the front yard. As a child in Montana, I'd helped grow produce in our one-acre garden. I could maintain a California yard.

Without Antonio there to discourage me, I made the changes to the house I wanted. Dad used his masonry skills to construct a three-foot-high stone wall on the two open sides of our patio. I helped install the screens above it, and we had a useful room outside our kitchen–family room. Too late I saw that the enclosure blocked much of sunlight to the kitchen. Antonio had predicted this before when he'd opposed enclosing the patio. Still, the patio was a handy place for the kids to play. When I'd not heard of plans for our family to live in Peru, I applied for a new job.

A full-time psychology position became available in one of the district's elementary schools. As in San Francisco, I preferred to have as much time in one school as possible. With five days a week in one school, I could provide counseling to students. The school had a high percentage of Hispanic students, so my fluency in Spanish put me in a good position for the job. But I wasn't selected. The interviewers said they thought I'd be leaving soon for Peru. I thought so, too. All of us were wrong.

The school year in Peru concluded in mid-December and Antonio came home for six weeks. He was thin and disoriented—caught between his two different worlds. He didn't talk much to anyone, including his Italian friend. Michele returned the Fiat, but Antonio didn't do much driving. He had nowhere to go. I wondered where we'd go—and if it would be together.

∾

Christmas with my parents was a joyous affair for me. We celebrated with my five siblings and their partners, my parents, my boys, their father, and Michele. Our Italian visitor showed more affection for Tony and Timmy than Antonio. Regardless, the boys loved having Antonio back.

Tony had been studying a special unit on health in his class. Typical of my serious son, he took the program to heart. He told his father he didn't want him to smoke anymore, and drew a poster showing a man lying on his back on the floor with a caption coming from his mouth that said, "I wish I'd never smoked." He posted his picture on the family room wall. I'd already insisted that Antonio smoke his few cigarettes per day outdoors in the enclosed patio he hadn't approved of. Between banishment outdoors to smoke and Tony's colorful admonition, Antonio stopped smoking.

His university contract obligated him to return to Cusco to continue teaching on February 1. I didn't object. I'd coped fine without him. Besides, a year's teaching experience would look better on his resume than four months. Although my husband assured me he'd continue his search for living accommodations for our family, I had my doubts.

Just after the boys and I bid Antonio good-bye, a friend in Peru informed me about an open position for director of the English Language Institute in Cusco. If I were awarded the job, our family could be together again. I applied and informed Antonio about the position.

In his March letter, Antonio encouraged me to take the post if the institute offered it. Instead of news about apartments where we could live, he said he was pursuing the documents I'd need to become a Peruvian citizen. And he'd searched for a plot of land where we could build a house. I interpreted his letter to mean he preferred to live in his homeland and wanted us to live there too. My original enthusiasm for moving to Cusco had waned over the past six months. The boys and I were doing fine where we were.

But my mother's admonition that a wife must live where her husband decided hung over me like a dark cloud. I loved Peru, but a gnawing feeling in my gut told me our situation might not be for the better if we lived there permanently. Antonio hadn't found us a place to stay nor said if his salary could support the family. Once again, we had a failure to communicate about a major decision.

"Kiss the boys for me and remember I love you all," he wrote at the bottom of his March letter. His words comforted me a bit knowing he thought of us for the moment it took to write the sentence. But I no longer knew what living arrangement would be best for our children, Cusco or California. Nor did I know what I wanted. I preferred to continue some meaningful work, but I'd grown weary of my bread-winner status. I'd hoped our work situation would be reversed in Peru, with Antonio supporting the family and me working part-time. But I had no confidence of that happening. If I accepted the language insti-tute directorship, I'd likely continue to shoulder the primary financial responsibility for our family. Not what I wanted. Antonio should be the primary provider if we lived in his country. My current living sit-uation, but with more intellectual growth, would be more to my liking now. I turned down the position in Cusco.

I wanted what I'd helped our Italian friend, Michele, get—a doctoral degree. He'd worked toward his PhD when we were students at UC Berkeley and during his five-month stay there in the fall of 1975. In April 1976, Michele called from Italy to ask if I would get his advisor's signature on his dissertation and submit it to the university. I would.

The day after Michele's treasure arrived, I took a sick day off from work and drove to Berkeley in the pouring rain. I stashed my umbrella on the professor's porch and went inside. I handed the gray-haired economics professor the box containing Michele's typed dissertation and watched him sign the approval page. Then, I delivered Michele's opus to UCB's graduate studies office. *Someday I might deliver my own doctoral dissertation to a university.*

∿

April arrived, without any word from Antonio about where the boys and I should plan to live the following year. I called his Aunt Lastenia's house in Cusco. The undependable phone service hadn't improved much since I'd lived in Peru, so I was surprised to reach my husband.

"You've been there almost a year," I said, trying not to sound too upset by his inaction to date, "and I'd like to know your plans."

"I'm at the beginning of the school year here," he said, animated. "I thought you would come take that director's job they offered you."

"But you haven't found the kids and me a place to live, so that's not possible," I said, my voice rising.

"I asked you to send down the house plans," my husband said accusingly, "for the Mission Estates house we saw in Fremont. We could build it down here much cheaper than in the States."

Had he forgotten again that where we lived should be a joint decision? If he wanted us to live in Cusco, why hadn't he found us a place there? An apartment must exist someplace in that city. I hated being in limbo not knowing where our family would be.

"I think you need to get busy and seriously search for a place for your family and not spend your time dreaming of the house you might build there some day."

"I've been trying, so it's not my fault I haven't found the right place for you and the kids."

"But you're not even helping support the boys with what you earn. So why stay there?"

I pounded the wall with my fist. How inconsiderate of him to be living where he didn't have to concern himself with our children or me. He probably loved his freedom from responsibility. We continued to shout accusations at one another for another five minutes. This time, the phone lines were uncharacteristically clear.

The call cost sixty-five dollars and accomplished nothing except wounded feelings. The exasperation had come from the physical and emotional distance that separated us.

I was uncertain what to do. Maybe I didn't need him, and he should stay in his home country where he seemed happy and fulfilled. My marriage, begun with so much love and passion, seemed to be at an end. Not even the *Ladies Home Journal* could tell me, "Can this marriage be saved?"

Antonio had been in Peru for the better part of a year. I regretted our hasty decision for him to stay and teach there. Full-time college teaching experience might look good on his resume and increase his chances of a professorship at a California college, but it had done nothing for our family's unity or finances.

When he'd taken the professorship, Antonio had promised to find us a place to live. But he hadn't followed through, so the family wasn't together in Peru. I imagined my husband enjoying his single status, unencumbered by family responsibilities. He relished being at the same university where he'd been a student ten years before—and as free as when I'd first met him. By June 1976, our tenth wedding anniversary, our marriage was in trouble. I was ready to call it quits.

One day, looking for a project to quell my anxieties, I found a dusty box of family photos that had accumulated over several years. They needed a more permanent, orderly home. I located some empty photo albums and spread out the fifty or so snapshots on the nine-foot table in the combo kitchen–family room. I arranged them chronologically, ready to place our lives neatly into the waiting plastic inserts.

I peered down at the smiling faces of Antonio and his sons: Timmy building sandcastles with him at the Santa Cruz beach; Tony showing his father an eel at the Steinhart Aquarium; the boys and their father building a fire at the Standish-Hickey State Park campground. Antonio looked so appealing and fatherly in the photographs. Tears came to my eyes. Photographs Antonio had taken of Timmy on the pitcher's mound at Little League games and Tony jumping off the diving board at swim lessons tugged at my heart. I couldn't imagine him no longer part of our family.

I couldn't erase Antonio from my family memories any more than I could erase him from our lives. As I placed the last picture into a slot, I decided I'd bide my time. Maybe our family life would improve, though I didn't know how. Too bad our real lives couldn't be arranged as orderly as the photos in the albums.

My upcoming summer vacation allowed a way to help resolve our separation. I could visit Antonio. But airfare would cost $500 round trip and I wasn't sure I should spend the money. My mother recognized the rift between my husband and me. She believed that families belonged together, regardless of the obstacles. Her Catholic religion said divorce was a mortal sin. Mom hinted that our family's separation wasn't good for the boys or me. She offered to care for my nine- and five-year-old sons if I went to see Antonio in Peru. I took money from our meager savings account and booked a flight to Cusco.

Much to my amazement and delight, Antonio had reserved a pleasant hotel room for us near Cusco's center. He greeted me with loving arms. Most days he managed time off from his teaching duties. When he had to work, I spent the time shopping—using most of the salary he'd accumulated. I bought jewelry, unique fabrics, alpaca rugs, and sweaters—to take out of Peru in place of his earnings. We were in sync, and life was good again.

We took an eight-hour bus trip from Cusco to Abancay where we'd first met eleven years before. This time we stayed the night in the Tourist Hotel, then visited friends, now also married. Over tea, we admired photos of their children. Like two lovebirds, Antonio and I revisited our favorite places from years before. I felt special again with his arm encircling my waist. This was the honeymoon we'd never had. I fell in love with my husband all over again.

We needed to visit Arequipa, in southern Peru, where Antonio's parents continued to live. After riding the train for ten hours to Puno, we stayed overnight on an island in the highest navigable lake in the world, Lake Titicaca. We huddled together at 12,507 feet to keep warm on top of the cold *totora* reeds the island was made of. The following morning, we caught the bus to Arequipa, and bumped southward over gravel and dirt roads for eight hours. We held hands during the entire dusty trip.

Antonio's family welcomed us. They hadn't seen me in the past year because I lived fifteen hours and five thousand miles away. They hadn't laid eyes on Antonio either, even though he lived just three hundred miles away by land. Traveling in Peru was as difficult as when I'd lived there.

My month-long trip to visit Antonio was worth more than the $500 airfare. I returned to Fremont, content to continue my marriage. However, once more, I parented alone.

My sons had fared well in the care of my mother. Neither one seemed to have missed me. Mom had organized Timothy's July birthday party and a full schedule of the boys' activities. She'd transported them to their swimming lessons, sports practices, and baseball and soccer games. They now took showers instead of tub baths. Mom had managed the boys better than I did.

The July I spent with my husband reignited the love I'd felt for him eleven years before. Antonio remained the gentle, loving, supportive, and caring man I'd married. Before I flew home, we determined that the boys and I would not move to Cusco to be with him. He would continue teaching at the university until the end of his school year in December. Whatever happened after that, we'd face together.

A Major Decision

Sustained by Antonio's warmth, I resumed my counseling and testing duties at four elementary schools in Fremont. I enrolled both boys in gifted classes at Chadbourne Elementary, near their babysitter and my parents. And I discovered home maintenance skills I didn't know I had.

November of 1976 was exceptionally cold, and the wall heater in our wood frame house didn't keep us warm. Burning wood in the fireplace, I assumed, would remedy that. I commandeered a friend to load his pickup with twenty discarded wooden pallets the school district was giving away. We stacked them by the side of our house. When the house needed extra heat, I plugged in Antonio's electric saw and cut a pallet into two-foot pieces. It was like slicing a ham. My physical exertion warmed me, but not my house. The slabs burned bright in the living room fireplace for five to ten minutes without producing the warmth I anticipated. Most of the heat went up the chimney. Nevertheless, I added power saw handling to my list of achievements.

I let the boys adopt a gray kitten we found in a box in front of our local grocery store. Timmy named her "Sausage" because her color was the same as the meat I cooked for breakfast. Months later, when the kitten had matured, or maybe before, I heard a faint meowing in the garage. The distressed whimpers came from the open box that stored our artificial Christmas tree next to a few stairs. I looked in to

Tony, Timothy, and Sausage

see two tiny, newborn kittens clinging to the white flocking on the fake tree's branches. Sausage had given birth there because I had neglected to close the storage box. I called the boys and we set up a proper bed for the cat and her offspring. The father must have been the orange tabby I'd seen lurking around. A trip to the animal spaying clinic assured us there'd be no repeat of Sausage giving birth on Christmas trees or elsewhere.

Mom and Dad's support had helped me weather my eighteen months of parenting without my partner. My father repaired the garbage disposal and my mother invited us for meals. They entertained the boys if I had a weekend seminar to attend. With my parents' help, we survived and even flourished. Yet, I had problems.

I found it difficult to maintain peace between my two sons. Tony bossed around his younger brother. He liked to write out schedules for Timmy's activities. When my youngest ignored the regimen his brother had set up for feeding the cat or watching TV, they argued and sometimes wrestled. They disagreed about what fast food each preferred on the special days when I suggested we eat out. Tony wanted Kentucky Fried Chicken and Timothy insisted on a McDonald's hamburger. If I had money-saving coupons for the two places, we'd go to both, and the arguing ceased.

Tony, an organizer, glued envelopes with removable cards to the inside cover of his many books like he'd observed at the city library we frequented. His brother had to write his name on a card and check out the book if he wanted to read it. Tony recorded the date his brother signed his name on the card and when he needed to return the book. Timothy, a spontaneous kid, balked at his older brother's directives. Perhaps Tony wanted to parent Timothy in Antonio's absence.

Tony also organized the neighborhood. He set up "The Kids' Events." He was inspired by the 1976 Summer Olympics he viewed on TV. He calculated handicaps and varied the distance contestants had to run or jump, according to their ages. That way, younger kids could compete fairly against the older ones. Every entrant from the Creekside Park development had an equal chance of winning. He orchestrated his Olympics over several weeks. By charging a few pennies per entry, he had funds to purchase first-, second-, and third-place ribbons. He organized a final awards ceremony when the competitions concluded.

One thing Tony and Timothy didn't have to fight over was a cat. I let them each keep one of Sausage's two kittens. Tony named his orange striped kitten "Tigre," and Timothy named his orange kitten "Carrot." I wasn't certain what Antonio would think about a house full of cats when he returned.

Antonio's university break in December 1976 brought him flying back to us. We were happy to be with him again. I assumed he'd returned to stay. He didn't seem so sure.

One day I noticed the booklet from the airline on top of the dresser. I picked it up to file it away. When the booklet opened, I saw there was a return ticket to Peru. I gaped at the valid ticket and my heart thumped. When I'd left him in July, I thought we'd agreed our family would continue our lives in Fremont—together. Now, although he didn't say so, it looked as though my husband might not be staying with us. I'd not recognized the depth of his desire to live in his native country. Had the past months in Peru changed his mind about living in California with us? I knew he felt more pressure living here than in Peru. But I'd planned that we'd continue our lives just like before his long absence. Only now, I expected that Antonio would find a job to support his family. I confronted him about the plane ticket.

"Do you intend to use the return portion of your plane ticket?" I asked, my chest tightening.

"Do you want me to stay?" Antonio asked, staring at the open booklet.

It was impossible to tell from his serious expression what he was thinking. We needed to discuss our family's future—and if it had one. I recalled my mother's warning.

Mom had said many times that children often suffer when they have stepfathers, especially young boys. Antonio loved his sons and they loved him—when he was around. I did too, most of the time. Didn't Antonio want to be involved in raising our children? He'd not made it possible for us to join him in Peru and hadn't said that's where he preferred us to live. I knew where I stood.

"I need your help," I said, looking him in the eye, "raising our boys here."

Could Antonio be truly happy living his life away from his country of origin? If not, where did I stand? Antonio had missed his chance for me to follow him when he didn't find us a place to live in Cusco. Now he'd have to readapt to the fast pace of California life. He'd need to begin searching for work again. After his relaxing, culture-filled year-and-a-half in his homeland, could he do that? My breath caught in my chest awaiting his answer.

"Okay," Antonio said, "then I'll stay. But those two new cats have to go."

I breathed easier. The boys were heartbroken when strangers adopted their cats. But they were happy to have their dad home permanently. I was too.

A Busy Life

From January to June 1977, Antonio again made the rounds of the community colleges applying for teaching jobs in math and physics. We'd sacrificed a year-and-a-half's family separation hoping his full-time teaching in Peru would garner him a well-paying job in the US. We expected his experience in Peru to result in offers of a full-time position at a community college. It didn't. Like before, the only offers he received were for part-time math instructor. A heaviness entered my body. Would this torture of waiting for him to find meaningful, full-time work in the US ever end?

Antonio accepted every offer he received and, once again, began teaching part-time. On alternate days, four days a week, he commuted to two community colleges: twenty-five miles to De Anza in Cupertino, and four miles to Ohlone in Fremont. His income helped buy food but didn't pay the mortgage.

In the fall of 1977, I returned as a full-time school psychologist with the Fremont Unified School District. The boys were older, and I'd become accustomed to full-time work, so I didn't complain as much about supporting the family. I arranged for our sons to attend gifted classes at Chadbourne Elementary again. Then I took on more responsibilities.

❧

The teachers' union hadn't fought hard enough during collective bargaining to keep all the district's counselors. Many were in danger of being laid off. The counselors asked the psychologists to join them in forming our own bargaining unit, separate from that of the teachers. My father believed in unions, so I did too. I promoted the advantages of unionizing among my colleagues. The psychologists joined the counselors to become the Fremont Counseling and Guidance Association (FCGA). I became vice-president and, besides participating in collective bargaining sessions, I organized the group's professional development. I welcomed the challenge.

My mind buzzed with ideas when exposed to new books. A recent one, *The Open Classroom* by Herb Kohl, had inspired me. I contacted Dr. Kohl and invited the National Book Award winner to bring his message to FUSD. I was delighted when he accepted my invitation.

The auditorium of American High School filled to capacity with parents and educators the afternoon of January 26, 1978, to hear Dr. Kohl speak on "Motivating the Unmotivated Learner." I introduced the renowned speaker and listened in rapt attention to his words. He explained how labeling students stigmatizes them and channels many into an inflexible school track. I knew his viewpoint would be controversial in our conservative community, but the talk accomplished what I wanted. It stirred minds and stimulated discussion.

The director of student services complimented me on the thought-provoking presentation. I stood proud but wondered why his department had never sponsored an in-service like this one. I believed FUSD personnel and students benefitted from exposure to voices from outside the district.

❧

That summer, the boys and I took the train from California over the beautiful tree-filled Sierras to Denver, Colorado. For a week we visited Annette, a close friend with whom I'd attended Sacred Heart High in Miles City, Montana, some twenty years before. Her two children were near my boys' ages. Antonio stayed home to teach Spanish part-time at the Berlitz Language Center in Oakland.

Annette and I reminisced about old times and began organizing a twenty-year class reunion of Sacred Heart High's class of 1960. My friend's son and my two boys made a horror film with the movie camera I'd purchased for our trip. Life was so pleasant in Denver, close to the picturesque Rocky Mountains, that I thought maybe our family should move there. So I applied for an open position as a school social worker with the Denver schools before flying on to Montana. Unfortunately, we had to leave before I could be interviewed.

In Montana and North Dakota, I introduced Tony and Timmy to the friends and relatives whom I hadn't seen since my last visit in 1962. They fawned over the boys. We received more invitations for home-cooked meals of beef, potatoes, and delicious apple pie than we could accept.

Romualdo, Antonio's best friend from our UC Berkeley days, planned to meet us in New England, North Dakota, at my uncle Joe's farm. He, his wife Judy, their two elementary-school-aged children, Pedro and Natalie, and their cat, Miguel, had lived in New Jersey for the past two years where Romualdo taught physics at Princeton University. Our friends wanted to tour the US between coasts in their Volkswagen bus before shipping it, the cat, and themselves back to their home country of Chile. After picking the boys and me up at Joe's farm, they'd transport us back to California through the southwestern national parks and Disneyland. Perfect. A free ride home via a scenic route with friends.

࿙

Romualdo arrived in New England on schedule but was puzzled by the location. He said he couldn't envision me in a town of only eight hundred people. He asked in one of the local bars if there might be a larger town named New England somewhere else. There wasn't. This was the one and only New England, North Dakota, my birthplace. When everyone in the tavern pointed him in the direction of Joe's farm, east of New England, he had to believe he'd arrived in the right place. I could have told him that the inhabitants of small Midwestern places know who lives in their vicinity and what they've been doing.

For two days the kids rode horses, milked cows, and chased cats. We dined on homemade bread and beef raised by my father's oldest brother. When we were ready to depart, the cat wasn't. We looked everywhere and couldn't locate him. I suggested we leave without our friends' pet. But then, Joe discovered Miguel lying in the shade under a tractor. Miguel exhibited the relaxed Midwestern style of life I craved.

The next day we stopped in Miles City, Montana, to visit my younger brother, Buddy. He'd moved from busy California to settle in tranquil Montana. We planned to stay with Bud for three days. This time, however, the cat didn't cause a delay. I did.

Buddy introduced me to his next-door neighbor, John, a psychologist for the local school district. We had occupations in common. And as in Denver, I became enamored of the local ambiance.

"I don't suppose," I said to John, "there are any openings for school psychologists here, are there?"

"Funny you should ask," John said, surprised. "The school district just approved the hiring of a second psychologist. They'll be holding interviews next week. You should apply."

Each day in gentle Miles City, where I'd gone to high school, my desire increased to raise my boys close to nature and away from

California's hectic, crowded cities. I wanted them to bask in the people's warmth where I'd grown up and later rediscovered in Peru. The generous Montanans treated my boys to hearty meals, horseback rides, and friendly animals. I yearned for this simple and less harried life among rolling green hills and productive farmlands. In California, our family experienced too much stress. Big Sky Montana might be a better place to bring up my boys—and a place their father and I could both find jobs.

I applied for the school psychologist opening. The personnel administrator scheduled an interview date for the following Monday. In the meantime, I looked for teaching positions Antonio might apply for at the local community college.

"The head of the math department," the college secretary said pointing down the hall, "is in his office, painting."

A professor who uses his artistic talents to paint pictures—how cultured. I ventured toward the chairman's office to check out openings in his math department and see his artwork. His painting surprised me.

"Oh, you're painting your walls," I said trying not to sound shocked.

"Yes," the professor said, stepping down from his ladder and putting the paint roller in a pan. "Around here one has to have many talents. How can I help you?"

"My husband has degrees in physics and math," I said, "and has taught math for several years at community colleges in California and physics in Peru. Are there any teaching jobs in those subjects here?"

The professor threw me a sympathetic smile. He wiped light green paint from his hand before extending it toward me. I envisioned our slow-paced lives in this cow town surrounded by cattle ranches and wheat farms. Time and life here was measured by the change of seasons and nature, as in rural Peru.

"I'm afraid the most work he might get in this town would be some kind of accounting job in a local bank. And there aren't many of those right now."

Crestfallen, I thanked the professor, and left him to paint another wall. What did it matter? Antonio could be underemployed here as well as in California. Raising our boys in the clean air and peaceful atmosphere of Miles City might be healthier for all of us.

I'd still go to my job interview. But there was a problem. I'd hold up Romualdo and Judy on their drive to California if we all waited for my Monday interview. So we agreed the van would head on to Billings with Tony and Timmy, and I'd take a plane to meet the entourage there after my interview.

ᗡ

For over an hour, five male school administrators peppered me with questions about identifying and planning for blind, deaf, severely delayed, and learning-disabled students. Every scenario they presented I'd experienced. My California school district's larger population had given me extensive knowledge about the entire spectrum of students needing special classes. The director said I should phone him two days later from wherever I was for the interview results.

Sensing success, I began to make housing arrangements. My brother suggested I take over the payments on the mobile home his wife's brother was about to lose. My plans were falling into place. This move to Montana was meant to be.

The VW bus picked me up at the Billings airport and we headed south toward West Yellowstone to camp. On the appointed day, some-where along the road, I found a pay phone and called the special edu-cation director in Miles City.

"We'd like to offer you the job," the voice at the other end said.

"I'd like to accept it," I said, feeling victorious. "But I have to talk to my husband in California. I'll give you my answer as soon as I've reached him."

I called Antonio to tell him the good news. I felt lighthearted. I'd found a slower-paced living arrangement like that in Peru. However, my husband wasn't enthused.

"That's fine, dear," Antonio said. "You go right ahead, but I'm staying right where I am."

Nothing I said convinced him of the great life I'd planned for us in beautiful Montana. I turned the phone over to Romualdo, who missed having his old friend on this Western adventure.

"You've got to come join us," I heard Romualdo say. "We're making our way to most of the major parks between West Yellowstone and Disneyland."

"But I'm teaching at Berlitz in Oakland," Antonio said.

Romualdo took one last shot. He missed his good friend. I missed him too.

"You've got to join me," he pleaded. "I'm here with only women and children and need a man's help to build the campfires and drive."

Antonio flew to West Yellowstone, and I turned down the Montana job. We enjoyed two more weeks of playing the board game Clue, as we sped down the road in the VW bus to see Zion and Bryce Canyons, Las Vegas, and Disneyland. Antonio helped build the campfires and drive. We never missed the income from his part-time summer job.

We enjoyed the company of our friends back home in Fremont for another week. Then, Antonio and Romualdo drove to San Francisco and put the VW bus on a ship headed to Chile. Soon after, we bade good-bye to our friends at the airport. A week after seeing them off, we packed up their cat and shipped it to Chile.

That winter, Montana experienced some of the coldest temperatures in decades. We would have frozen inside the thin walls of the trailer house I'd wanted to buy. Antonio's choice of warm California over cold Montana had been a wise one.

And I had an *aha* moment. I realized that I applied for jobs wherever I vacationed, thinking we'd be happier moving to greener pastures. It wasn't the places I loved—it was being on vacation.

Productive Kids, Productive Party

For the past several years, Romualdo had discouraged Antonio from seeking employment in physics. Both had majored in the subject at UCB. Romualdo counseled Antonio to take classes in computer programming if he wanted a full-time job. So Antonio had earned an *A* grade in a computer course at Cal State Hayward in the spring of 1977. In succeeding quarters, he completed eight more computer classes while he taught math at nearby community colleges. Romualdo had been right.

In April 1979, the software company Informatics hired Antonio as a computer programmer. I was ecstatic. After thirteen years of marriage, we had the income and routine of a normal American family.

Antonio drove his Fiat twenty-five miles down the 880 Nimitz Freeway to the Informatics building at Moffett Field every day. I saw Timmy off to second grade and Tony to sixth grade at Warwick Elementary, our newly opened neighborhood school. Then, I too headed to work at one of my four assigned Fremont schools. The year before, the boys had been in gifted classes in a more affluent school near my parents. That school had higher academic standards, but my sons wanted to go to the same school as the other neighborhood children. So I'd enrolled them in regular classes nearby. I hoped I hadn't stunted their academic growth.

Tony, Timmy, and the other neighborhood kids caught tadpoles after school in the mud puddles of nearby Alameda Creek. Antonio and I went to the creek for another purpose. We arose early each morning to jog for half an hour along the creek's paved pathway. I left something—buttermilk biscuits, muffins, cinnamon rolls, or a coffee cake I'd made—baking in the oven. After we finished our run, I added eggs, bacon, and fruit to my family's plates to start their day with a hearty breakfast. We needed good nutrition for all our pursuits.

Timmy was one of the first to be named "Student of the Week" for good behavior and completing his homework in his second-grade class. He often won the maximum number of points toward a prize at the end of each week. No wonder he liked his teacher, Mrs. Higbie. The class chose Timmy as their representative to the student government council. His interpretation of what went on at the meetings made me laugh. Like when he requested the students all to go to a KISS rock concert. I didn't laugh at the information he shared with his class after Easter vacation, however. His teacher recounted the exchange at our spring parent-teacher conference.

"I asked the class, how each spent his or her Easter vacation," Mrs. Higbie said. "Timmy was excited to share your family news."

"'My mommy had an operation,'" his teacher said repeating my son's words, "'so she can't have more babies.'"

My face turned red in front of the chuckling, pregnant teacher. Antonio and I wished to limit our family to two children. The birth control pills I'd been taking messed with my emotions, and the intra-uterine device infected my body. So, during Easter vacation, I'd spent a day in the hospital recovering from a tubal ligation. I hadn't realized my operation impacted my youngest child enough to share the information. Maybe he wanted to impress this teacher that he liked so much. Mrs. Higbie and I agreed that if Timmy had a fault, it was talking too much.

Some evenings, with their homework completed, the boys and I

Tony and Timothy playing cards

played card games like Scan, Concentration, Animal Rummy or Crazy Eights. One day a neighbor asked Timmy who his favorite author was. My seven-year-old answered, "Robert Lewis Stevenson." The neighbor was impressed. Timmy had learned the names of famous American and English authors from playing the card game Authors, where he had to match four author cards to make a "book."

Timmy also had impressive math skills. If he heard a word problem requiring arithmetic calculations, he'd determine which mathematical process to use, then perform the operation in his head. He could subtract eleven from twenty-five in an instant. He'd learned to read at age five and enjoyed books. But he preferred riding his bike and playing soccer and baseball. He was constantly active.

Tony played on sports teams and enjoyed board games like Risk and chess that used strategic skills. Antonio had taught him chess moves at age six. Tony won first prize in the game at age ten at the Mentally Gifted Minors Faire. When he joined the Fremont City chess club, he often beat the adult members. I prided myself that we had intelligent, well-rounded sons.

Each evening at bedtime, I read the boys classics like *Treasure Island, James and the Giant Peach,* and *The Mouse and the Motorcycle*— until they reached their teens. My reading selections for them were unlike my mother's. In Montana, she'd read *The Lives of the Saints* and religious newsletters to her children. The stories of persecution, penances, and sudden apparitions had created frightening scenes in my fertile imagination. I nurtured my sons' imaginations with fiction and life adventures.

Afternoons, Antonio or I took one or both boys to soccer or baseball practice and attended their games on Saturdays. Antonio volunteered to coach Tony's soccer team of eleven-year-olds. But a few games into the season, he almost came to blows with the husband of his female assistant coach. She and her husband disagreed with Antonio's Latin American style practice sessions designed for fun and improved skills. By contrast, the assistant coach adhered to a serious set of rules enforced by her commands and those of her interfering husband. Both overrode Antonio's directives. After Antonio quit in disgust, the team lost many of its games.

Timmy asked to join our neighborhood Cub Scout pack. He and Antonio worked long hours to put together his entry for the Pine Car Derby. Other scouts' cars looked like they'd had professional paint jobs. Timmy painted his car himself. Someone advised him to tape a few quarters to the top of his car for weight and use graphite lubrication on the wheel bearings. Antonio, Timmy and I cheered as his ugly car zoomed down the ramp to place among the top three.

Timmy received our neighbor's assistance for the Cub Scouts' cake-decorating contest. Together they fashioned his entry like an Indian teepee, complete with spaghetti lodge poles at the top. It won first place. There was no end to my children's talents.

When Tony heard me playing the piano one day, he asked for lessons. Timmy followed suit. I found an instructor, and before long I heard simple, recognizable tunes coming from the living room. We had to squeeze piano practice and lessons in between sports team training. As I listened from the kitchen to the piano exercises, I often heard the piano go silent. When I checked, I found the young pianist,

Timmy and his prize-winning cake

arms folded on the keyboard, fast asleep. Piano practice couldn't survive a hard day playing sports. We discontinued the piano lessons. Sports had won over music.

Swim classes, camping trips, zoo visits, and summer school filled our June to August vacations. During winter breaks, the boys wanted to go to the snow. I'd had my fill of the cold white stuff growing up in Montana and had no desire to drive for hours from Fremont to the Sierra to play in it. I'd become friends with Douglas and his Costa Rican wife, Orfa, when I'd worked in the Alum Rock School District in East San Jose. They and their two elementary-school-aged children had moved to the top of Mount Hamilton, near the Lick Observatory, where Doug taught multiple grades in the one-room school. The few times it snowed on the mountain each winter, our friends gave us a call and invited us up to play in the cold stuff. We grabbed our warm coats and boots and drove forty miles up the two-lane winding road. At the top, the children played while I stayed inside our friends' cozy warm home helping put a meal together. Driving to Mount Hamilton took a bit over an hour and cost less than staying overnight at a resort.

It's good that we hadn't splurged on excursions to the resorts of Squaw Valley or Pine Ridge for snow play. We needed to curtail our spending in February 1981. Lockheed's government contract expired, and Informatics laid off Antonio. He applied for unemployment, which money I put into savings. We'd lived on my income alone before. We could do it again.

Antonio returned to applying for work, this time as an experienced computer programmer. For two months he had interviews but received no job offers. Our entertainment consisted of visiting friends. We'd met a few Peruvians living in Fremont, and one couple invited us to their pre-Lenten party.

Delicious Peruvian dishes filled the table at the Leons' cozy home. They had moved from Lima, Peru, to the Bay Area several years before. Herman Leon worked at the General Motors plant on the edge of Fremont, and his wife worked at the same company's local office building downtown. As my potluck dish, I'd made my specialty, *ceviche*—fish marinated in lime juice. A few couples danced to the peppy *cumbia* piece playing on the stereo. The crowded family room allowed little of the hip swaying the rhythm provoked. The voices of the thirty Americans and Peruvians, speaking mainly Spanish, rose in a crescendo over the music. I sat on the living room sofa wedged between the hostess and a lively Peruvian woman.

"Evelyn, this is Nelly," Rosa, our hostess said. "She lives in Union City."

"Nice to meet you," I said, exchanging pleasantries.

"Where does your husband work?" Nelly asked.

"He's just been laid off," I said. "He was working as a computer programmer at Moffett Field."

"Hmmm," Nelly said, her dark eyes dancing. "My husband, Ron, works as a programmer at United Grocers and receives a hundred-dollar bonus for each qualified programmer he finds to work for them."

We got our two husbands together, and they talked the rest of the evening. Ron arranged for an interview, and soon Antonio was commuting to the United Grocer's Oakland campus on BART, our rapid transit system. I learned that parties are excellent for networking. Once again, we were an intact, two-income family, and I could become political at work and maybe even study for another college degree.

Years of Aspiration

The Fremont Counseling and Guidance Association's membership of forty was small by comparison to the much larger teachers' union. But FCGA was mighty. Under the leadership of president Dottie, and the energetic bargaining unit, our members continued to receive the same salary increases as the teachers. And the school district ceased proposing to save money by decreasing the number of school counselors.

In the middle of her term as FCGA president, Dottie said she would need to curtail some of her union duties to write her doctoral dissertation. Her announcement piqued my interest and came at a critical juncture in my work life. My brain needed feeding.

In seven years of work as a school psychologist, I'd become competent, and bored. I could administer the IQ tests in my sleep—and sometimes did. I needed more cerebral stimulation than my job provided. My supervisor, Mrs. McGee, disliked my intellectual curiosity almost as much as my FCGA union participation. I spent a Saturday in Palo Alto learning how to develop individual education plans (IEPs) for learning disabled students. When Mrs. McGee discovered what I'd done, she called me in to her office for questioning. Her brash manner made her intimidating.

"Why would you go out of the area to a class?" the portly woman said, frowning, hands on her hips. "My department will teach you what you need to know about the recent laws."

"My understanding," I said, hands in my pockets, rarely looking at her, "is that psychologists will have some responsibility in developing IEPs, and I was eager to learn what our role would be."

I'd spent my own time and money to learn the upcoming legal requirements for IEPs. Meanwhile, no one in Mrs. McGee's special education department had mentioned the law to those of us responsible for carrying out its mandates. I knew I'd done nothing wrong, yet I cowered under the glare of the director's authority.

Antonio had cared for our boys when I'd taken the Saturday class. He encouraged me to learn whatever I wanted. He took in new information from his books and didn't seek to climb a career ladder the way I did. My desire to take on new challenges motivated my learning. His satisfaction came from solving difficult computer programming problems. He didn't mind repetitive work, especially as he became better and better at it. He was a loyal employee. But he counseled me to seek the level of responsibility and stimulation I desired in my job.

"The California commission is awarding the administrative credential," fellow school psychologist Ed had announced at our monthly meeting. "By just passing a written exam you can get it. You should accumulate as many of these pieces of paper as you can, when you can. You never know when they might be needed."

Usually, it took two years of university classes, including a year in a practicum, to qualify as a school administrator. I'd never planned to be a principal or an administrator, but I agreed with Ed—one could never have enough credentials. I passed the test and received the document.

Then, because I had the required administrative credential, my Fremont Unified colleagues convinced me to apply for the department's assistant director of special services job. I hadn't really wanted to be Mrs. McGee's second in command. I'd be a thorn in her side. But going for the administrative job might make the higher-ups notice my skills.

However, after applying, I suffered through a humiliating interview with a hostile hiring committee. They asked questions like, "Where do you see yourself in five years?" and "Who do you think you are?" Maybe not this last question, but it was implied. As expected, I didn't get the administrative job.

The school district's lack of advancement opportunities stifled me. Earning a doctoral degree might fulfill my desire for accomplishment and move me up the pay scale. Antonio had once mentioned working for his own doctoral degree.

"I'd like to continue studying for a PhD in physics," Antonio had announced as he completed his master's degree in 1974. "I could earn it in four or five years if I study full time."

His plan hadn't sat well with me. I'd already supported him through his bachelor's and master's degrees. Moreover, each academic degree raised my salary more than it did my husband's. In school districts, the more academic credits and degrees one accrued, the higher pay one earned each year. In terms of salary payoff, if one of us went for a doctorate, it should be me.

"Whoa," I'd said. "Four or five years is a long stretch. I'd have to continue being the major breadwinner if you didn't work full-time."

I'd left unsaid my speculation that he liked to study more than he liked to look for a job. Books didn't reject him like interviewers did. I was glad my husband aspired to higher education like I did, but it was time for Antonio to use the education he'd already gained.

"No," I'd said, my jaw tightening, "I won't support you through another degree. If anyone goes for a doctorate, it will be me."

I'd sympathized with my husband's dislike of searching for work. But I was tired of being our family's main wage earner, year after year, with no end in sight. Neither of us brought up the subject of an advanced degree again, until the summer of 1979 when I decided I would work toward a doctorate. Antonio didn't show enthusiasm, but he didn't discourage me. I inquired into the program Dottie, our FCGA president, was enrolled in at the University of San Francisco.

The Education Department's newest program, Multicultural Studies, excited me. Most of the students, like the professors, were from a variety of cultures—Vietnam, Cuba, the Philippines, and several Latin American countries. Foreign countries and their people had interested me ever since I'd moved from all-Anglo Montana to polyglot California. I'd lived and traveled in Mexico and Peru and married a Peruvian. Multicultural studies appeared designed for my interests. As one of the few Anglo students in the department, I'd be a minority. That was fine with me.

The university organized its doctoral program for working professionals. The required courses were scheduled on Saturdays and during school holiday breaks and summer vacations. The Jesuit university, being private, charged an expensive $145 per unit. However, I saved a year's tuition costs when USF said many of my previous graduate-level units fulfilled some of their requirements. When I couldn't afford a class, I audited it, allowing me to gain information I wanted and avoid the $500 cost.

The private university tuition strained our family budget, so I continued to hold down a full-time job. Mom helped out, as she always did. Now that the boys were twelve and eight years old, they didn't need me as much as when they were six and two. My mother reminded me that my primary work was to raise the boys, not study for a higher degree. Still, she transported Tony and Timmy to their activities when neither Antonio nor I were available. I promised myself that my family wouldn't suffer because of my studies. I hoped I could keep my word.

My mind soaked up the new information about bilingualism, other countries' customs, and language learning like a drought-plagued desert. Professors who visited from Chile, Puerto Rico, and around the US taught me to appreciate the diverse linguistic, political, and economic underpinnings of the world's many cultures. The foreign backgrounds of my instructors and fellow students fascinated me. I never missed a class.

The professor stood at the bottom of the large auditorium-style classroom after a required USF class one Saturday. He had a stack of the final exams from the previous semester's class ready to hand back. I was surprised to hear him call my name.

"Top student in the class after the final exam," he shouted, "is Evelyn LaTorre."

I lowered my head in embarrassment, then skipped down the stairs to collect my test amid clapping from the other students. My chest swelled. I knew how to study, write papers, and pass tests.

I enjoyed the intellectual challenge of my classes, especially those of Dr. Cohen, a demanding professor of educational research. He advised students to write each class paper as if it were a chapter for their final doctoral dissertation. That way, he said, at the end of the coursework we'd only need to put the papers together to have the final requirement for the doctoral degree.

But I didn't follow his advice. My interests were too diverse to focus on a single topic. Like my life, the subjects of my papers weren't neatly organized. My curiosity somersaulted from early language learning to how adults learn a second language and back again. I needed novelty—and money—to pay the mounting tuition costs. I applied for a Title VII scholarship that would defray my expenses. Then I became sidetracked and began to pursue other potential money-making activities.

When I was two years old and my parents' only offspring, my mother had decided I was pretty enough to be a child model. She'd used money she earned from caring for others' children to pay for eight-by-ten-inch professional glossy photos of me. Alas, she had no time to submit the photos to Seattle modeling agencies before the US Navy sent my dad to electricians' school in Chicago. I never became the next Shirley Temple.

Now, my youngest son's big brown eyes, long eyelashes, and wavy light brown hair gave me the idea that he could be a model. I had eight-by-ten-inch professional glossy photos taken and signed him with the Brebner Agency in San Francisco. Not long thereafter, they called Timmy in for an audition. A lunchmeat company selected him for their commercial and I began fanaticizing about his showbiz career.

Timmy's commercial was filmed with area funny man Ronnie Schell, somewhere in Marin County on a weekday. We both had to skip school to be there. As the shoot began, the director told Timmy to stand in the background with a group of young boys. He instructed the lead youth to bite into a bologna sandwich and look like he enjoyed it. But the boy didn't like lunchmeat. After a brief conference with the boy's mother, the kid faked his pleasure and the commercial was made. I found the entire episode fascinating.

A week later, when the agency called Timmy in for more auditions, he balked. My eight-year-old said he feared his friends might see him on TV. Then, my interest also waned. I had difficulty leaving work to transport my son to interviews. I wasn't as dedicated as the overbearing stage mothers I saw at the tryouts and filmings. Like me at age two, my son's showbiz career ended. I deposited $181 for Timmy's one day of work in his bank account. Then, I wandered into another way to add to our family's coffers—real estate.

The value of houses in California increased by over 18 percent in 1979 and 1980. I encouraged my parents to invest their extra cash in rental housing. But Dad had grown up during the depression and would only put his money into savings accounts and treasury notes, not housing speculation. I didn't have my dad's cash or his financial apprehensions.

Larry, a real estate broker, showed me how the price of houses had doubled in the past ten years. Several friends bragged about how their real estate investments had paid off. I too wanted to counteract the 12 percent inflation rate and turn a 30 percent profit. Antonio opposed my ventures and wanted no part of the financial risk. He said houses in Peru were purchased with cash and not bought as investments. I had no capital with which to purchase a single-family dwelling, so I found a townhouse I might afford, with financial help. Mom encouraged me to approach Dad.

"Your dad thinks you can do no wrong," my mother said after I'd shown her the specs on the first townhouse. "Ask him to lend you the money to purchase the property."

I'd never before asked my parents for money. But I would now. I felt certain the housing market would yield great profits.

Dad didn't trust real estate to continue rising, but unlike my husband, he had faith in my judgment and lent me the $18,000 down payment. Antonio signed quitclaims to the two places I purchased. Whenever repairs were needed on my rentals, Dad came to the rescue. He fixed leaks and painted walls, often with my husband's help. After three years, my profit didn't amount to a great deal, but it helped beat the high inflation rate and increased our tax deductions. I more than broke even.

A year into my doctoral studies, I made a major change. In September 1980, at the first psychologists' meeting of the school year, a colleague mentioned that San Jose Unified School District was looking for a bilingual school psychologist. He thought I might be interested. I was, but I also was wary. The teachers in the San Jose district were on strike. Regardless, I applied. Fremont Unified and I were no longer a good match. An enlightened acquaintance, Dr. Olivia Martinez, headed SJUSD's Special Education Department. I'd replaced her at San

Francisco Unified ten years before. Olivia offered me the job at San Jose Unified, and I took it. Whenever our paths crossed, I benefited.

The more hospitable work environment was worth the twenty-mile commute through traffic from Fremont to San Jose. Olivia looked with favor upon my doctoral studies at USF, where she'd completed her EdD. Mrs. McGee was not happy when I left Fremont Unified at the beginning of the school year. But I was ecstatic to be out from under her supervision and into a work environment that encouraged learning. I searched for new opportunities wherever I could find them. I found one perfect for me.

The bulletin board in the USF Education Department announced Fulbright Scholarships that would pay for living abroad. I could use the award to complete the research for my doctoral dissertation. To qualify, I had to have high academic achievement, an interesting project, and a statement of purpose. My grade point average was 4.0 and I knew a project I could pursue. I applied for the Fulbright to study bilingualism in a couple of schools in Cusco, Peru, where Antonio's parents had moved.

Bilingual theory said that when taught to read in his/her first language, a child would more easily learn to read in his/her second language. The study I proposed would see if Cusco's first and second grade children, when taught to read and write in their native Quechua language, could then more easily learn to read and write in Spanish. I envisioned our family living in Peru while I studied there. Antonio hadn't arranged for us to live in Cusco five years before, but I would now.

I asked my Peruvian father-in-law to obtain a letter that established my connection with the University in Cusco. Adolfo sent me an official statement from the director of the School of Education at Cusco's Antonio Abad National University supporting my proposed study. My children would finally become fluent in Spanish. In addition, I'd have data for my doctoral dissertation.

I needed letters of recommendation to vouch that I could accomplish the study I proposed. I asked Dr. Cohen. The first sentence of his letter surprised me.

"Evelyn is impulsive, but impulsive people account for most of the world's achievements. Evelyn accomplishes what she sets her mind to."

Applying for the Fulbright may have been impulsive, but the possibility of living in Peru again excited me. However, a move back to Cusco didn't excite my Peruvian husband. He said no way would he leave the computer program job he'd finally landed. Our ideas of where we should live, once again, did not synchronize.

After days of discussions, Antonio agreed he would rent an apartment near Pleasanton, where his company had moved. Our house could be rented out while the boys and I lived in Peru. Once again, we risked another family separation.

But then, after a summer trip, I was inundated with more opportunities than I could plan for or handle.

Too Many Opportunities

I'd completed two-thirds of the graduate courses needed for my doctoral degree by the summer of 1981. So, after sending in the Fulbright application, I rewarded my boys, now fourteen and ten, and myself with a trip to my home state of Montana. Antonio stayed home to work in his computer programmer-analyst job.

The kids and I flew into Billings where my father collected us in his fifth-wheel camper. He had spent three weeks with friends and family in Montana and North Dakota. Mom hadn't accompanied him because she disliked camper living. "Just another house I'd have to clean," she said. Unlike Mom, Tony and Timmy were eager travelers.

We drove over the Rockies through Glacier Park looking for the rare bighorn sheep that live there. The eleven-thousand-foot, snow-capped peaks awed me, as mountains always did. The Montana pinnacles were half the height of the twenty-two-thousand-foot Andes, but still inspiring. I recalled seeing the Rockies for the first time when I'd been a year older than Tony was now. I'd stood in awe of their enormity then. The Montana mountains still impressed me and my boys. We spied the white rump of a big brown ram close to a snow-covered peak. Timmy pointed with excitement at its heavy curled horns almost scraping the grass as it grazed. Spying wild animals in their natural habitats boosted my adrenaline. In Peru, I'd seen deer but not big rams. I loved exploring hills, streams, and mountains wherever I found them.

Crossing into Canada on July 12, we discovered we could attend the final day of the Calgary Stampede. Cowboys in Western gear trotted around town on their handsome horses. The four of us, along with a million other attendees, toured the exhibition halls and admired displays of prize-winning farm produce and show animals.

The next morning, we drove to Banff and Lake Louise, where I snapped photos of the aqua-colored lake, tranquil beneath snow-striped mountains. We motored on westward to Victoria, BC, where Dad took the boys to a local park while I hopped on the ferry to the Butchart Gardens. There, I walked among lush green lawns and colorful blooms—a welcome respite away from the highway and city traffic. Then we created a traffic problem of our own. The fifth wheeler broke down on the highway on our way to Seattle.

We were within reach of Renton, Washington, where Dad's brother, Matt, and his family lived. So Dad had the vehicle hauled there— good for everyone but me. I had made an appointment to visit Arla Jeanne, my former Sacred Heart High roommate. She now worked as an airline hostess, and I'd been fortunate to catch her at her Seattle home between flights. Arla Jeanne had two days to spend with me. Dad arranged for the boys and him to stay with my uncle while our transportation was being fixed. I could have my two-day visit with my high school best friend. My mood picked up.

I'd last seen the auburn-haired Arla Jeanne in Miles City, Montana, at the 1962 wedding of one of our classmates. Arla's green eyes sparkled as we reminisced over cups of tea in her fashionable all-black kitchen that had once been featured in *Architectural Digest*. After refreshments in the dark and unusual room, we bounced out of her lakeside place to tour the overcast city. The sun came out at four in the afternoon as we stood at the top of the Space Needle.

"What a perfectly sunny day," Arla Jeanne pronounced. At least our spirits were bright.

❧

The trip to Montana, Canada, and down the West Coast had been my reward for a hectic year of classes and work. With my energy renewed, I braced for the stress to come—writing my doctoral dissertation. This would be the final and most difficult step in attaining the advanced degree I desired.

I hadn't heard from the Fulbright Commission about my application to conduct doctoral research in Peru, so I began writing the background chapters that would begin my opus. I needed extra time to read, contemplate, and compose my thesis. So, like I'd done twice before in my career, I asked the district if I could work part-time— three days a week instead of five. The district granted my request, and my school year started at a more relaxed pace. But true to my nature, I became sidetracked by other interests.

Over the past years, Antonio and I had wanted a larger home. We'd toured the Mission Estates model homes in southern Fremont in 1973 when looking for our first house. Antonio was studying at San Francisco State then, so provided little income. The $87,000 price of the Mission Estates homes was too expensive for my salary alone. We had settled for the more affordable $31,000 place in northern Fremont.

In 1966, my parents had moved to the historic Mission San Jose area in southern Fremont, two miles from the Mission Estates homes. They loved being close to the old Mission. Now, eight years after our original home purchase, and with Antonio working full-time, we told Larry, our realtor, that he could start the search for our dream home. I didn't think the right house could be found. The inflation rate in 1981 had spiked to 10 percent, and interest rates were twice that. Few houses were for sale. Besides, I wanted to be off to Peru for a year, compliments of the prestigious Fulbright scholarship. I only lacked the award letter.

Surprise, tinged with a bit of chagrin, greeted me in late November. Larry found a house we loved at a price we could almost afford. The 2,700-square-foot Kimber Park home measured twice the size of our Darwin Drive house. Its two stories sported four bedrooms, three bathrooms, two fireplaces, formal dining and living rooms, a huge cathedral-ceiling family room, a three-car garage, and a bar we wouldn't use. Our boys said the landing at the top of the stairs was perfect for launching paper airplanes. The house stood on a quarter acre and had a wall of sliding glass doors that looked out onto two huge redwood decks and a professionally landscaped backyard. This was a real estate venture Antonio and I could agree on.

Then, the letter I'd been waiting for arrived from the Fulbright Commission. I'd been awarded their scholarship and would need to begin my research in Peru by February. My initial pride at winning such a coveted prize was tempered by my new reality. When I'd requested the Fulbright, I'd wanted to live in another country, not buy another house.

My father-in-law in Peru wrote that the $450-a-month Fulbright stipend would be insufficient to support the boys and me in Cusco. He added that a bomb set off by the Shining Path terrorists had recently exploded in the local post office. Hearing that, Antonio said it was too dangerous for me to take Tony and Timmy to live in his hometown. I reminded him that he'd not supported my decision even before news of the bomb. My husband seemed to think this venture looked like my decision in 1978 when I'd wanted to move to Montana. Despite the dangers from rebel Peruvian terrorists, I still hoped to gather my dissertation data there.

Tony had done so well at our local junior high school that in the fall of 1980 we'd decided he should go to Bellarmine College Prep, a private Jesuit Boys' High School in San Jose. I drove him to his new school on my way to my new job with San Jose Unified and picked him up most evenings. In November of Tony's sophomore year, I made an appointment with Bellarmine's principal to discuss taking my son to Peru.

"Father, I've been awarded a Fulbright scholarship," I said to the prelate. "I'll be removing Tony from school for the next year."

"Congratulations," he said, "but I don't think taking your son away from his studies here is a good idea."

"But he'd have an opportunity to become fluent in Spanish," I said. "He'd get the kind of education few children get by living in another country."

"Leaving now would deprive a bright student of the new learning he's getting in his math, science, and English classes. It would be detrimental to his future."

"I'd enroll him in high school in Cusco where he'd be exposed to other points of view."

"Tony is a good student here. If he goes to Peru at all, I think it should be during his summer vacation."

Timmy was up for any new adventure and ready to go. But I delayed accepting the Fulbright while I contemplated what to do. I'd have to choose between a new home or a Fulbright scholarship. I wanted both. I weighed the pros and cons of my competing opportunities. A Fulbright doctoral study would provide me data for my dissertation and open the possibility of a future college professorship. But, if I accepted the Fulbright, we couldn't afford the bigger house in the classier area of Fremont because the monthly payments would require two salaries. Buying the expensive home meant not conducting research abroad and my children not becoming bilingual. Then again, Tony didn't seem any more enthusiastic about living in Peru now than he'd been in 1975.

How could I choose between the house of my dreams and intellectual advancement through adventure? I usually figured out a way to achieve most of what I wanted. Not this time. If I chose the more elegant house, I'd give up a year in Peru and the prestige of the scholarship. This turning point would decide my future career and life direction.

I maneuvered through freeway traffic on Highway 680 to my job in San Jose in November 1981. I heard a voice in my head make my decision. *I want that house, no matter the consequences.* Such a bargain might never come again, and Antonio didn't want me to take our children to live in his dangerous homeland. He preferred the house purchase. I called Larry and instructed him to bargain for the house.

Due to the exorbitantly high interest rates and the holidays, we were the only bidders. We could purchase the big house from the original owner for $241,000—if we assumed his loan with a 21 percent interest rate. He'd obtained the loan to pay the wife he was divorcing for her half of the property. Our realtor said we were playing Monopoly—trading in our Darwin Drive and rental townhouses for a Park Avenue-type property.

My desire for the house triumphed over my plan to study in a foreign country. With a heavy heart I informed the Fulbright Commission that I would decline their award. My boys wouldn't spend a year in their father's country and become fluent in Spanish. No dissertation or professorships would result from my research in Peru. I might someday regret passing up this once-in-a-lifetime opportunity.

Hardest of all was seeing the truth of who I was. Material good had triumphed over my higher ideals of intellectual improvement and foreign living. Before, adventure had defined me. Now, materialism did.

I turned my attention to the mercenary details of financing the house. The $12,000 down payment couldn't come from the sale of our Darwin Drive home. Larry couldn't sell the house because mortgage interest rates were the highest they'd ever been. Instead, he rented it out at a rate that just covered the mortgage.

I secured a $5,000 student loan from a bank at three percent interest. I needed the Title VII scholarship I'd applied for the previous spring to complete the money package. If awarded, it would cover a year's tuition and give me a $5,000 stipend. I'd submitted the required documents for the award months ago and hadn't received word if I was still in the running. For the money to do me any good, I needed it soon. I took action.

I phoned the director of the Multicultural Department. Silence. I received no response about my status. I knew my grades qualified me, but as one of the few Anglos in the department, I didn't think I stood much chance of being given the award. I sent the director a certified letter requesting to know my status. He couldn't ignore me because he had to sign for the letter. A week later I received a response.

I jumped with joy. The director informed me that I'd been granted tuition for thirty units of classes I didn't need, and the $5,000 stipend I did need. Now, added to the $5,000 low-interest loan, and our $2,000 in savings, we had our down payment. Lady Luck was still with me.

We assumed two high-interest loans: one for 17 percent and the second for 21 percent. This made our house payments in excess of $2,500 a month, a bit less than our combined take-home pay. We'd have to curtail all spending until we refinanced the mortgages. For the first time in our marriage, our house payment required both our salaries. Our financial exposure was high. Antonio and I hoped that neither of us would get sick, lose our jobs, or have some other expensive mishap. We were in hock to the banks up to our ears.

I returned to full-time work. Working part-time had had minimal impact on my dissertation-writing time. I had little written work to show for my extra two days a week off. Rather than read and write, I'd spent time performing mundane household tasks like cleaning and organizing. This resulted in a clean house but little progress on my dissertation. Time pressures made me more efficient. That's when the job change from Fremont to San Jose Unified paid big dividends.

My new supervisor welcomed my dissertation proposal to conduct research with students from the district. So, in the summer of 1982, using two questionnaires I developed, I interviewed nineteen mothers regarding their Spanish-speaking four-to-six-year-old children. Ten children, who had been identified as communicatively handicapped, were in the experimental group. Nine others, with the same ages and backgrounds and selected at random, were in the control group. I compared the pace of language development of the two groups and found a significant difference in their language milestones. I concluded that illnesses, usually ear infections, had delayed the identified children's early language growth. By fall 1982, my doctoral degree was in sight.

From September to December, I spent weekends and vacations compiling and writing my results. I accepted no social invitations and never attended a movie. Antonio accompanied Timmy to his baseball games and Tony to his soccer games. I still drove my oldest son to his speech debates and chess matches in the San Jose area until he earned his driver's license. My mother pitched in to provide meals and patch our clothes when I had no time to do either. Coworkers covered for me if I had to leave work early to confer in person with my statistician or meet with my dissertation committee. The pressures grew.

Antonio purchased our first computer and encouraged me to use its word processing program to edit my writing. Completed chapters often disappeared when I hit the wrong command. The lost chapters miraculously reappeared after I'd spent hours late into the night reconstructing them. The university informed me that our dot matrix printer's writing wasn't acceptable for my final dissertation document. So I hired a professional typist in San Francisco to produce the quality of printing they'd accept.

Many Friday nights I motored an hour to San Francisco and tossed an envelope with my latest precious chapter through the locked gate of my typist's apartment building. I wouldn't relax until I received her call informing me that my work was safely in her hands. On my way, I passed college-age revelers partying and drinking into the night. At my all-women's college, I'd never celebrated like that. Pangs of envy hit me as I sped by these San Francisco college students enjoying their carefree lives.

By December 1982 I'd analyzed the data, written my findings, and presented the volume of completed work to my dissertation committee. But from January through April 1983, I received contradictory requests from two dissertation committee members about the correct terminology to use in my written work. I couldn't satisfy both. In the end, my committee chairman stepped in and convinced the disagreeing professors to accept my work.

Just as I'd delivered my friend Michele's dissertation to the University of California nine years before, this time I delivered my own signed dissertation to the University of San Francisco. I breathed a sigh of relief. I had achieved another difficult goal.

On May 28, 1983 my parents, sons, husband, and my high school girlfriend Annette, who'd come from Denver, watched me walk across the University of San Francisco stage and accept my doctoral diploma. The flowing black graduation gown disguised another unanticipated achievement—I'd lost thirty pounds from the stress. The doctorate though, was the more important goal. I'd achieved it, despite the distractions and odds—and received the satisfaction of another victory and another piece of paper.

Tony with Evelyn and her doctoral diploma

Progress and Pitfalls by Degree

One day in June of 1983, I was clearing piles of notes and stacks of dissertation drafts from my desk when the phone rang. Hoping for a social engagement, I answered.

"Dr. LaTorre?" an official-sounding voice asked. I quivered with pride at the use of my new title.

"Yes," I answered, "This is Dr. LaTorre." I felt a bit uncomfortable referring to myself that way.

"The Special Education division of the California State Department of Education is sponsoring a five-week program in Southern California to update bilingual personnel on the latest educational research and practices. I thought you might want to attend."

"What is the cost and where will it be held?" I asked.

I enjoyed learning new information and techniques that I could use as a bilingual psychologist. But I'd just spent four years and considerable money on multicultural education classes. I'd written numerous papers and completed a dissertation about bilingual students. More of the same didn't sound appealing.

"It will be held at Cal State Northridge," the official said. "The state is paying for all education, travel, and housing expenses. And there will be a week of field experience in Ensenada, Mexico."

"Please send me an application," I said. "I'm definitely interested."

Four weeks in Southern California didn't sound as enticing as the week in Mexico. However, I couldn't pass up the prospect of a paid trip. I'd have the chance to connect with others in my field and earn the new Certificate of Bilingual Competence. This new certificate might be handy to add to my others.

I had earned the BA, MSW, and EdD degrees from attending ten years of classes and writing stacks of scholarly papers. The LCSW (Licensed Clinical Social Worker), MFT (Marriage and Family Therapist), and LEP (Licensed Educational Psychologist) licenses had required the signatures of supervisors who vouched that I'd performed hours of counseling and test administration. Teaching boys PE in the Peace Corps and passing a course in the new math curriculum had qualified me for a California Standard Teaching Credential. Two Pupil Personnel authorizations resulted from studying two years at UC Berkeley and one at Cal State Hayward. The Administrative Credential came when I heeded the advice of a colleague and passed an exam that was offered only once. My degrees and credentials overflowed like a bowl of alphabet soup.

"Due to the state's growing number of Spanish-speaking pupils referred by their teachers for learning difficulties," explained the papers admitting me to the July 17 to August 20 program, "the California State Department of Education needs to train bilingual psychologists and speech therapists in appropriate evaluation procedures."

"Can I leave you guys on your own?" I asked Antonio and the boys at a June dinner.

It seemed I left them too frequently. Though I'd promised myself that I wouldn't neglect my family during my doctoral studies, I'd spent many weekends and evenings writing my dissertation and not with them. Maybe I needed to make it up to my family.

"I believe you should do whatever you want," said my understanding husband. "Just like I take the classes I want. People are happier and more productive when others don't keep them from getting more education. We'll manage."

Maybe Antonio hadn't always shouldered our family's financial and child-care responsibilities equitably, but he didn't stand in the way when I needed to diminish my role to further my career. We had taken turns managing our little family. I'd taken full charge during the eighteen months of Antonio's absence in Peru. Now it was his turn to be in charge of the household.

"Mom," Tony said, "I'm in high school. I don't need a babysitter."

My sixteen-year-old was right. He now had his driver's license and a part-time job at a fruit stand. He could drive himself and his brother to their summer swimming and sports activities. And if he couldn't, my mother said she would.

The first week we all did fine. But, after that, I missed my boys terribly. I wondered if they missed me. A letter from twelve-year-old Timmy confirmed that he longed for me too. He wrote that he was trying to have fun but was curious about where I was and when they could come join me. I knew what I had to do. I flew back home from L.A. the Saturday before my final week of classes, collected my sons, and drove four hundred miles back to Cal State Northridge in Antonio's red two-door Fiat coupe.

I loved being reunited with my boys, and Antonio welcomed the reprieve. Tony didn't mind taking a leave from the copy store, and both boys were eager for a new adventure. Our first undertaking wasn't to Tony's liking.

"Tony, lift your end higher," I said pulling the fifty-pound microwave oven up the stairway backward toward my second-floor apartment in the Cal State dormitory.

"Mom," my nearly five-foot-eight son said, panting and hanging onto the heavy appliance with all the strength of his adolescent arms, "Maybe we should leave this in the car trunk."

"No," I said, "we need it mornings to heat up your cocoa and evenings to warm our TV dinners. Just another few stairs and we'll be in the apartment."

We didn't yet have a microwave oven at home in Fremont. Most households had had one for a couple of years. A friend recommended a Panasonic model. I discovered one at a bargain price in a San Fernando Valley appliance store and bought it.

Struggling, Tony and I managed to get the oven into my small residence damaging nothing more than my thumb. I bent the appendage backward, nearly out of its socket, to keep from dropping the heavy appliance. My consolation was having found the new microwave at a lower price than in the Bay Area. That problem solved, I faced the next one.

I had no one to check on the boys the mornings I attended classes. They had to entertain themselves alone inside my student-housing flat while I was in class. I worried that they'd be bored on their own. A fire could start in another apartment or my boys might go outside and get lost. Bringing them to the Cal State campus might not have been well thought out. I comforted myself knowing they usually showed good judgment and had become used to taking care of themselves. I left them with television and snacks and hoped for the best. Then afternoons, we enjoyed ourselves seeing the Los Angeles sites.

I drove to places that would entertain two active boys. At Marineland, we sat in the first row and got splashed by jumping orca whales. Already wet, the boys headed over to a pond and went snorkeling. We rode the train around Knott's Berry Farm and afterward slurped triple-decker ice cream cones. One afternoon we revisited the boys' favorite place, Universal Studios. They loved all the movie sets and startled when the *Jaws* shark jumped out of the water.

At the end of the week, we drove 230 miles down highway 405, crossed the border, and arrived in Ensenada, Mexico. The town of 139,000 didn't look at all like when Antonio and I had visited it in 1973. The population had increased 60 percent and spread out every which way.

The state program had arranged for the three of us to live with a Mexican family that had an eleven-year-old boy. Tony and Timmy were captivated by the family's litter of fat, tan-and-white German shepherd puppies. Timmy became attached to the whitest one and begged to take her home with us. I inquired how to do that and discovered that transporting the puppy to the US required documentation and a quarantine period. I called Antonio.

He shouted an adamant *"No!"* over the phone, when I asked him if we could bring a dog into the family. Pets, he believed, required more care than we could provide. However, he agreed that I could have the worn-out seats of the Fiat recovered in Ensenada where labor was cheap. We arrived back in Fremont without a dog, but with new cherry-red vinyl seat covers on the Fiat.

I returned to work in September 1983 to a surprise. San Jose Unified's superintendent announced that the district was near bankruptcy and would take drastic measures to save money. All psychologists would be assigned to schools and serve in the dual roles of vice-principal and psychologist. For two years, I'd been the psychologist at Markham Middle School and loved working with the staff. Now I'd be their school psychologist and one of two vice-principals.

Many of my colleagues weren't as pleased about their new roles because the positions required an administrative credential, which they didn't have. They had to return to college to obtain the specialization. Most of them enrolled at San Jose State College for a two-year program of classes. I recalled the similar situation when I'd worked for San Francisco Unified Schools. Credential requirements cropped up frequently in education. This time I escaped even more easily than I had in San Francisco. I had the required credential, thanks to the exam I'd passed in 1978.

My fellow San Jose Unified psychologists left work to attend evening classes while I drove home to my family. I silently thanked Ed for his advice five years before. Having this additional piece of paper had come in handy. However, having credentials and degrees counted for little in some situations.

At times I was called upon to simultaneously reward a student as a psychologist and punish him as the vice-principal. For example, a pupil's behavior plan called for him to receive a reward from me, the psychologist, for getting to class on time. But then, on the same day, he got into a fight. So he also needed to be punished by me, the VP. Which hat should I wear, rewarder or punisher? After puzzling over the dilemma, I concluded it was like being a parent. If the student and I had built a relationship, he would see how he'd earned both the reward and the punishment.

In a second situation, I was tasked with leading a meeting of parents whose children had shown little or no progress in their classes and had failed standardized tests. At the evening engagement, I listened to a room of forty irate mothers and fathers hurl blame at the school's teachers and administrators for their children's deficiencies. I came armed with suggestions of how to improve study habits at home. But these parents weren't interested in my ideas and continued to complain with increasing volume. I lost my voice trying to be heard over their shouts. When the disastrous meeting finally ended, I uttered a soft curse to myself. My degrees and credentials counted for little when trying to reason with disgruntled parents. Luckily, the year ended with an invitation to travel far away from them.

Summer Break

I sat in my kitchen the spring of 1984 making plans for another eventful summer. As I was contemplating a return trip to Montana, my phone rang, and I heard an unfamiliar voice.

"I'm with the National Hispanic University and was given your name by the State Special Education Department," the woman said. "I understand that you participated in their bilingual assessment program at Cal State Northridge last year."

I answered in the affirmative, curious about what this university I'd never heard of needed from me. I didn't plan to take more coursework.

"We are now in charge of the program," the woman continued, "and would like you to teach the six-week bilingual assessment course to twenty or so school psychologists. A bilingual speech therapist will teach the speech therapists. To reinforce use of Spanish, this year the program will be held in Guadalajara, Mexico, and taught in Spanish."

I sat up straight and alert. A new crop of Spanish-speaking assessment personnel from California school districts needed to learn current evaluation tools. I could teach them how to determine whether a Spanish-speaking student qualified for placement in special education. And I'd be paid to live in Mexico. Of course, I would teach in Guadalajara.

I again asked my mother to usher Timmy to his daytime summer activities—swimming lessons, baseball and soccer games. Mom, like my husband and sons, seemed to expect my usual summer departure. Tony was busy working at the Winchester Repeater copy store and unable to play chauffer. Antonio said they could survive without me—and besides, this time, I'd be earning money. We could all tolerate the six-week separation just fine. My thirteen- and seventeen-year-old sons had activities they didn't want to miss, and I'd be busy planning lessons. I started making arrangements.

First, I had to find twenty Spanish-language test kits to take across the border. I convinced an administrator I knew from the Alameda County Department of Special Education to lend me the equipment I needed. Next, I crammed the five-pound manuals into a couple of suitcases. Then, I ushered them all through customs into Mexico without a mishap.

I was delighted to be back in the colorful colonial city of Guadalajara. I'd first visited it in 1963 on my way to Central Mexico, where I volunteered with Amigos Anonymous. This attractive, bustling city had grown by a million inhabitants since I'd last seen it.

Louisa, a Spanish-speaking speech therapist from the Oakland Unified School District, taught the speech therapists. This friendly and fun-loving instructor and I became fast friends the first week. Our classrooms were next door to one another at the Universidad Autónomo. We agreed on the importance of a program like ours for public school personnel—and the challenge of teaching the group in a language many couldn't comprehend.

Louisa's family had come from Uruapan, Mexico, three hours south of Guadalajara. One of our first weekends, she hosted eight students and instructors from the program at her grandparents' home in this second largest city in the state of Michoacán. We spent hours walking on paths among the ancient trees, natural waterfalls, and springs in the city's impressive nearby national park. From there, we traveled by bus to the city of Pátzcuaro with its indigenous Indian atmosphere and flower-filled balconies. Discovering new cultures excited me.

Surrounded by vibrant colors, unique crafts, and interesting people—this was my kind of summer.

Two weeks before our teaching duties ended, Louisa suggested that our group spend the weekend at the Barra de Navidad coastal beach, a four-hour bus ride west of Guadalajara. I loved exploring new places and was eager to go. Teaching adult students with limited Spanish skills required almost more patience than I possessed. I hadn't spoken Spanish for a six-hour stretch since my Peace Corps days in Peru and was ready to relax on the sand.

We packed snacks, bought bus tickets, and Friday after classes set out across the state of Jalisco for the two-hundred-mile journey. Louisa had reserved a room for the two of us in a resort hotel on a hill with a view of the ocean. We arrived in time for a quick dip in the Pacific and a fish dinner afterward. We spent Saturday touring the town where we admired the curvy wrought-iron balconies, the mariachis in the plaza, and the forested path to the beach.

Sunday morning dawned clear and perfect for another day at the beach. There wouldn't be a place to change there, so I dressed in white shorts and a black-and-white-striped T-shirt, with my bathing suit underneath. I was ready for fun in the sun.

I tiptoed to the picture window of our room, careful not to awaken the still-sleeping Louisa. Down below on the burnt-orange clay tennis courts I saw eight dark-haired, muscular young men attempting to play tennis. I was irresistibly drawn to dark-haired, handsome Latin men like my husband.

Back home in Fremont, I played weekly on competitive singles and doubles teams at the local tennis club. Between games, I practiced several times a week. I hadn't hit a tennis ball now in over a month and was itching to get onto the courts below. The urge overtook any shyness I felt. I bounded downstairs to where I'd seen the guys.

I hadn't brought my tennis racket to Mexico and had never played tennis on clay courts. So, at first, I sat and watched the twenty-something young men, critiquing how poorly they played my favorite sport. These handsome youths missed the ball more than they hit it. And they never connected hard. Their lack of tennis skills was pathetic. I knew I played better than they did—and longed to show them. So I challenged them to a game.

Laughing, a slim, dark-haired man with muscular legs handed me his racket, and I took my place across the net from an equally fit guy. My athletic opponent hit the first ball high into the air to my side. I'd learned how to spot the ball by pointing at it with my left index finger, then whacking it back with my racket when it reached just above my head. *I had this. I would show them the correct way to play.* I spotted the ball, jumped high off the ground and threw all my weight behind the anticipated shot. The racket and ball didn't connect but I did—with the clay court.

Crash, bang! I came down hard—onto my rear. Orange dust covered the back of my white shorts. I had seen the water on the court near my feet but didn't know that clay courts become slippery when wet. I landed with my right hand still wrapped around the handle of the wooden racket. Dang, I'd failed the shot. Worse, a pain, like a sharp poker, radiated through my wrist and up my arm. Now, besides sitting on my rump, I couldn't lift the racket. My hand wouldn't move. It seemed disconnected from my arm. A new concern overshadowed my humiliation at missing the ball.

A dark-haired man, even more handsome than the others, ran up from somewhere as the guys gathered around with concern on their faces. The man from the sidelines said he was the Monterrey Mexico soccer team's orthopedist and had seen me fall. He felt my wrist. It hurt.

"I think you've broken it," he said in Spanish. "I need to set it in place right away. Do you have a room here?"

"I have a room above in the hotel," I said, in shock from what had just happened.

I'd never before broken anything but my teeth in a fall. That too was because of tennis when I'd attempted to jump over a net in college. Tennis was bad for my health.

Louisa was surprised when I entered our hotel room with the handsome physician. I explained what had happened. The doctor told me to lie down on my bed and knelt beside me.

"I need to manipulate your hand," he said, concern in his dark brown eyes.

Did I see moisture in his long, black eyelashes? Louisa stood by my bedside in almost as much shock as me. The good doctor directed us both.

"Please get a washcloth from the bathroom," he said to my roommate.

"You will feel pain and can bite on this." The doctor said to me, handing me the cloth. "You can scream or anything because it will hurt. But I have to do this."

I'd heard these directions in a movie somewhere and knew what he was about to do. With a quick jerk, he pulled my hand to realign it with my arm. I felt excruciating pain for a moment but didn't scream. I wanted to impress him with how brave I was. The doctor was the orthopedist for one of the best professional soccer teams in Mexico. That was the team I'd challenged. I trusted that this physician knew what to do. He did. My wrist bones connected and once more I could move my hand.

"I think I know where the break is," my savior said, standing. "But to be sure, we should have it X-rayed before I set it."

He could do whatever he wanted. I was in a daze, partly from shock and partly from being with one of the handsomest Latin guys I'd ever seen. And I hadn't been with my own handsome Latin husband in a month.

It was Sunday and most clinics were closed. But Louisa knew of a man who had an X-ray machine in his home office. The three of us took a taxi to the place.

The X-ray showed the break where the doctor had suspected. I paid for the film with the few pesos I'd brought with me. With the last of my money, we stopped at a pharmacy to purchase *yeso* (plaster), and bandages. The orthopedist structured a cast around my right wrist and finished by fashioning a sling for my arm. He looked proud of his work.

When I was again in one piece, I borrowed $150 in pesos from Louisa and paid the kind doctor. He advised me that my wrist would hurt more as it healed but should be okay. We returned to the hotel where the *futbol* team waited. The team signed my cast and wished me well while Louisa took photos with my Instamatic camara. Then, I said good-bye to the team and the town. I left with a painful reminder of getting to know both.

Futbol team's doctor signing Evelyn's cast

When my adrenaline wore off, the pain from my injury increased as the bus bumped along the road back to Guadalajara. The ride gave me four hours to contemplate my impulsive behavior. I shouldn't have expected men skilled at hitting balls with their feet to be adept at hitting them using their hands. Now, how would I teach without the use of my writing hand?

Monday at the university, the program director from the National Hispanic University visiting from California said he'd be returning to the States the next day. He offered to take back any written communication we wanted mailed in the US. I had Louisa write a quick postcard from me to my former Peace Corps roommate, Marie. Marie worked as a school psychologist in a Pontiac, Michigan, district. She would be off work for the summer and liked to travel.

In her early childhood, Marie had lived for twelve years near Guadalajara with her American parents. She spoke fluent Spanish. We regularly compared notes on our lives and work. My postcard informed her about my broken wrist and my inability to write on the blackboard. I invited her to come stay in the extra bed in my free apartment and help me teach my class. She didn't need much coaxing.

Thank heavens the US had an efficient postal system. Marie arrived by my side on Sunday. For the next week she accompanied me to my classes, helped me dress, cook, and perform everyday tasks that I couldn't do using my nondominant hand. Laughing and talking together took my mind off my hurting, healing wrist. Marie taught my class, telling the students about the research she'd done to understand the learning difficulties of the Spanish-speaking students where she worked. I thanked her by helping her track down friends with whom she'd gone to school near Guadalajara thirty years before. We enjoyed the colorful city and one another up to the last day of my teaching contract.

Unfortunately, Marie couldn't accompany me to the airport the Sunday I left for home. I was set to board my flight when a man blocked the doorway in front of the ramp to my airplane. He held out his hand and said he needed my visa. I remembered seeing the officially stamped piece of paper when I'd entered the country. But I didn't have it now. It must have fallen out of my passport somewhere between the apartment and the airport.

"You are required to present proof of when and where you entered Mexico," the man said giving me a stern look.

"But I have my passport," I pleaded. My heart beat fast.

"Without that paper," he said again holding out his hand, "you aren't allowed to leave."

"I can't miss my plane," I said, beginning to panic.

"Sorry," the man said, gesturing with his greedy palm, "without that visa, you'll need to stay the night in town and apply for a duplicate visa at the US consulate tomorrow."

From his stance, I guessed that this man wanted a bribe. Paying bribes went against my principles. Besides, I had no money to pay for a hotel in town or give to this corrupt gatekeeper. As usual, I'd spent every last peso.

I began to sweat, and my body tensed. This person was trying to take advantage of a woman with a broken, hurting, wrist—all because of a thin little piece of paper with a stamp on it. I wanted to cry but wouldn't give this guy the satisfaction. I took a deep breath and stared him in the eye.

"I have to see my doctor in the States tomorrow morning," I said with authority. "He has to look at my wrist, which I broke here. If I can't make it to my appointment and am permanently disfigured, I'll blame you."

Without another word he let me pass. I gathered up my passport and marched onto the plane where I collapsed into my seat.

I returned to my VP-psychologist job at Markham that fall with my right wrist immobile and my arm in a sling. Writing class schedules and psychology reports was impossible until the cast came off. Nevertheless, my time in Mexico had refreshed my Spanish-speaking ability enough to pass another test that gave me a new piece of paper—the Advanced Bilingual Assessment Credential. I added it to my pile.

By the spring of 1985, San Jose Unified's finances were solvent and the school district offered its psychologists a choice to go back to their original roles or remain assistant principals. All the psychologists including me chose to return to their original jobs of serving four schools a week—a testament to the difficulty of the VP job.

I'd accomplished a great deal during my past summers. Now I deserved a real vacation. I'd never been to Europe and decided to go. I asked Antonio and our boys if they wanted to accompany me. Their answers surprised me.

Off to Europe

I'd loved to travel ever since my parents took us five children on a train trip from our home in Southeastern Montana to the West Coast when I was fifteen years old. For the first time, I saw mountains and the ocean and realized what an amazing world existed outside my hill town of two hundred people. I never wanted to stop exploring after experiencing the joy of that first discovery.

Before marrying and having children, I satisfied my wanderlust by journeying about Mexico with Barbara, my college friend from the Amigos Anonymous group. In the Peace Corps I'd explored Peru and Chile with my roommate, Marie. My international travels, after marriage and having children, had been to visit Antonio and his family in Peru and to whichever country I'd won an all-expenses paid trip.

When Tony and Tim were small, I fantasized that during my summer hiatus from school, I would pack up my preschoolers, hop on a bus, and visit my home state of Montana. But when Antonio said he couldn't be away for more than a weekend because of his summer job, I had to face reality. A lengthy trip alone with our youngsters would be more hassle than pleasure. I didn't have enough energy to wrestle two little ones for long distances. I'd need to pack bags full of diapers, clothes, and baby food for Timmy. And Tony needed to have regular meals, or he got cranky. I realized then I'd need to wait until the boys were older to take them on long trips. Antonio didn't dream of travel like I did.

During Antonio's first eight years in California, he'd never expressed a desire to travel outside the state, so the four of us had visited a few state and national parks within California. He'd not even suggested returning to his Peruvian homeland until I convinced him that his mother would like to meet our sons. When Antonio remained in Peru for eighteen months to teach, I almost regretted having insisted that he travel with us.

The summer of 1978, Antonio's best friend, Romualdo, had to coax Antonio to accompany him, his family, and us through the US Southwestern parks in his VW bus. Antonio reluctantly agreed. What joy adventuring for two weeks through the West's unique mountain and valley formations with Antonio and our friends. But Antonio had reached his limit. He had no wanderlust—and mine couldn't be satisfied.

He chose not to accompany the boys and me on our camping trip through Canada with my father in 1981. My sons and I had returned several times to my home state of Montana without Antonio. Therefore, I expected him to decline my invitation to travel to Europe, which he did. The kids and I were used to traveling without Antonio.

I wanted to visit as many European countries as possible during my ten-week summer vacation. With Tim almost fourteen, and Tony eighteen, travel abroad would be educational for them, and something they'd likely remember later in life. Finances were not an obstacle because we'd received an unexpected windfall.

The high interest rates on our new house had resulted in a $3,000 income tax refund. I said I'd use the unexpected bonus to pay for a European adventure for any member of the family who wanted to go. Antonio couldn't get away from work, but he didn't object to my going. Tony said he needed to prepare for entry into the university in the fall. Only Tim was enthusiastic to accompany me.

I hadn't made detailed travel arrangements in several years and didn't know where to begin. Where should we stay in Paris and Athens? How many hours did we need to see the ruins of Pompeii—and how would we get there? I wasn't even certain which cities in what countries we should visit. When I saw an ad for a three-week, $3,000 tour for two through France and Greece, I signed up Tim and me. When Tim saw the colorful brochure, he could hardly wait to stay at the Blue Lagoon Hotel on the cover.

A week after committing to the tour, I was on the phone with Barbara, the Amigos Anonymous friend with whom I'd traveled around Mexico. Barbara was incredulous when I told her I'd signed up for a European tour.

"Evelyn," Barbara said, as if she were older than me instead of younger, "if you can travel in Mexico and Peru on your own, you certainly can travel in Europe without a tour guide."

I thought long and hard about Barbara's words. She had traveled to Italy so knew about European travel. I hated paying $3,000 for two people to spend three weeks in two countries. There were so many more places to see. Barbara was right. But I'd have to get out of the "no cancellations" travel agency contract I'd signed. And, maybe more challenging—explain the change of plans to my eager young son.

One Saturday morning in April, Tim and I lay on our stomachs on the orange carpet of our large family room looking at a map of Europe. Sunshine streamed through the sliding glass patio doors and warmed our backs. It felt like we were already lying on a beach in Greece. Tim looked at the worn brochure with the picture of the sparkling blue pool at the Blue Lagoon Hotel.

"Tim," I said in a gentle voice, "I'm going to cancel our tour and we'll figure out how to travel in Europe on our own."

"But Mom," my son said, a pout of disappointment spreading over his face, "if we cancel the tour, we can't stay at the Blue Lagoon Hotel with the pretty swimming pool."

"Hmmm," I said, putting my arm around him, "we could follow the same route as the tour and add more countries and cities. We might even stay at the nice hotel in the picture."

My words seemed to pacify him, especially when I drew a route that over eight weeks went to England, France, Italy, Greece, Austria, Germany, and Holland. Now I just had to figure out how to get out of the travel agency's contract that stated only medical emergencies could nullify it. I didn't want to pay the hefty 25 percent penalty for canceling. I had to lie.

I held my breath when I called the agency to report that Tim had broken his arm and we'd have to cancel our trip with them. The woman from the travel company didn't ask for a doctor's statement as proof. My breathing returned to normal. I'd escaped the tour, but now I had to make plans. I started with two resources. I purchased a copy of Frommer's travel guide, *Europe on $5 Day* and I joined Intervac, a home exchange network.

On the Intervac form, I submitted the dates of the home stays we needed in Europe. I offered the dates between June 16 to August 17 for Europeans to stay in our home. If Antonio and Tony chose not to go with Tim and me, they might just have to entertain people from Europe whose houses we'd stay in. Antonio might object, so I didn't mention this potential home intrusion to him. As I often did, I trusted things would work out.

One May day at work, the Markham school secretary buzzed me on the intercom in a classroom where I was observing a student. The secretary said I had a call from England. Bewildered, I hurried to my office. Who would call me from so far away? The person must have calculated the eight-hour time-zone difference in order to reach me during work hours.

"My name is Mr. Miller," said a clipped, precise English voice on the other end of the phone. "I live in England and am responding to your Intervac Home Exchange ad."

"Do you live in London?" I asked,

"No, but we're just a half-hour train ride away," said the BBC-type accent, "in Hemel Hempstead, near St. Alban's. My wife and I have two daughters, ages six and eight."

I listened, hardly moving, waiting for Mr. Miller to tell me when his British family would come to stay in my California home. I wondered how the non-traveling half of the LaTorres would like hosting the Miller family of four.

"We won't stay at your place," Mr. Miller continued, "but we would like you to stay with us. We like our daughters to get to know people from other countries. The charge would be twenty-five pounds for the week, including breakfast."

I relaxed. I knew from reading the Frommer guide that the $40 price for a week's stay was more than reasonable. And better yet— Antonio and Tony wouldn't have to share our house with a family from England.

"That sounds fine," I said, overjoyed at the affordable price. "We arrive on June 17. Give me your phone number and address and, after all our transportation is confirmed, I'll let you know exactly what time we'll get there."

"Good," our future host said, "I'll pick you up at the train that comes from London."

We were off to a great start. This home-exchange thing was better than I'd anticipated. My opinion was reinforced when I received a second offer from a family who lived outside Bologna, Italy. The city was on our itinerary because we wanted to visit friends Angela and Michele, whom we'd known at UC Berkeley.

The Italian woman from the Intervac ad wrote in English that we could stay in her family's home for the week in July when she, her husband, and teenage son would be on vacation elsewhere in Italy. Better yet—her family wouldn't come to stay at our house. The signora wanted the option to send her son to stay with us in California for a week sometime in the future. Elated, I accepted her offer. Now

Antonio wouldn't have to share our house with an Italian family in my absence.

The more plans Tony heard Tim and me make, the more interested he became in the trip. My two sons were so different. Tony, like his father, usually stood back to analyze a situation for a long time before making a commitment. Tim, like me, jumped into opportunities trusting everything would work out. Soon, Tony offered his opinions about places to visit. Then, he decided to accompany us.

I purchased three round-trip tickets on a charter flight to London for $1,000, then found out where to purchase Eurail passes. These official permits would allow us to ride trains for two months in most European countries. I notified our Italian friends of the July dates we'd be in Bologna. We packed three small suitcases and three empty carryon bags for future souvenirs. We were ready.

Antonio drove us to the San Francisco International Airport the evening of June 16 and kissed us good-bye. I felt a bit guilty that he'd have to return to an empty house. The smile on his face, however, told me that being away from our noise and activity might be something he looked forward to.

For two months Tony, Tim, and I followed the seven-country itinerary I'd planned. We only had to call Antonio once and ask him to send us more money. We had scores of adventures.

Tony almost got lost from Tim and me when, after our tour to London's East End, he went off on his own to retrace the murders of Jack the Ripper. In Paris we stayed in a cheap hotel on the left bank, whose four stories leaned toward the street and smelled of urine. The boys refused to use the shared showers there, so I went to twenty-eight other hotels requesting *"une chambre avec deux lits et une salle de bain,"* before finding a two-bed room where they could finally take a shower.

Inside the celebrated Cemetery of the Capuchin Fathers in Paris, the boys were enthralled to see six rooms filled with monks' skulls and bones arranged in decorative motifs around arches and over every wall. The hall of mirrors at Versailles amazed me more. Tony was pick-pocketed on a bus in Rome. We forgot to grab the bag of music boxes we'd purchased in Sorrento when we got off our train in Munich. In an instant, Tim and I raced back, reboarded our train, and grabbed the bag a minute before the locomotive left for Vienna.

When we heard our Italian hosts, Angela and Michele, shouting at one another, we assumed it was just usual loud Italian talk, and tried to ignore it. Later, we learned the couple was on the verge of divorce and what we'd heard was anger. The ship we thought our Italian friends had booked for us to Greece, didn't have our names on the docket. The alternate ship we took went on strike and stranded us for a day in Corfu. We decided to go to a beach there, but women at the one we chose bathed topless—which shocked us all. In Greece, the Blue Lagoon Hotel turned out to be a dump. We stayed elsewhere.

By mid-August, the three of us had been educated in the art, music, language, food, and customs of seven foreign countries. Our luggage was loaded with more souvenirs than we could carry. At the San Francisco Airport, a big flat box moved down the baggage conveyer belt toward us. I told Antonio it was for him. When he looked inside, his mouth fell open. There was a sleek, red Italian racing bike—one like I'd heard him often say he wanted. He was almost as pleased as I was whenever I won a prize. And I did win more.

In May of 1986, I won an all-expense paid trip for two to the World's Fair in Vancouver, Canada. I stretched it into a trip for three so Tim could go too. As always, Tim and I were eager to explore a new country. We rejoiced when Antonio said he, too, wanted to see Canada. Finally, a trip I didn't have to beg him to take.

In April 1988, I entered a contest that required, "one entry per household." So I wrote my mother's name on one of the entry blanks. Weeks later, Mom recieved a call.

"Congratulations," said a woman from the fabric store to my sixty-eight-year-old mother. "You're going to the prom!"

After a good laugh, Mom and the woman transferred the "junior prom package"—free corsage, dinner, limousine, and tux rental—to Tim for his upcoming junior prom.

Reunion

I'd never been to Washington, DC. Fellow Peace Corps volunteer Karen, from my Peru group, suggested we go to the September 18, 1986, weekend celebration of the twenty-fifth anniversary of the Peace Corps. I agreed, but I couldn't convince my former Peace Corps roommate, Marie, to attend. She'd been to the capital many times and didn't want to go again. Too bad, she'd miss three days of merriment, reminiscing, and inspiration with four thousand other returned volunteers.

The first day, on a tour through the White House with Karen, I admired the different colored rooms that had been decorated by Jacqueline Kennedy. In her 1961 TV tour, Mrs. Kennedy had said that the White House belonged to the American people. Feelings of patriotism filled me as I viewed the antique furniture and gold-framed paintings of our forefathers in the elaborately decorated Red, Blue, and Green Rooms. I'd made a good choice to visit "my house" on the way to celebrate President Kennedy's Peace Corps.

Eight members from my original group of seventy-two attended a reunion dinner at a Peruvian restaurant on the first evening. It had been too long since I'd tasted Peru's marvelous cuisine. The *ceviche* with spices and onion produced a tartness that my tongue enjoyed. The taste lingered in my mouth until replaced by the cumin, *aji* pepper, and garlic of the marinated beef heart *anticuchos* served next.

It seemed like yesterday, instead of twenty years ago, that our group had been debriefed as we departed Lima in June 1966. Then, most had gone off to travel, attend graduate school, or began their careers. I'd returned to Cusco to marry Antonio. Now all eight of us who'd come to the reunion had careers, spouses, and children.

The second day, State Department personnel, the Peruvian Consul General, and a panel of returned volunteers provided an update of recent events in the country of my husband's birth. Antonio and I already knew the bad news—hyperinflation with 55 percent of the country in poverty. My in-laws had fallen into the "poor" category, and we did what many immigrants did. We'd sent Antonio's parents money to help whenever we could.

The final day at the Arlington Cemetery Memorial Amphitheater, we heard the first Peace Corps director, Sargent Shriver, joke about the free spirits who'd help set up the organization. The founders began with no market research, experience, or definition of the Peace Corps. They'd managed with interim policies that changed as the group learned. As of September 1986, the director said the Peace Corps had sent and returned 120,000 volunteers and currently had 5,600 volunteers serving overseas in fifty-two countries. His entertaining and informative speech at the Sunday memorial service, focused on the beginnings and vision of the Peace Corps.

> . . . no one in 1961 would have predicted that the Peace Corps would last five years, let alone twenty-five. Most of us just hoped we would get approval from one Congress and survive to the next. . . . We cannot police the world. But we can begin to liberate it from despair and fear and anger by making economic development and mutual service the hard core of our foreign policy, and of our national defense!

A host of renowned speakers such as CBS commentator Bill Moyers and Cory Aquino, the newly elected president of the Philippines, reminded us of how our more idealistic and humanitarian values differed from those of many of our non-volunteer peers.

Pride welled in my chest as I listened to the stirring speeches. The Peace Corps had forever altered my life and outlook on the world. I'd experienced how caring and generous another culture can be, even without conveniences like the roads, potable water, and electricity that we in the US took for granted.

Later, I encountered Sargent Shriver, accompanied by an assistant, coming toward me in a hallway. I pulled out my camera, and the Peace Corps director stopped.

"Can I take your photograph?" I asked, in awe of this energetic leader.

"Better yet," Sarge said, with a broad smile, "give your camera to my aide and he'll get one of the both of us." A quick snap, and I had a photo of the gregarious and thoughtful director next to his grinning admirer.

Evelyn with Peace Corp Director Sargent Shriver

The events of the weekend reaffirmed my belief in the Peace Corps' mission to promote world peace and friendship. I felt tempted to rejoin. But I had family responsibilities now and had become dependent on too many material comforts.

When I returned home to Fremont, the local newspaper interviewed me. It quoted me as saying, "It's hard not to get caught up in the material world. The hardest choice of my life was turning down a Fulbright grant to return to Peru in 1982. Not enough money to live on, much less hang on to my Fremont home."

I often questioned contentment based on accumulating material wealth. An unexpected tragic event soon reminded me that wealth is of minimal importance when compared to a human life.

Buddy

My brother Bud was a man's man, well suited to live in the cattle country of Eastern Montana. He and we four Kohl sisters traced our earliest childhood memories to that flat Montana landscape of white-shedding cottonwood trees in the spring and whiter drifting snow in the winter.

Buddy was born on May 28, 1948, in Miles City, Montana, when Mom and Dad were twenty-eight. He was the fourth child born in the space of six years. As the only male, he received loads of attention from everyone, including us three girls. We called him "little man" when he was dressed in a little fedora hat and the suit jacket Mom had sewn for him. The boy Mom and Dad had hoped for had finally arrived. I was six years old and loved having a baby brother—one who might eventually take my place collecting the dropped nails from under my father's ladder.

We called the new boy "Buddy" instead of his given name, Leon Donald. At age five he was old enough to be my dad's companion instead of me. Besides picking up Dad's stray nails, he took over my job of running to get a tool Dad had forgotten for his latest home remodeling project. Buddy even rode on Dad's little railroad motorcar when Dad checked the crossing signals for the Milwaukee Railroad in and around Ismay. I didn't mind being replaced. At age eleven, my interests had turned to clothes, hairstyles, and earning money. Dad needed a pal with more interest than I had in hunting, fishing, and building.

In Montana, Buddy was outgoing, talkative, and happy-go-lucky. When he was eleven and our family moved to California, he changed. He and I argued when he insulted me about my weight and other unimportant topics. I'd finally have peace when he retired to his room. Through the open door I'd see him lying on his bunk, spending hours tracing imaginary figures on the ceiling with his index finger. Few of us noticed how unhappy he'd become.

Still, Bud had a real work ethic. He got up early seven days a week to deliver newspapers. When he couldn't do it, we girls had to service his route—so I knew the job was hard. Bud had a hobby of capturing pigeons, which he fed, then released. He related to vulnerable beings. He coasted through school earning A and B grades without studying.

The year after he graduated from Newark High School, he befriended Lezlee, an attractive blond, pregnant, and unmarried senior who walked by my parents' house on her way home from school. Someone else had fathered the baby, but Bud remained by Lezlee's side throughout her pregnancy. He stood by her when she gave the baby up for adoption. He had a fondness for people and creatures that needed him.

As he grew into adulthood, Bud remained relatively short at five foot five. His appearance favored the dark hair of our father and the brown eyes of our mother. He wasn't heavyset or athletic looking, just muscular. He had many friends who liked him.

Bud attended Laney Community College where he was in a four-year electrical apprenticeship program. He became an electrician and, as a member of the electrical workers union, never lacked for work. He saved enough money to take flying lessons, obtain a pilot's license, and buy a small airplane. He was an active guy.

He enjoyed other activities like welding, repairing automobiles, and hunting deer. He joined the Navy Reserve, where he learned to smoke marijuana. Happiness for him was driving down the freeway on his motorcycle with the wind blowing in his early-thinning brown hair. I don't know if he drove high, but he never had an accident or got arrested.

In his early twenties, with his electrical expertise, he helped us select our first stereo. He also helped Dad and Antonio install double-paned windows throughout our house. I fixed lunch for the men, and we joked around. My brother seemed fun-loving and carefree, so the question he asked me in the midst of the window-replacement work seemed strange.

"Evelyn," he asked, "how do you figure out what makes life worth living?"

"I have my children, husband, and many interests that fill my life," I said.

Always the optimist, I had no problem answering. My brother looked at me puzzled. He seemed sad and, for once, had no smart comeback.

On December 30, 1972, he and Lezlee eloped to Reno. A few years later, they had a baby girl. After that, Bud's little family wandered from town to town, looking for a place where they could be happy. Over the next few years, they lived in Sparks, Nevada; Mandan, North Dakota; and Phoenix, Arizona. Finally, they returned to his birthplace, Miles City, Montana, where they added a son to their family.

The little boy was born with his intestines on the outside of his abdomen, a birth defect called, gastroschisis. Bud and Lezlee stayed at the Children's Hospital in Denver, Colorado for the baby's operation. My parents provided emotional support to them and cared for their daughter back in Miles City. Bud and Lezlee returned to Miles City during the three months their son was hospitalized. The baby recovered but needed a great deal of care.

Bud worked then as a welder and an electrician at the coal mines in Colstrip, Montana. He reduced his eighty-mile highway commute by flying his plane between home and work. Long work hours kept him busy and near exhaustion. But he wasn't content.

His restlessness made it appear to me that neither work, family, nor marijuana satisfied Bud. In his search for meaning, he joined a fundamentalist Christian sect in his thirties. He became intolerant of anyone who had a religious practice unlike his and hadn't been "saved." My mother, a devout Catholic, took the brunt of his badgering, which I overheard on her phone calls to Bud. She complained to me about some of their conversations that transpired when my parents visited my brother in Montana and whenever he came to visit them in California.

"Your Catholic religion," Bud said, taunting, "won't save you from the fires of hell."

"My religion," Mom said with conviction, "has been around longer than yours."

"But mine is based on the Bible." Bud sneered. "Yours only uses it when it wants."

"My religion comforts me," Mom said exasperated, "and has proven its legitimacy."

Bud preferred to tear down others' beliefs rather than coexist in a world of many religious faiths. His words struck blows that hurt my Protestant-turned-Catholic mother. But she remained as steadfast in her beliefs as Bud. No amount of his insults or Mom's reasoning persuaded either of them to change their opinions on religion.

On my trip with my boys to Miles City in 1978, we stayed at my brother's home. He lent me his car to drive to see relatives in North Dakota. Upon my return, I cleaned it inside and out, then made the family a meal in appreciation. Later, my mother reported that Bud had complained to her that I'd not thanked him for his hospitality. I was dumbfounded. I realized then that nothing anyone ever said or did would be enough to lessen the discontent my brother felt.

The next time Bud visited Fremont I asked my mother to invite him to my place for a meal. He didn't show up or return my phone calls to him. He told Mom he resented her attempts to get us together.

When Bud finally responded to my calls, I told him how much I'd like to see him. His response surprised me.

"I don't want to talk to you," he said, angrily. "Why should I see you?"

"I really had hoped to reconnect so—" I said, softly, before he cut me off.

"We have nothing to talk about," he snapped, "and nothing in common."

He sounded like he wanted to hang up, but I managed to keep him on the line. I wanted to know what had upset him. He indicated he hadn't wanted Mom to try to bring us together for that lunch. But he hadn't answered my calls, so there had been no other way to invite him.

"If that's truly how you feel," I said hurt and angry, "then I don't see what I can do. I'm sorry you feel that way," I said, and hung up.

Having nothing in common may have been how he interpreted my lack of interest in the religion he seemed to cling to like a life raft. My heart went out to my brother, but I didn't know how to help him. He lived in Montana, and I lived in California, and he wasn't speaking to me. Mom encouraged Bud to see a psychiatrist, which he did. Lezlee agreed he needed counseling but wouldn't accompany him to his therapy sessions. He told Mom that the psychiatrist said he was depressed and prescribed medication. He was reluctant to have to depend on anyone or anything, including medication.

His depression deepened with each job he lost or didn't get. Mom and Dad traveled to Montana several times to give him pep talks, advice, and money. They comforted Lezlee and the children. No one enjoyed my brother's constant proselytizing, but at least he still talked to Mom and Dad.

Bud ceased hunting, fishing, and flying, activities he had loved. The bank repossessed his plane. Then he began to lose his wife. Lezlee's svelte body, sparkling blue eyes, long blond hair, and year-round tan made her attractive. Bud became convinced that other men lusted after her. He accused her of infidelity, which she denied. He had always been a super strict parent to his two children. Now my parents heard rumors from people they knew that my brother had become an abusive husband.

In November 1986, Lezlee came into their living room to find Bud with a gun to his head. She talked him out of killing himself. Then Lezlee took the children, moved out, and filed for divorce. She said she was fearful her husband could harm her or the children. She found a job in a local store and said she was happier and safer on her own.

Whereas Bud had once had a challenging job, fulfilling activities, an attractive wife, and well-behaved children, he now had none of these. As his life continued to spiral downward, he became more and more despondent. He commented to our parents that life had become a chore and held no joy. It seemed nothing could fill his inner void.

With each financial and emotional crisis, Mom and Dad made urgent trips to Montana. On one of their visits, Lezlee reported that Bud had threatened to kill her with his rifle. Dad talked to Bud at length about how it was one thing to take his own life, but quite another to take the life of someone else.

Bud celebrated Christmas 1986 with us at our parents' home in Fremont. He was on antidepressants, and I was able to talk with him. He continued his insistence that I needed to be born again. We sparred by throwing Bible quotations at one another. He still didn't buy my version of religion any more than I bought his. I told him that he now functioned like the kind adult he'd once been. He agreed he performed better with medication but didn't want to be dependent upon it for the rest of his life.

∾

On Monday morning, November 16, 1987, a special education secretary at San Jose Unified's headquarters gestured to me in my office
cubicle.

"You have an urgent call," the secretary said.

"Yes," I said, lifting the receiver and hearing someone take a long
breath, "Who's this?"

It was my mother's neighbor Marian calling. She had never called
me at work. Mom must have given her my office number. I wondered
if something was wrong with my parents.

"Are you sitting down?" Marian asked, an uncharacteristic tremor
in her voice.

"I am now," I said. "What is it? Are Mom and Dad okay?"

"They are in shock. They received a call this morning that your
brother Bud shot himself in his house in Miles City. He's dead."

"Oh no," I said.

"Your parents need you with them as soon as you can get to
Fremont."

I dropped the phone and stared straight ahead. Other psychologists poked their heads above their cubicles with looks of concern.
Kathy, a fellow psychologist, must have seen the blood drain from my
face. She rushed to my side. I mentioned briefly what I'd learned. After
condolences from my workmates, I requested a week's bereavement
leave and rushed to be with my parents.

At home, Antonio embraced me. I let him comfort me but I
couldn't cry. Instead, I sprang into action. I dialed airlines and found
flights to Billings, Montana, for my parents, two of my sisters, and
myself. Antonio opted to stay home with Tim. I arranged for Dad's
sister Mickey to pick us up and transport us the three hours from
Billings to Miles City.

Mickey lent us her station wagon for the week. Family friends
invited us to stay in their extra house in Miles City, the town where
Bud had been born, lived, and died.

I stared at Bud's round, motionless face in the casket at the Stevenson Funeral Home, owned by friends of his. I wondered what it had been like for his pals to tend to Bud's remains while also grieving for the loss of their friend. Here lay a member of my family, who despite having young children, died by his own hand. How could that happen when he had so many more years to live? I'd not yet mourned my thirty-nine-year-old brother because I had busied myself organizing the family's trip. The brave front I'd had for the past week crumbled. Tears erupted from my eyes like two gushing faucets I couldn't turn off. A deep sadness engulfed me.

At the November 19 service, two of my sisters read letters they'd received from our brother. A four-girl guitar group sang "Amazing Grace." I heard none of it. I sat in the pew of Bud's fundamentalist church and cried uncontrollably.

Bud's many friends filed by after the service offering their condolences while sobs wracked my body. I had no energy to thank any of them. Savory homemade sandwiches, hot dishes, gelatins, and desserts, typical of small-town fare, spread out over several tables at the luncheon after the funeral. The food the considerate local women prepared went uneaten by me. When I finally stopped weeping, I picked myself up and went searching for answers.

I arranged a meeting with my brother's psychiatrist. She had prescribed his medications and talked with him whenever he kept his appointments. She invited any family members who wished, to meet with her in her office. My parents, three sisters, our remaining brother, and I listened while Buddy's psychiatrist shed light on his mental state in his final months.

The drugs she'd prescribed had improved his outlook, the therapist told us, but he didn't always take them. And they didn't do much for his unemployed status. A proud man, Bud said he deserved better jobs than the ones offered him. He'd only consider doing work that required his electrical or welding skills. He refused to take on handyman repair work he considered beneath him. His strong work ethic and pride didn't allow him to delay payments, have his debts forgiven by generous benefactors, or accept charity. This put him in an impossible bind of being financially bankrupt, yet too scrupulous to obtain the help he desperately needed.

His therapist arranged for Bud to pay for his medication and therapy by doing odd jobs for her. He resisted, saying he wouldn't be "just a handyman." He cut his medication dosage in half—a fact his therapist learned too late. Buddy defined himself by what he produced. He could no longer work at the level he thought he should, and his despondency deepened.

For a year after Lezlee filed for divorce, Bud's church had threatened to expel him. The fundamentalist religion prohibited divorce but kept Bud in its fold while trying to restore his marriage. In mid-October 1987, the pastor took Bud to Billings to see a counselor connected with the church. That "therapist" mentioned that guilt is often a reason for depression.

The pastor and a church committee held a hearing where they chastised Lezlee for seeking the divorce and Bud for not making his wife happy enough to stay married. Questioning his manhood must have been a final blow to his fragile ego. The morning his divorce became final, Bud put his shotgun in his mouth and blew out his brains.

The plaque on the rose-colored marble headstone with doves in flight read, "Bud Kohl, May 28, 1948–November 16, 1987, Beloved Son, Brother, and Father." The upright marker was a final gift from my siblings and me to our brother.

My parents transported the stone in the bed of their truck from California to Miles City, on their way to a July 1988 family reunion.

On a sunny morning we gathered at the Custer County Cemetery around the headstone to recite prayers. The cheery green countryside and warm summer sun contrasted with the somberness of the occasion. As I mourned my brother's premature death, I reviewed his path.

His choices reflected his values: needing to be saved by a religion, accepting only high-paying work, and a wife who didn't seem suited for him. Antonio and I, too, had been unhappy with one another and with our low-income status. But our work did not measure our worth. Some of the poorest people I'd known in Peru were the most content. Their satisfaction came from not being tortured by desires for a superior religion or a higher income.

With volunteer work in foreign countries, an immigrant husband, and higher education—my passions—I'd reaped the unexpected rewards of meaningful relationships, personal growth, and adventure. My brother's final passion became religion. By worshiping at the altar of pride and religion, he had forfeited fulfillment, happiness, and ultimately his life.

Divorce

Antonio and I had been married for fourteen years when our good friends Federico and Monica divorced in 1980, after thirteen years together. Then, our Italian friends Angela and Michele divorced, and we heard both versions of who was at fault. Years later, two of my sisters went through divorces—one angry, the other heartbreaking. Each announcement caught me off guard and frightened me with how precarious marital relationships could be.

The divorce rate in the US hovered around 50 percent. And that doesn't count the thousands who live together unmarried for years, then separate. When I contemplated my own up-and-down marriage, I wasn't surprised that 50 percent of the couples I knew had divorced.

Monica and I had married Latin American men after meeting them in their home countries while serving in the Peace Corps. In many ways, the marriage of Federico and Monica mirrored my marriage to Antonio. Like me, Monica had taken charge of their lives in the US and worked to support their growing family. She had controlled Federico's life path in their first years of marriage. Monica chose which classes Federico should take to complete his teaching credential and with whom the couple socialized. Monica had insisted that her husband work while he studied.

In 1977, the couple added to their family the twelve-year-old son

Federico had fathered in Costa Rica years before. Monica had welcomed the boy and treated him as one of her own. She helped him settle into his new country and chose his school and the classes he should take. But as her husband went from earning $2.25 an hour in the cookie factory to $35 an hour teaching at a community college, he demanded more say in family decisions. Their relationship began to falter.

We shared meals with Federico's family once a month or more, so I witnessed Monica's growing discontent with her husband. In the kitchen, before and after our dinners, Monica complained about her husband's failings. He didn't communicate with her, help discipline the children, or take care of household repairs. These were criticisms I also had about Antonio, in addition to not earning an income. Discussions with Monica began to make me think that I, too, should have her same dissatisfactions. Then, Federico and Monica moved fifty miles north to a home closer to their work and her parents. Our interactions became less frequent, and I returned to relative marital contentment. I was fine doing much of the disciplining, and Dad was teaching Antonio to do household repairs. Their situation, however, became worse once Federico's income surpassed Monica's and he asserted his opinions more.

One Saturday we were invited to their new home. Upon arrival, our children went off to play, and Antonio found Federico by the bar in the family's dining room, filling and refilling his glass of scotch. Monica cornered me in the kitchen.

"I don't know what I'm going to do," she said, a worried look on her face. "Federico drinks too much."

"That doesn't sound like him," I said, putting on my psychologist's hat. "When did this develop?"

"It became a problem shortly after we moved here," she said leaning in closely with a furrowed brow. "Every night when he comes home from work and every weekend, he drinks until he falls asleep."

"Maybe it's the stress of all you've been doing to fix up your new house," I said, meeting her green eyes. Trying to lighten her mood I added, "I love the pool you put in, but it must have been expensive. Bet the kids like it though."

"I have the same amount of stress I've always had," my friend said, twisting a lock of her reddish hair, "arranging schools for my family and trying to teach math to classes of junior high kids who'd rather act out than learn."

"Have you thought of marital counseling?" I said, fidgeting on my stool. "For you and Federico, I mean."

Monica whispered as she looked at her husband in the other room. He was leaning in talking to Antonio. I hoped my husband was helping Federico more than I seemed to be helping Monica.

"I've suggested seeing our priest, but Federico says because priests never marry, he wouldn't be able to help us."

My heart went out to our friends. I recognized the pressures she and Federico were under with the purchase of their third house and move in ten years. Their last move put them closer to her work and family, which I thought was beneficial. Apparently, cutting down her commute had led to other problems. Back home that evening, Antonio and I exchanged the information we'd heard separately.

"Monica says Federico drinks too much," I said, as Antonio and I lay in bed.

"He tells me," Antonio said, putting his hand on mine before I could go further, "the liquor doesn't affect him in a bad way. It just buries his sadness about their deteriorating relationship."

"What does he say his problems are?" I asked, curious to hear Federico's side.

"Monica gives him no say in any decisions. Now that they live closer to her family, Monica spends most of her time with them, and not with him."

"I know she cut her commute time to work in half," I said, yawning, "so she should have more family time."

"Now that he's begun teaching at the community college," Antonio said, ready to sleep, "he brings in more income, but she never says she appreciates it."

We were too sleepy to verbalize any parallels to our marriage. But I did some analysis as I drifted off. Initially I had complained about what I saw as Antonio's shortcomings. However, I had learned that my husband's opinions and desires were valuable and should be respected. He treated me the same, so we worked out family challenges together.

Shortly after this visit, Federico called Antonio to give him his new address. Monica had asked him to leave. The four children continued to live with Monica, and the kids visited Federico whenever their activities allowed. We rarely saw either of them after their divorce.

The situation of Angela and Michele was similar. We'd met the couple in 1968 when we all attended the University of California at Berkeley. When Tony, Tim, and I stayed at their home in Bologna, Italy, on our European trip in 1985, we often heard them shouting at one another. Angela visited us in California the following year and, over breakfast one morning, said the couple had been having serious disagreements for years and finally decided to divorce.

Shouting was nonstop between my younger sister, Patti and her husband, Mark, when we visited them in 1995 at their Santa Fe home. It started as soon as they poured their morning coffee and continued past their last beers of the day. My blood pressure rose whenever I heard their voices crescendo. This middle sister and her husband agreed on one thing: they needed a good fight to feel better. Mark often disparaged the low pay of Patti's occupation as a teacher. She retorted by criticizing Mark's insistence that he could be the successful novelist he dreamed of being instead of the carpet cleaner he was. My sister had hung their marriage license behind their toilet as a symbol of their deteriorating relationship. Then she arranged for their high school-aged daughter to live with a family in Costa Rica for a year, to protect her from Mark's abusive outbursts. When their only child left for college, Patti divorced Mark.

I could see from these couples that shouting hadn't led to communication that might ease their marital problems. Antonio and I disagreed but rarely shouted at one another. We preferred to reason our way through our arguments. Raising our voices just created more anxiety. In time, I chose to influence my husband rather than try to control him. We developed a sense of ease and compatibility that helped us tolerate our differences.

My youngest sister and her husband were loving parents to their two children. But my brother-in-law became enamored of a woman who worked in his classroom. He told my sister that he wanted to have an affair with the woman. My sister was devastated. During their thirty-one-year marriage she'd given in to most of what her husband wanted. But not this time. Divorce was her only recourse.

Antonio found it difficult to believe that a man would stray like my brother-in-law had. I felt fortunate that he believed in monogamy as I did. Besides, infidelity required deception and planning, and Antonio was too honest and irresolute to plan and carry out a secret affair.

I accompanied my sobbing youngest sister to the mediation session that marked the finality of her marriage. She was in such emotional pain that she could barely function and speak up. My sympathy went out to this sister I loved and whom I saw so overwhelmed. I wanted her to demand the remuneration she deserved and ordered her to "snap out of it right now." Through her grief, she managed to obtain a just settlement. Her husband married the woman, and eventually my sister remarried too.

I appreciated that Antonio didn't have a wandering eye. I vowed to complain less about shortcomings I saw in him. I could overlook his seeming lack of employment goals and love him for the loyal person he was.

I began to think that everyone around me was heading towards break-ups and new relationships. Even my Peace Corps roommate, Marie, and her German-born American businessman husband divorced after twenty years. His corporate job had allowed them to live well in Europe, which she'd always said she wanted. For ten years they pursued what sounded like an idyllic life wining and dining executives in France and Germany. However, several years after returning to the US, they divorced. Marie wrote very little about the breakup, but she soon remarried someone she saw as more passionate and caring than her first husband. Antonio and I tried to keep the passion in our marriage by being considerate of one another.

The divorce rate in Peru was 80 percent lower than in the United States. I suspected that was because Peru's major religion, Catholicism, prohibited divorce. Yet, the marriages of Antonio's cousin Elsa, his two brothers, his sister, and several cousins in Peru all ended early. They were private people who didn't communicate with us often, so we didn't always know the reasons for the demise of these marriages.

The divorcing couples had entered their marriages "the right way," with their parents' blessings, husbands with jobs, and not expecting a baby before tying the knot. But that had not guaranteed marital success. Antonio and I had broken the rules and followed our hearts and desires. Yet our leap of faith had led to a more permanent coupling than 50 percent of the paired-up population.

Despite our efforts, divorce had been mentioned a time or two during our marriage, usually when we argued over a lack of income. In spite of the shortcomings I saw in Antonio, I knew him to be a good person who did the best he could. We allowed each other to pursue the work and travel we wanted. We collaborated and stayed together.

Mom had married Dad, in part, she said, because his religion forbade divorce. They celebrated their fiftieth anniversary in 1991. But Antonio and I had stopped adhering to Catholic rules. So it wasn't religious beliefs that kept us together.

Of course, we knew many couples who, like us, had successful, long-term marriages. Many were also of mixed cultures. Our Mount Hamilton friends, the Costa Rican wife and Anglo husband, stayed together as did another Peace Corps volunteer who had served in Brazil and married a Brazilian. That couple tried to live in his homeland for a few years but returned to live permanently in California. Three couples with an Anglo wife and Latino husband, who'd spent the entirety of their married lives in a Latin American country, continued married for five decades like Antonio and me. Maybe we all knew from living in another country that there are many paths to happiness.

Each partner in a committed relationship brings his or her own culture with them, regardless of their country of origin. Sometimes the customs, values, and religions combine well, and the couple live in relative harmony. Sometimes they don't, and the partnership ends. It appeared to me that divorces often occur when finding a satisfying life is difficult inside the marriage.

I believed my happiness depended in large part on me, not my mate. Antonio didn't discourage the majority of my ever-changing interests. Rather, he encouraged me to pursue my goals. That respect fueled our relationship. I admired him for his family values and kind ways, and he valued me for my fortitude and ambition. Our marriage was built on mutual respect. Though I might not always feel completely satisfied in love or work, as long as I was happy 50 percent of the time, I continued on my path forward.

New Beginnings

In 1959, my family had moved to Northern California from Montana, and I enrolled as a senior at Washington Union High School. Mr. Roberts was the high school's popular activities director then. From the Washington High alumni news in 1990, I saw that he had a doctoral degree and now taught at San Jose State College. Dr. Roberts found out where I worked and that I too now had a doctorate. We hadn't kept in contact, so I was surprised by his phone call inviting me to lunch.

On a sunny California June 1990 afternoon, the rotund, balding professor met me at a Thai restaurant near the SJSC campus. After exchanging pleasantries and ordering bowls of the restaurant's famed noodle soup, he explained why he'd wanted to meet.

"Our Department of Education at San Jose State has an opening for a tenure-track professor," he said between slurps of the delicious broth. "We need someone who knows bilingual education. You should apply."

"When I got my doctorate seven years ago," I said, excited at the prospect, "I saw myself teaching at a state college. I like exchanging ideas with others in higher education. I've enjoyed the courses I've taught for the National Hispanic University."

For four years I'd worked for the California Department of Special Education's summer programs on bilingual assessment. I'd passed the state's exam and had a Bilingual Certificate of Competence. I'd taught a range of classes from Bilingual Assessment to Child and Adolescent Development for future teachers during five quarters at the National Hispanic University. Teaching stimulated my mind and forced me to keep abreast of the latest research. Sharing my experiences and expertise with aspiring educators gave me a shot of adrenaline that made me feel alive.

But my work as a full-time school psychologist, part-time college lecturer, and bilingual consultant to neighboring districts had me spread thin. There seemed to not be enough hours in the day to fulfill all my commitments. Planning lessons, correcting papers, and writing reports left me no time for a social life. I accepted each new opportunity fearing it might never be offered again. Dr. Roberts's invitation to apply for a full-time college teaching position presented a better alternative. Perhaps if I taught full-time, I could dedicate myself to one major occupation.

"Kathy," I said to my fellow psychologist, "would you write me a letter of recommendation? I'm applying for a teaching position at San Jose State."

"Sure," Kathy said, across our cubicles at the school district's central office, "if it's to say how we've worked together on cases of children's behavior disorders."

"That works," I said, "and you could add that I've conducted classes for parents and for county psychologists. I want to emphasize my ability to teach."

"What type of position is it?" fellow psychologist, Silvia, asked, poking her head up from the cubicle next to mine.

"A tenure track teaching position," I said, "in the Education Department at San Jose State."

Silvia, who'd recently completed a PhD at UC Berkeley, listened in rapt attention. She was married to one of her undergraduate professors from San Jose State, so it surprised me that she hadn't learned of the open position from her husband.

That evening Antonio and I discussed whether I should change jobs.

"I enjoyed the years I spent teaching here and in Peru," Antonio said.

"I like having to learn about the latest research," I said, "so I can answer students' questions."

"If that's what you want," my husband said, smiling, "I think that's what you should go for."

I appreciated his support. He had faith that I could achieve the teaching career denied him in the US, if that's what I wanted. I did.

No candidates from other parts of the US submitted applications. The high cost of housing in the Bay Area prohibited qualified candidates from moving here. So I was one of two applicants invited to spend a day in interviews and teach sample classes. I prepared for both. At the end of the trial day, I felt I'd done well. I was optimistic that I'd soon be a full-time university professor at SJSC.

A week later Dr. Roberts called to tell me who'd been offered the job. As I listened, my mouth and heart dropped. It was Silvia. I didn't have to go far to congratulate the winner of the professorship.

I was devastated. Silvia should have had the decency to tell me she was going for the job I wanted. When I thought about the college's decision logically, I understood why it may have happened. Silvia's PhD degree was from a higher-ranked university than mine. Having a SJSC professor husband put in a good word for her would also have helped.

She'd had as much right to apply for the position as I did. But I'd become accustomed to getting whatever I pursued. I consoled myself with my belief that when I didn't get what I wanted, something better usually came along. That's when my loss took an unexpected and ironic twist.

Career Opportunity

I began my tenth year as a San Jose Unified psychologist in September 1990 licking my wounds from San Jose State's rejection of me for their professorship. Antonio said it was my own fault I'd not been hired. I'd harmed my opportunity for the job when I talked about it at my office. My extremely introverted husband never understood my extroverted ways. I rarely attempted to hide any news. I doubted I would curtail my talkative behavior, even if my husband thought it advisable.

On our first day back at the school district's central office, Silvia entered her cubicle next to mine. I did a doubletake. It didn't look like she was there to clean out her desk.

"What are you doing here?" I asked, trying not to look as surprised as I was. "I thought by now you'd be lecturing in the hallowed halls of academia." I didn't add, ". . . where I should be."

"I negotiated all summer for a decent salary," Silvia said, in a low tone, "but the head of the university's Education Department wouldn't budge."

"What?" I stammered. "You mean San Jose State's salary is too low?"

"Yes," said Silvia, now raising her voice. "Their salary isn't nearly what I make here. Go figure."

I couldn't fault Silvia for wanting the teaching position at SJSC. She too had worked hard for her doctoral degree. I only questioned how secretive she'd been about going after the job and then turning it down.

The same month Silvia and I returned to our former positions as school psychologists, San Jose Unified's director of special education, Jack Elzroth, decided to retire. Our young superintendent, Jim Baughman, asked fellow psychologist Caroline to fill Jack's position. She turned him down. Maybe Caroline didn't want to face the school board's pressure to cut the department's $18,000,000 budget that was needed to instruct the district's 3,200 special education students. Most likely, the power wielded by special education teachers within the teachers' union frightened her. They had a reputation of demanding costly changes to their working conditions.

Then too, a special ed director had to hire and evaluate scores of psychologists, program specialists, speech therapists, occupational therapists, and other specialists. The intense competition among the twenty-nine Santa Clara County school districts for a limited number of specially credentialed personnel could be intimidating. Equally daunting was the indirect supervision, in conjunction with school principals, of over five hundred teachers and their assistants. And most trying—the special education office had seven secretaries, often at odds with one another. The director was expected to keep the peace among them. With all the responsibilities, I understood why Caroline didn't want the job.

Jack had remained in his position until a new director could be found. However, I saw no announcements for his job. One day in mid-September, Jack approached my cubicle.

"The superintendent wants to meet with you," Jack said.

I gave my boss a quizzical look. I'd never had a private meeting in

Dr. Baughman's office. However, I often attended assemblies where our charismatic superintendent spoke to district employees. I liked what I saw.

"Do I go alone," I asked, "or are you or another department representative supposed to go with me?"

"Just you," Jack said, a gleam in his eye.

Formerly a district principal, Dr. Baughman had turned more than one high school into a top academic performer. With his dedication and energy as superintendent, he'd averted an almost certain teachers' strike when hired in the fall of 1989. As the superintendent of the thirty-thousand-pupil district, he'd inspired teachers and parents alike with his vision for the future of education.

"Our students have to be trained in math and science," Baughman had said, "for jobs coming in the future."

He initiated an education foundation and obtained outside funding to begin introducing staff and students to the new computer technology just starting in Silicon Valley. He seemed ahead of his time. I looked forward to personally meeting the thirty-seven-year-old, boyish-looking, dynamic leader.

"Come on in," Dr. Baughman said, extending his hand and meeting my eyes with his piercing brown ones.

I entered the superintendent's office and sat down in the plush chair across the desk from the head of the district. My personnel file lay open between us. I wondered what was up.

"I don't believe I've met you directly," Dr. Baughman said. "We met from a distance when you received that California Outstanding Psychologist Award at the school board meeting last June."

"It was kind of you to write me that letter of congratulations," I said, feeling my face flush with slight embarrassment and a little guilt. A colleague had turned the tables and nominated me for the award after I'd suggested nominating her for it. As a result, the board of Santa Clara County's school psychology organization had named me a California Outstanding Psychologist from our region. I felt proud to be recognized by my peers. The accolade looked good on my resume.

"I'd like to offer you the position of manager of special education," said the sandy-haired leader. "Jack Elzroth highly recommends you and, from the looks of your file, you are well qualified."

Now my face felt hot—with delight. I silently reviewed the rumors I'd heard. Someone else had been the administration's first choice. They had pressured her so hard to accept the difficult job that she'd quit and taken a vice-principal position in a neighboring district. I, too, had trepidation about the difficulties that lay ahead. But my arm didn't need to be twisted. I welcomed challenges. Her refusal would be my gain. Though their second choice, I apparently had the support of important district leaders.

"Yes, I'll accept the job," I said. "I know I'm filling some big shoes. I'd love to be director of my department, but I'll need someone to show me the ropes."

"Jack will stay on to train you for as long as you need," Dr. Baughman said.

I could hardly believe my ears. Just when I needed more stimulation, I'd been offered an exciting new opportunity. I'd have major responsibilities and get a sizable raise in pay. And I hadn't had to go through the usual application and interview process. I thanked my former fellow Fremont psychologist Ed. He had suggested I take the exam for the administrative credential. And Silvia. If she hadn't applied for the San Jose State job, I might now be teaching there—at a much lower salary.

Silvia had been a psychologist with the district longer than me. She was quiet and didn't talk as much as I did. However, if I had a question about a test instrument or needed advice about what program to suggest for a student, Silvia took time to give me her opinion. How ironic. Now I'd be Silvia's boss.

∾

In 1975, the US Congress had passed the Education of All Handicapped Children's Act but didn't fully fund it. As a result, most school districts had to use increasing amounts of general education funds to pay for their growing number of special education students. This meant less money available for regular education students. I wanted to make certain my superintendent knew how the laws wouldn't allow me to significantly reduce my budget.

In one of my first actions, I wrote a letter to Dr. Baughman demanding to meet with him monthly to discuss my department's problems and requirements. I knew the school board was likely to put me on the defensive by demanding I reduce the amount of general education funds needed to educate students with academic, behavioral, and physical disabilities who required specially trained teachers and therapists. I'm uncertain what Dr. Baughman thought of my rather brazen letter, because he never again met with me.

After Jack departed, I proceeded confidently on my own with the assistance of a long-time secretary who knew everything about the department. I set about learning as much as I could in areas where I lacked knowledge and experience, like legal filings.

Part of the 1975 Disabilities Act allowed parents to seek judicial review if they disagreed with a school district's decision about the special education services their child should receive. Since the district's lawyers didn't specialize in special education law, they couldn't help with the fair hearings. Instead, I, along with a couple of my best psychologists, attended legal workshops led by a special education lawyer well versed in courtroom procedures. We soon put our new knowledge into practice.

A month into my administration, I received notice from a fourth-grader's parents that their son, Johnny, needed to be placed in an expensive private school. Dr. Rob Jones, a psychologist in private practice in San Jose, had tested Johnny and recommended he be placed in the private Guiding Light School, something the private psychologist suggested for many of the students referred to him. The more testing and advocacy he provided, the more money he made.

District psychologists, whom I supervised, had also tested Johnny. They recommended placement in one of the district's special education programs that would meet his needs. If we lost the hearing, San Jose Unified would have to pay the $13,000 a year cost for the special school. At Dr. Jones's urging, Johnny's parents filed for a fair hearing against my department because we'd denied paying for their son's private school placement.

Mediators from the McGeorge School of Law handled the legal proceeding. We met in one of our vacated wood-paneled schoolrooms. My hands perspired and my heart pounded as I entered my first day in court. My new black suit made me feel confident. I closed my eyes and took a calming breath. I not only had to control my department's expenses, but I also needed to consider what was best for Johnny. The hearing began with explanations of the process and reading of the complaint.

Dr. Jones sat across the wood table from my staff and me. He had extensive paperwork spread out in front of him. He testified first.

"My tests of this student, indicate without a doubt," Dr. Jones said, after reviewing his data, "that he should be placed in the Guiding Light School as soon as possible."

Two district psychologists, a special education teacher, and I listened and took notes. Dr. Jones droned on about his test rationale for placing the fourth grader in the expensive school. When our turn came, my psychologists presented their interpretation of more current and reliable tests that contradicted what Dr. Jones had found. Then it was my turn.

"Isn't it true, Rob," I said, first looking down, then up at our adversary and using his first name, as I'd been trained to do, "that you administered an older, less reliable version of the Wide Range Achievement Test and have never observed our more-suitable district class?"

Caught off guard, Dr. Jones muttered something about how his test was accurate and that he knew about the Guiding Light classes but not ours. I watched with interest Dr. Jones's discomfort, which our legal counsel had predicted. My team and I had this.

We won that fair hearing and all the others where out-of-district placements were requested. My staff's abilities and experience were superior to those of many private practitioners. Not having to pay for expensive private schools saved the district money and placed our students in classes where we were confident they could succeed. My experience as an administrator, in charge of a large school district's special education programs, caught the attention of local private and public universities.

The National Hispanic University and the US International University employed me part-time to teach classes in counseling, adolescent development, and behavior disorders. In succeeding semesters, three other private universities hired me to teach their undergraduate and graduate classes in bilingual assessment and psychology. San Jose State asked me to teach several classes in their special education department. *Back where I'd planned to be,* I thought. Contacts with so many talented educators enabled me to recruit quality personnel to staff my district programs.

Our youngest son, Tim, had graduated from high school in June 1989 and was now a sophomore at the University of California at Los Angeles. Tony had graduated from UCLA and worked in motion picture marketing in Los Angeles. With both boys on their own, I no longer had to rush home to make dinner. Finally, I could use my teaching skills at the university level. So I accepted many offers to teach and consult on evenings and weekends. What I earned helped pay for Tim's college expenses. Antonio applauded my efforts and often helped with household duties.

In December 1990, my youngest sister and her husband completed their special education credentials at Western Oregon University. Their training in behavioral techniques and the use of academic data to make educational plans was superior to that of many of my locally trained teachers. But they found no special education jobs available midyear in Oregon. I needed credentialed special education teachers for my programs in San Jose. I had an idea.

I arranged for my sister and brother-in-law to interview with a district committee for two open positions being taught by non-credentialed, substitute instructors. My sister and her husband were hired so quickly they had little time to pack up their belongings and move to California with their two children by December 10. I felt fortunate to add the two talented and credentialed teachers to my staff.

From conversations and questions of SJUSD administrators and the school board, I knew those in charge didn't understand how my special education staff provided specialized instruction. Verbal explanations didn't convey my staff's dedication. So I looked for ways to educate others about my department. A short film might do that. My twenty-six-year-old son, Tony, had studied filmmaking at UCLA. I contracted with him to produce a video about my department. Over a period of two weeks, he shot many hours of video footage in the classrooms of some of my department's most innovative teachers. It took him many months to digitize and edit the videotape. The twenty-minute end product highlighted the talents of our teachers and explained the nature of special education. In the end, I had a quality video I could use to educate the school board and the public. My family had benefited from my administrative position.

❧

I encouraged my teachers, students, and parents to take part in studies conducted by the American Institutes for Research (AIR). With my staff, AIR explored teacher retention and attrition, self-determination in students with disabilities, and early intervention for infants and toddlers with disabilities. The studies advanced scientific knowledge of special education personnel and programs. They also allowed district participants to earn extra money.

I planned staff development with presenters who taught about appropriate interventions for disruptive student behavior, bilingual education, crisis management, and innovative teaching practices. Exposure to outside experts increased my special educators' knowledge base. It also stimulated the development of more effective programs for our students.

As director of SJUSD's special education department, I searched the country for, and then hired, the best personnel I could find. Workshops at the district and county levels offered my staff opportunities to acquire new skills and earn college credit. And I promoted open and frequent communications with parents and employees through regular meetings and newsletters. Every challenge became an opportunity to learn something new.

When I began my tenure as San Jose Unified's manager of special education, I'd anticipated daily confrontations with angry, demanding parents and school personnel. In two years on the job, that hadn't happened. On occasion, I tangled with members of the administration in defense of my classes and personnel. I loved coming to work every day. Then, in October 1992, the bubble burst.

Caught in the Fall

My boss, Jim Baughman, when hired at age thirty-six in 1989, was San Jose Unified's youngest ever superintendent. In his first three years, he saved the district from a major teachers' strike and restored teachers' trust in administration. Baughman believed that the rate of change in US society would continue to accelerate so that our students would need to switch occupations three or four times before they retired. So he reorganized the curriculum to include the latest technology.

"We need to fashion the curriculum for children in a sequential way so the skills students acquire will enable them to deal with change," he said. "How do you make decisions? How do you work with people? How do you obtain and analyze information? Those skills can't be taught in a short course where you go to understand about change. But they can be integrated into a school's curriculum."

Baughman wanted to fashion a program that didn't fragment the learning process. He desired to decrease the number of specialists required for the numerous categories of students ranging from gifted to special ed. He reorganized the district's traditionally male management staff and placed many women, including me, into administrative positions. I'd been noticing greater opportunities for women in education since 1974, but Baughman advanced the cause one hundred percent.

In early October of 1992, the man whom the local newspaper touted as the "man of vision with wonderful ideas," and whom everyone in the community and the district admired, found himself in deep trouble. When he'd applied for the superintendent position three years before, his application said he'd completed his doctoral degree at Stanford University in 1984. At the time, no one in the personnel department bothered to check with Stanford. After all, Baughman displayed a diploma and a needlepoint image of the university's insignia on his office wall. Everyone referred to him as Dr. Baughman. But he'd lied about having a PhD.

He hadn't needed a doctoral degree to apply for the superintendent's position, though having the diploma enhanced his resume. Baughman had already proven his leadership abilities when serving as a principal at two previous secondary schools in two school districts. Most likely, he would have been hired for the superintendent's job with just his master's degree. How had he deceived so many about having a PhD?

Colleagues from his days as a principal at Live Oak High in Morgan Hill in the early '80s said Baughman often left meetings early claiming he had to get to his classes on the Stanford campus. Apparently, he would drive up to the university in Palo Alto and sit in the library. Or he'd walk into a class and stay until it was over. He did that so when a colleague or family member asked where he'd been, he could say, "I was up at Stanford working on my doctorate."

Revelations about the degree deception came out because San Jose Unified was under a court order to desegregate its schools. In preparation for an upcoming court hearing, the outside monitor asked the superintendent for a copy of his doctoral dissertation. Viewing Baughman's writing might help in their courtroom strategy. When asked, Baughman couldn't recall the title of his dissertation and he didn't supply it. So the Office of the Desegregation Compliance Monitor requested the dissertation from Stanford. None existed. Nor was there any evidence of Baughman's attendance there. That was the end of the charade. And it got worse.

Baughman hadn't just listed a doctorate on his resume, he'd forged transcripts from Stanford and inserted them into his personnel file. He'd awarded himself a generous number of As with a smattering of A-minus grades and one B-plus to give him a 3.96 grade-point average. The forged doctorate entitled him to a yearly stipend of $1,200 a year from the district. Upon discovery of his deceit, he promptly repaid San Jose Unified $7,775 to which he'd not been entitled. But his forgery could not be forgiven.

The school board deliberated nearly eight hours before asking Jim Baughman to resign or be fired. They gave him accolades for the leadership he'd provided, and then accepted his immediate resignation.

Then, the board launched an investigation into Baughman's time as principal at San Jose Unified's Leland High School. That uncovered further misdeeds. He had misused credit cards to the tune of $6,200 and falsified receipts for school signs changing them from $240 to $2,400 for reimbursement. In the end, the fake doctor pleaded guilty to five felony charges, one count of forgery and four counts of grand theft. He served four months in the county jail. According to prosecutors, he'd also failed to pay his taxes for eleven years.

Mr. Baughman said he didn't think he had hurt anyone but himself. A letter to the editor in *The San Jose Mercury News* for January 24, 1993, from Santa Clara University ethics professor Ted Mazur, stated: ". . . for someone who asserts that the only way to prepare students for a life of change is to teach them how to change, Jim Baughman should realize that forging academic records and lying on resumes will instead prepare students for a life of deceit by teaching them how to cheat."

I agreed. Lying about his PhD felt like a slap in the face to those of us who had completed the hard work required to earn our doctorates. I had labored long and hard for my EdD. He'd bypassed hours of researching, writing, and defending a dissertation by forging transcripts. But why would Baughman jeopardize his educational future by lying?

A local reporter interviewed Jim for the *West* magazine. John Hubner discovered that as a boy, Baughman was a model student. As an adult, he became a model administrator because he sacrificed his private life for his job. He must have decided that his hard work justified his cutting corners where he saw fit. Jim said he always meant to enroll in a PhD program but never had the time.

His sister related that Jim never developed any serious romantic relationships because, being married to his job, he worked twelve to sixteen hours a day, seven days a week. His office door stood open if a parent, teacher, or staff member needed to see him. And he listened to all of them and tried to solve every major problem in new, creative ways. He often succeeded.

I mourned the loss of our charismatic leader like many in the district. Baughman's appointees to leadership positions remained, but with their leader gone, the 1992–93 school year twisted and turned along like a snake without a head. With a temporary, acting superintendent in charge, the excitement of innovative programs ended. Everyone waited with anticipation for the hiring of a new superintendent, a process that would take the rest of the school year.

A new female superintendent came on board over the summer of 1993. She brought many of her own people with her and began reassigning administrators, including the assistant superintendent to whom I reported. My office was relocated to a separate, older building away from the main office where I'd been. Not knowing what my future held, I began sending my resume to other school districts that advertised for directors of special education. My interviews didn't result in any job offers. I continued my previous commitments, including collaborating with the American Institutes for Research.

One day in the fall of 1993, the head of AIR sent a huge bouquet of flowers in an elaborate glass vase to the building where my office had been the previous year. My new boss's office was now located there. The building change resulted in an awkward phone call.

"An enormous arrangement of beautiful flowers for you has ended up in my office," my new boss said, sounding annoyed and envious at the same time.

"I'll be right over," I said.

"Who are these from?" asked the former preschool teacher, now one of the new assistant superintendents, as I gathered my flowers.

"The American Institutes for Research sent them," I said looking at the attached card, "as an expression of appreciation for my cooperation. I've encouraged my teachers to participate in AIR studies. That way they influence research findings and can earn extra money. It's a learning situation for all involved."

My new supervisor didn't have a doctorate. Her skeptical look told me she might not value research the way I did. She said nothing and cast a covetous gaze at my big vase of flowers.

༄

When my long-time head secretary announced her retirement, I sought to replace her with a secretary who could speak Spanish. I found Marta, who had been the office manager at one of the district's schools with a large Hispanic population. A few months after I'd hired her, Marta entered my office shaking.

"Mr. Hiroshima summoned me to his office," she said trying to hold back tears, "and read me the riot act."

"Whatever for?" I asked, upset that the assistant superintendent would reprimand my secretary without my knowing the reason beforehand so I could accompany her.

"He said I forged his name on Bonnie's request to take out her retirement money," Marta said, shaking her head as if trying to purge the experience from her mind.

In between Marta's long sighs, I learned that Bonnie, one of the psychologists under my supervision, had requested early disbursement of her retirement contributions. Payroll had granted the advance based on the assistant superintendent's signature. Now Mr. Hiroshima needed to blame someone for his error, and my Hispanic secretary seemed a good target.

"Don't worry," I said, and ushered my still-shaking secretary to her office chair. "I'll take care of this right now."

I flew down the corridor of my building to the main structure that housed the Human Resources Department. I didn't know what I would say when I arrived on Mr. Hiroshima's turf, but he had overstepped his boundaries by accusing my Hispanic secretary of forgery. Since the new superintendent's arrival, he'd gained favor with her and used his authority like a whip. His office door was open.

"I understand you just met with my secretary," I said, entering his inner sanctum and closing the door behind me. I looked straight at the dark-haired, rotund department head.

"Yes," Mr. H said, his mouth open in surprise. Regaining his composure, he smiled and approached me. "And may I say how that green dress makes your eyes look a pretty green instead of the usual blue."

Ignoring my glare, he neared me, his dark eyes gleaming. I hoped he wouldn't put his arm around my back, as he'd done a time or two before.

"Marta forged my name on the papers that Bonnie submitted," Mr. H said, he turned and found the offending form on his desk.

"And just what proof do you have of that?" I said, my voice rising.

"The superintendent questioned why I would authorize the premature payment to one of your psychologists," he said, his face beginning to get red. "I didn't sign it, so someone in your office must have. Marta probably—"

"Marta would have no motivation to do such a thing, nor would anyone in my office." I cut him short. "She wouldn't even recognize what that form meant. And that signature looks exactly like yours."

"She signed it like I would have. That's what forgers do." Mr. Hiroshima's face now had turned completely red and his nostrils flared.

"And why did you call her to your office without me present? You know that puts her in a very vulnerable position and is highly irregular. Don't you ever do that again. You owe Marta an apology."

Mr. H, with his too-liberal hands, had lost my respect long ago. Not interested in any explanation he might offer, I turned around, opened the door, and marched triumphantly back to my building. I'd made my point—and most likely sealed my fate.

A proud man, I knew Mr. H wouldn't stand for being corrected—especially by a woman. He'd figure out some penalty for my confronting him. He had more power than I did and would certainly use it to demote or fire me. But I had my self-respect and knew that I'd stood up for the rights of my lower-ranking secretary. Satisfaction for my actions came the following afternoon.

"Guess who came over to our building when you were out at a school yesterday?" Marta said, greeting me with a big smile. Without waiting for my answer, she continued. "Mr. H himself came walking down the hallway toward our office when I was on my way to another room. When he saw me coming, he got down on one knee and apologized for having accused me of forging his name."

I'd been vindicated. My sense of justice told me I'd done the right thing. Antonio agreed. Now I'd have to accept the consequences.

Aftermath

As the 1993–94 school year came to an end, the new superintendent announced a new organizational plan. Baughman-appointed district office managers were reassigned as principals to district schools. Some took early retirement, and many resigned.

I was out as director of special education. The decision might have been jealousy over the flowers or my tirade with Mr. H, or both. Upper-level administrators decided that my position would be filled by one of the district's school principals. I could return to my former job of school psychologist. I didn't want that.

I arranged a quick debut of the film my son had put together. The school board didn't have time to view it, but my teachers applauded when they saw their classrooms spotlighted in a professionally made film. The movie looked good and I was excited to show it to the Board of Education at their next meeting. But I didn't get the chance.

I'd been fortunate in 1990 to land in a management job that had challenged me. For the next four years, I'd used more of my negotiating, organizing, and psychological skills than ever before—and I loved it. The variety of responsibilities made every day an adventure I looked forward to. My work life was never boring. I'd learned legal skills and how to play the power game. My voice had been heard by those in the upper administrative structure, and I'd had a greater positive impact on the lives of students and staff than in any previous position I'd had. I would not return to my former school psychologist job. It would be a step backward in my career. I loved being an administrator and wanted to find another such position. I couldn't retire at age fifty-one. I had few options.

I applied for and was interviewed by half a dozen Bay Area school districts for special education administrative positions. No offers came my way. I became adept at recognizing when an interview panel had already decided on another candidate. They asked their assigned questions on autopilot, weren't interested in my answers, and rarely asked follow-up questions. I could predict after each interview that the committees would choose another candidate. Now I knew how Antonio must have felt during his numerous fruitless interviews early in our marriage. My chances to leave San Jose Unified decreased with each rejection.

Antonio traveled to Peru to visit his family for his three-week vacation in August 1994. I stayed home to continue my search for a new administrative position. Antonio had never objected to my working to support our family. I'd done so now for twenty-eight years, ever since we'd married. In the late 1970s other wives had joined me when their households needed two incomes. Both Antonio and my incomes had been required for our larger home and to pay for our sons' college educations.

By August 1, most educational agencies had concluded their hiring for the 1994–95 school year. A feeling of hopelessness entered my soul. One day in early August, with Antonio still in Peru, I sat alone with no one to comfort me in my job-hunting misery. I again empathized with how difficult it must have been for my husband twenty years before when he'd been denied the many positions he sought. However, I could return to my former job, an advantage Antonio hadn't had. I came to an important reckoning. *I am not identified by my work alone. I am a still a worthwhile human being apart from my job.*

I picked up my pride and prepared to begin the school year as a bilingual school psychologist for the district that had demoted me. Disappointment filled my soul. I'd try to be content returning to a job I could do but didn't want to.

In mid-August, the Special Education Local Plan Area (SELPA) of Contra Costa County announced the semi-administrative job of program specialist. I completed the application and sent it in. When called to interview, I debated whether I should go. The job paid the same as the psychologist position in San Jose, and I had little familiarity with that part of the East Bay. On the other hand, this might be the last administrative opportunity available to me. I decided to give the interview a try. I would have to teach a lesson. Teaching hadn't been a requirement since my audition at San Jose State, and never for school psychologist positions. Nevertheless, I had an idea what lesson I would teach.

The previous June, while still in my administrative job, I'd taken a class on California's general education curriculum areas. I often enrolled in courses to obtain new knowledge that interested me or might advance my career. I knew little about the mainstream general education curriculum because I'd always worked with special education's unique programs. The first day of class we formed teams to demonstrate a class lesson. Though I'd worked with the language arts team, the demo given by the science group had mesmerized me. I'd use their presentation for my SELPA demo.

I dressed in my navy-blue business suit and white blouse and left the house early for my interview in Concord. Unfamiliar traffic wouldn't delay me for this chance to leave SJUSD. I arrived at the SELPA office an hour early.

My eyes opened wide with surprise when I saw Cathy waiting outside the SELPA interview room. She was a competing candidate whom I knew. She had tested my oldest son when she'd interned as a school psychologist in Albany, twenty years before. We chatted. I learned that she'd been working as a private contractor for the SELPA for the past couple years. An hour later she emerged with a smile from her interview. I suspected that she had an inside track for the job. I went in next.

The interview committee consisted of the SELPA director, two parents, a couple of administrators from surrounding districts, and three program specialists. After a few questions, it was time to give my lesson. I stood at the head of the table with my bag of props next to me and cleared my throat.

"I have chosen to teach a high school science class the properties of two common foods—bananas and almonds."

I felt my heart pumping in my chest. Why had I chosen this risky demonstration? The interview team, in their dark suits, looked too conservative for my wild ways. I charged ahead undeterred.

"The banana is botanically a berry," I said, and pulled a peeled, half banana from my bag. "It belongs to the genus Musa and goes by a variety of names in different countries."

I passed around pictures of the herbaceous flowering plant and placed the banana piece on a plate in front of me. The audience looked puzzled. I doubted that any of the previous interviewees had begun their presentations with a banana. Next, I removed a lemon and a small jar of lemon juice from my bag and explained.

"Lemon juice has a pH of two-point-two, and its high vitamin C content was used to prevent scurvy on long ocean voyages centuries ago. Its phytochemicals can neutralize the amines in fish by converting them to ammonium salts. Because its acid denatures enzymes, it also serves as a short-term preservative of food that tends to turn brown after slicing. This banana was dipped in lemon juice two hours ago."

The interviewers leaned forward. The director rubbed his chin. I hoped the next step would work.

"Almonds are native to Iran and Central Asia. They contain important vitamins, minerals, and healthy fats."

I pushed a slivered almond into the top of the banana and lit it with a lighter. The almond produced a lovely flame on the first try. Then, in one deft movement, I put the 'candle' in my mouth and took a bite. The science team I'd witnessed when I'd first seen this demonstration must have orchestrated that part to keep high schoolers' attention. I had the interviewers' attention now.

The committee gasped and their mouths dropped open as if I'd eaten a real candle. For my part, I burned my tongue because I'd forgotten to blow out the flame before taking the bite. Despite my theatrics, I didn't get the job. Cathy did. But the interview team said I'd made an impression they wouldn't soon forget.

∽

Three weeks into August, I spied an announcement for a Program Administrator II position with the Special Education Division of the Contra Costa County Office of Education (CCCOE). The late announcement surprised me, but grateful for another chance, I submitted an application. I'd become more familiar with Contra Costa County because of the SELPA interview. This would be a final stab at an administrative job for the coming year. If not selected, I'd have to content myself with a permanent return to my school psychologist job.

I whispered a silent "thank you" when CCCOE's office of Human Resources called to set up an interview for August 31. Antonio was still in Peru, and I missed him. But I could function on my own without his support. I relaxed a bit when the HR secretary assured me I'd wouldn't have to teach a lesson.

However, I paused to consider if this job would be better than the one I had in San Jose. The administrative office would be at Liberty High School in Brentwood—an hour from Fremont. For eighteen of my twenty-four years in education, I'd commuted to work. To reach the Liberty High office I'd have to drive an hour each way navigating Vasco Road, a curvy, two-lane highway that had a high rate of fatal accidents. I was weary of driving to work. Regardless of the danger, cost, and commute time, I knew my answer. *Better to spend time and money driving than return to employment that doesn't fulfill me.*

I reviewed the information I'd been sent about the position. "The Program Administrator for the Far East County Regional Special Education Programs directly supervises teachers, instructional assistants, and other educational specialists who provide services for severely handicapped and severely multiple handicapped students from birth to age twenty-two. Twenty-two classes are located in school and community sites in five surrounding school districts."

I reread the materials from the curriculum class I'd taken. Then, I dressed in my interview uniform, slid my feet into a pair of navy heels, and drove to the CCCOE Human Resources Department in Pleasant Hill.

The HR director greeted me with a friendly smile and handed me the list of questions I'd be asked. *How considerate and unusual to have the interview questions ahead of time,* I thought. This would give me a chance to compose my answers. I gave the HR director a weak smile, then glanced at the list. *What a stroke of luck. I could answer all of them.*

I entered the window-filled room to find five relaxed, casually dressed interviewers around the table. They introduced themselves as fellow administrators, the HR director, and the head of the Special Education Department. Before them lay the letters of recommendation I'd obtained from the SELPA director for Santa Clara County, two principals I'd worked with, and the research institute's senior scientist with whom I'd collaborated. I felt confident.

"Name the state's general education curriculum categories," said Dr. Penning, the CCCOE's director of special education with question number one. I aced the answer because of the curriculum class I'd taken. Dr. Penning explained the importance of the question.

"Knowing California's curriculum areas is important because our county will be the first to develop special education curricula in line with the state's general education curriculum."

"What makes you qualified," another questioner asked in a pleasant tone, "to head a county program?"

"You can see from my file," I said, "as director of special education for a large school district, I worked with county programs and supervised severely handicapped classes."

I relaxed and enjoyed answering the rest of the committee's questions. I had this. Not only did I sail through the interview with ease, but I sensed rapport with the team of interviewers.

As we concluded, the committee expressed admiration for my bilingual abilities, my volunteer activities, and awards. Everything about this innovative county matched my value system. I'd love to work with these people—and they didn't seem to already have selected another candidate.

The day after my interview, Dr. Penning, called me.

"We'd like you to come work with us," he said, "as the next administrator for the Far East County Special Education Programs."

"I'd love to," I said, happier than I'd been in months. "When would I need to start?"

"Your appointment should be approved by the County Board of Education when they meet on September fourteenth," Dr. Penning said. "But before that, I want you to spend a few days meeting others at the district office and at the Liberty High site."

"Oh," I said, "I'm not free to do so right now. San Jose Unified is expecting me to return to work as a psychologist tomorrow. I think it would be best to come after my appointment is official."

"Do what you need to," said my new supervisor, "but the staff is eager to meet you."

I didn't wish to lose half a month's salary while I waited for official approval. My resignation letter requested release from San Jose Unified effective September 15, when I'd be placed on Contra Costa County's payroll after their board's approval. For the two weeks in between, I resumed the psychologist position that I'd had four years before.

I felt awkward attending the beginning-year orientation in schools I'd soon leave. However, returning to SJUSD gave me an opportunity to bid good-bye to those I'd worked with for the past fourteen years. The special education department secretaries presented me with a beautiful, engraved crystal table clock. They had been supportive to the end.

My fellow SJUSD psychologists expressed delight at my good fortune when I told them about my new position. Some wanted to quit with me. All wished me well.

To appease Dr. Penning, and because I knew it would be important to acquaint myself with the people I'd soon be working with, I took several sick leave days the first part of September for events with Contra Costa County. The overlap between my present and future employers resulted in a problem. I received paychecks from both San Jose and Contra Costa County for the same days. Being on the payroll of two school districts at the same time was illegal. So I returned what I'd earned on the sick leave days I'd taken with San Jose Unified.

I greeted Antonio with my good news when I picked him up at the San Francisco airport. He was fine that my salary would increase just enough to pay my Volvo's gas bill. My benefits didn't include a medical plan, so Antonio added me to his. I had no regrets leaving San Jose Unified. The district had changed. I looked forward to new challenges.

Dream Job

Working for a county special education department, I didn't have to agonize over my school budget. The local school districts paid the county what it cost to educate their severely disabled students. My program didn't compete for limited resources with general education programs, and I didn't have to defend my expenditures to the school board. I no longer counted pennies or put used paper in the copy machine. My energies turned to enhancing the workplaces of my staff and resolving personnel problems.

Many of my program's students had the most serious intellectual and physical impairments that I had ever seen—the result of accidents, abuse, or birth defects. Special lifts and medical equipment filled many classrooms, making them look like hospital rooms. One-third of the secondary students lived in group foster homes because they'd become too big or unruly for their parents to manage at home. Many were nonverbal, in wheelchairs, or had spastic muscles, necessitating staff to feed and toilet them. Staff had to lift, carry, and diaper students of all ages. On occasion, we'd have a student hooked to an oxygen tank. Regardless of the disability, everyone who worked in the program treated each student as a respected human being who could be educated on some level.

Our program's able-bodied students helped decorate, then graced our float at the Liberty High homecoming parade. They went on a range of field trips. One class journeyed annually to the Monterey Bay

Aquarium on an overnight excursion. Experiences abounded to help students navigate around their communities. From the secretaries to the custodians—all loved our vulnerable population.

I supported students and staff by applying for MediCal monies to purchase vans equipped with wheelchair lifts, specially adapted playground equipment, and motorized lifts in the ceilings for moving the heavier, non-mobile students. I employed teachers and assistants with skills to teach our students how to grow a garden, run our own café, and work in sheltered employment situations. The staff's generosity toward the students was also bestowed on me. Several times I was called into a classroom for a special presentation.

"Every classroom has made something for you," the grinning instructional assistant said, "as a token of our appreciation."

"What a surprise," I said, often holding back tears of gratitude. "How could you arrange all of these presents without me knowing?"

I spent the next hour admiring the myriad of aprons, potholders, uniquely shaped paperweights, and monogramed canvas bags, made by the 180 students in the twenty-two classes I supervised. In return, on several holidays and always for Christmas, I gifted the one hundred members of my staff with candles, candy, photo albums, or wine glasses I found at bargain prices. When I traveled, I brought back unusual gifts for them—wooden parrot-headed letter openers from Brazil and pine ones from Mexico. In his woodshop, my father made recipe holders, letterboxes, and postage stamp dispensers for all of my employees.

The teachers especially liked the way I settled personnel problems. If two employees who worked together had a serious disagreement, I used my therapist skills to get to the root of the argument and mediate a compromise.

The psychologist, who'd been assigned to my area for many years, often saw potential problems before I did. Soon after I began my job, she alerted me to the fact that some veteran teachers consistently selected the most compliant pupils with the most cooperative parents and kept them in their ungraded classrooms year after year. Teachers argued over who would have to teach the student who had loud outbursts or bolted out of the classroom. As a result, a new or a less assertive teacher might end up with a room full of the unruliest students. In collaboration with the teachers, we arrived at a solution. We looked at the number of challenging students in each classroom, the personnel available to help, and the best fit age-wise for the student. I instituted a rule that no student could remain with the same teacher for more than two years. Though not a popular decision among some veteran teachers, all had to admit this was a fairer way to assign students.

For the first time in my educational career, my employer paid for enjoyable perks. There were holiday dinners and gifts, three-day planning retreats in the wine country, and even free appointment books and cell phones. Not since beginning my school career in San Francisco had I experienced such generosity, camaraderie, and affection at a job.

As a lifelong dedicated bargain-hunter, I searched for free and low-cost items. I outfitted my Liberty office and classrooms with usable, donated, outdated office furniture discarded by those with more modern tastes. I checked weekly with the county office general services manager to learn of leads for free items. One day, in 1997, I hit a goldmine of goodies.

The big covered county truck, called Big Blue, roared its approval as I threw it in reverse and backed up to the loading dock at the Kaiser Hospital facility in Concord. The general services manager had called me with an offer I couldn't refuse.

"I'm here from the county education office," I said, "to relieve you of your Mac computers."

"I'll get some workmen out right away," said the swarthy man on the dock.

Within an hour on a bright sunny day, we had filled the cavity of the big truck with over thirty new and used iMac computers. Kaiser had decided to switch to using HP computers. Their changeover was my staff's gain.

Every classroom benefited from Kaiser's largess. We set up a computer lab, headed by an instructional assistant who had extensive knowledge of Apple computers. I fought for and won a new position for her when we needed a full-time technician to keep the computers operating. My area's teachers learned to make movies, improve instruction, and streamline their record keeping using their new machines. One teacher centered his curriculum on student-made movies. At our annual Back-to-School parent event, he and his students proudly exhibited their latest movie complete with music and narration.

Driving Big Blue was easier than safely navigating the fifty-five miles each way of my commute to Brentwood from Fremont. Antonio worked in Pleasanton, so I could drop him off mornings on my way to my office and pick him up each evening upon my return. This arrangement worked well for us until our first accident.

A Multitude of Mishaps

The fifty-five-mile trek to my office involved driving half an hour on two major six- and eight-lane freeways and another half hour on the two-lane, twisting Vasco Road. My route passed Pleasanton near Antonio's computer programmer-analyst job. So, on most days, when neither of us had evening meetings, we commuted together to and from work to save gas. I enjoyed the hour a day of uninterrupted communication time with my husband. He drove the black Volvo we'd purchased for its safety record to his Pleasanton office at the United Grocers' headquarters. After dropping him off, I continued driving on to my office at Liberty High School. We reversed the procedure on our way back from our jobs.

The evening of August 26, 1996, I picked Antonio up at his office at seven o'clock. He climbed behind the wheel of the Volvo. After we entered Highway 680 going south, he moved to his preferred position in the far-right lane. We sped down the freeway at the 65-mph speed limit, eager to reach home for dinner. I saw the danger first—a Caltrans state highway maintenance vehicle moving in from a side road on the right.

"Antonio, watch out!" I screamed. "That Caltrans truck is going to hit us!"

Antonio too saw the truck moving in from a parking area on the right. He jerked the steering wheel sharply to the left to avoid contact. The long body of the Volvo 940 swerved to miss the moving Caltrans vehicle. The car rocked violently back and forth for what seemed like an eternity. Our bodies knocked left, then right, against the doors in the swirling vehicle now out of control. The car slid sideways, turned 180 degrees, then skidded across all three lanes of traffic before banging up against the center divider. The solid Volvo seats held us tight in the car that felt as if it would tip over any minute. Sounds of metal scraping on concrete screeched in my ears as my passenger side door banged into the immovable concrete divider. We came to a stop.

I looked around bewildered at what had happened. The traffic whizzed by, detouring around us. *Thank heavens we didn't hit anyone else and no one has hit us—yet.* I took out my employee cell phone and called my mother.

"Mom," I said, with my seat belt still fastened tight around me. "We were just in an accident on the freeway."

"If you hurt anyplace," Mom, the former police clerk, said, "call an ambulance."

Men from the Caltrans truck we'd swerved to avoid reached us. I gave them an accusative look. I wanted to blame them for our accident, but they had other concerns.

"Are you okay?" said one of them.

"I'm not sure," I said. "I think maybe you should call an ambulance."

At the hospital, I finally came to my senses. I had nothing wrong with me except an extreme adrenaline rush. Antonio had no complaints either except about the damn Caltrans drivers. We'd both escaped unscathed. The Volvo was totaled.

Antonio and I looked at one another amazed when we read the official traffic collision report. It said that the Caltrans truck had stopped to pick up one of the construction workers. We both knew it had been moving slowly toward us, not stopped. It also said our car had hit two orange cones in the right lane. Neither of us recalled seeing any orange cones, and we certainly hadn't hit any. When our car insurance increased, we knew whose version of the accident our insurance company believed. The report said the Volvo driver was 51 percent at fault for the accident. Antonio had his own version of what had happened.

"When you screamed," he said, a scowl on his face, "it rattled me so much that I crashed the car."

"But I saw that truck coming toward us on my side," I said, defensively. "You needed to get out of the way."

Antonio was right that I had screamed. What I'd forgotten was how extraordinarily sensitive he was to my motions and words. He often reacted fast to my slightest signal. I didn't know if that was good or bad. It just was. We stopped commuting together. Not dropping him off and picking him up saved me time. We could communicate at home, not in the car.

My Volvo couldn't be repaired. I bought another secondhand Volvo, an 850 model in a pretty burgundy color and shorter in length. I learned from my research that the shorter body of the 850 model lessened the loss of control problem we'd experienced with the longer-bodied 940 model. I shuddered every day for the next year whenever I passed where we'd had the dangerous bounce across three freeway lanes.

Four years later, on February 1, 2000, I was driving my burgundy-colored Volvo north on Highway 680, faster than the posted 60-mile-an-hour speed limit. It was always a race to arrive at my office in Brentwood before my bladder burst. I noticed a large object ahead in the middle of the fast lane I always drove in. I thought of steering my car into the center lane to avoid hitting it but there was no time. In a split second, I straddled the thing.

Pow, bang! Both of the Volvo's airbags activated. One blew up from my steering wheel and I was hit smack in the face. I heard the engine stop. I couldn't see where the car was headed because of the bag blocking my view. I steered to the right and crossed all three freeway lanes. The car came to a stop on the shoulder and I breathed a sigh of relief. Thank heavens I hadn't banged into other cars. Shaking, I stepped out to inspect the damage. Oil I'd had changed the day before streamed out from under my car leaving a black trail across the freeway. Whatever I hit must have wiped out the Volvo's oil pan.

Then, like magic, a California highway patrol car pulled up behind my car. A petite female CHP officer got out and walked toward me. I relaxed a bit.

"Are you okay?" the woman said.

"I think so," I said, getting out of my vehicle. "I hit something in the middle of the fast lane and all hell broke loose."

She stooped to examine the underside of my car. Just then, a tow truck stopped behind her vehicle. Two men got out. They greeted me, then joined the CHP officer to look under my broken-down car.

"We dropped a tow bar back there," one said. "Looks like your car hit it and carried it over to the side for us."

"We're sorry," said the second man. "We'll take it and get out of here."

"Not so fast," said the highway patrolwoman. "I'll need to get your information for my report."

I had my car towed to the nearest Volvo dealer—by a different tow truck. I called Antonio to tell him what had happened and let my office know I'd be late. Then I rented a car and drove to work in Brentwood. The front of my body felt hot. I thought it was due to the force of the air bag hitting me. It wasn't. The chemicals inside the air bag, not the force, had caused temporary burns and a rash on the front of my body. I sought treatment with a chiropractor recommended by one of my staff. I smiled reading the CHP officer's account of the accident when it came.

This time, the official report didn't blame the Volvo driver. The tow truck company admitted their big metal bar had caused the accident. I felt relief. At least my insurance rates wouldn't go up. I appreciated the tow truck driver's apology but wanted compensation for their mistake.

The new tires I'd just had installed on the wrecked car weren't damaged. My father and Antonio found four used ones, located where my car had been towed, took the new tires, and left the old ones on the wrecked Volvo. I had four new tires to use on my third used Volvo—a white one this time.

For months after the accident, I winced each time I came upon the oil stain on the northbound 680 spot where my accident had occurred. I had a second jolt when I realized that my most recent accident happened directly across the freeway from the southbound 680 location of the first accident.

Both accidents had occurred in the daytime. Nighttime trips felt even more perilous. More than once, I briefly fell asleep speeding toward home after an evening open house at school. By some miracle I hadn't been injured—yet. But my commute might kill me before I had a chance to enjoy retirement with Antonio.

I found a lawyer who helped me sue the tow truck company. But I had a weak case. I hadn't lost any workdays or sought traditional medical attention. My insurance company paid to replace my Volvo. I used the $7,000 settlement from the tow truck company to treat us to a restaurant dinner, foreign travel, and therapy.

Sights and Insights

The human psyche, including my own, always interested me. I majored in psychology and sociology in college so I could study how individuals and human societies develop and function. Throughout my life, I attended scores of evening classes, daylong seminars, and week-long retreats with the goal of self-understanding. Topics ranged from The Intensive Journal to Women's Mysteries. My search led me in many directions, but two experiences impacted me the most—investigation of personality types using the Myers-Briggs Type Indicator (MBTI) and attendance at a series of spiritual awakening workshops. Both heightened my understanding of myself and my marriage.

The MBTI personality assessment intrigued me when I first took it in 1985. The Bay Area Association for Psychological Type, (BAAPT), had recently formed to promote information about the forced-choice inventory. I joined and rarely missed the group's monthly Saturday morning meetings. There, professionals shared their expertise about temperament and interpersonal dynamics. I described the MBTI in an article I published in the Winter 1995, *Delta Kappa Gamma Bulletin* titled "Appreciation of Cultural Diversity Through Awareness of Personality Types."

The MBTI explains the filter through which we see things, not as things are but as we are. The instrument sorts out six-teen different personality types by the ways people approach information and decisions. It describes preferences on four scales, each consisting of two opposite poles—Introversion vs. Extroversion; Sensing vs. Intuition; Thinking vs. Feeling; Perceiving vs. Judging. Everyone has a natural preference for one of the two opposites on each of the four scales. Both of the poles on each scale may be used at different times but not with equal confidence. It is much like writing with one hand, either left or right, rather than developing both and being ambidextrous.

I completed the instrument numerous times, always with the same results. My preferences correctly described me—extroverted (E), intuitive (N), feeling (F), and perceiving (P). In general, I preferred action, avoided conflict, and drew energy from others. Antonio's preferences—introverted (I), intuitive (N), thinking (T), and perceiving (P), explained why he made decisions cautiously, needed quiet time for reflecting, and valued logical thinking.

What I interpreted as Antonio withholding information was his need to process data internally. He needed a much longer timeframe than I before deciding on a course of action. We both could focus on future possibilities and took a spontaneous and flexible approach to life. Understanding our differences made me more patient. Appreciation replaced accusation.

My two interests, personality type and the Latino culture, combined when the international women educators' organization I belonged to, Delta Kappa Gamma (DKG), chose me to be the international speaker at Jalisco State's Convention. In February 1994, the organization flew me to Guadalajara, Mexico. I was honored.

The planners of the two-day event requested that I administer, interpret, and give a talk in Spanish about the MBTI to 139 attendees in a half-day session. I asked Flora, a Spanish-speaking colleague from San Jose Unified, to accompany me. I packed my suitcase with booklets of the MBTI in Spanish and two sets of scoring templates. I loved traveling to foreign countries, especially ones where I'd lived before.

Mexico felt familiar the minute the plane descended. Cheerful buildings of bright yellow, orange, and green slid by my window to greet me. I heard lively Mariachi music coming from somewhere in the terminal. Only in Mexico would there be welcoming entertainment in an airline terminal. Flora and I disembarked and walked toward our smiling hosts.

"*Hola, bienvenidas*," said Hilda, the local DKG chapter president, said.

I greeted Hilda and her fellow DKG officer, Eva, with hugs and the same "Hello," in Spanish. I added, "Thank you for inviting me to your beautiful city."

We drove through the metropolis to the member's home where we would stay. I'd last visited Guadalajara in 1984, when I taught a bilingual assessment course at the Universidad Autónomo. The city's population had increased by almost one million to 3.3 million. I looked up admiring the many modern skyscrapers that had been added to the skyline of church steeples. The city was becoming a major center of business and finance for Latin America.

"Our program tomorrow morning, Education in the Twenty-First Century, Hilda said, "will feature a government official speaking for the first hour about the new North American Free Trade Agreement (NAFTA). You'll speak for the second hour and after lunch."

However, as often happened to me in Spanish-speaking countries, the day didn't unfold as planned. Two hundred and thirty participants appeared before me instead of the 139 I expected. The first speaker spoke for two and a half hours about the benefits the NAFTA agreement would bring to Mexico. His topic held the audience's interest an hour past his ending time. He'd encroached an hour into my allotted time. The loss of time for my talk meant I could explain far less about the MBTI than I'd planned. I hastily revised my schedule. In the forty-five minutes that remained before the lunch break, I explained what I could, then distributed the question booklets and inventory sheets for those present to take the assessment. There weren't enough pencils or booklets. From somewhere we obtained more pencils and I asked the participants to silently share question booklets with each other. That broke the required test protocol, but I needed to get through this.

"*Doctora*," came a voice from the middle of the auditorium, "what do we do with the sheet full of circles?"

"Yes," said another teacher, "I've never seen a page like this. What is this page of zeros for?"

Caught off guard, I searched my Spanish vocabulary to explain the concept of filling in a bubble to correspond with an answer. It had never occurred to me that my audience wouldn't know how to use this type of fill-in-the-bubble answer form, a staple in US schools for tests. I defined the bubble-filling concept and the group got down to completing its task. Next, I organized how six of us would score the inventories during the lunch break.

No time to fill our plates with the delicious-smelling tacos, beans, and rice served for lunch. During the allotted hour, Flora and four others I recruited hand-scored with me the 137 forms turned in. I thanked the heavens that I'd thought to pack two sets of templates. It helped that one hundred participants hadn't returned their inventory sheets. The smaller number of answer sheets allowed us to finish scoring all 137 within the hour. As the group took the last bite of their flan dessert, I jotted down the total number of individuals in each of the sixteen personality categories based on their completed inventories. A bit frazzled, I hurried to return to the stage.

Using a series of overhead transparencies, I explained the importance of understanding personality differences at home, in school, and at work. I emphasized the instrument's usefulness for successful communication and learning. Flora changed the overheads as I spoke in my best Spanish. If I didn't know a word, Flora, helped me find one.

"Why do some people love their jobs and others dislike them?" I asked. "It could be that your personality type makes you feel more confident to perform some tasks rather than others. For example, do you prefer to develop a work schedule more than plan a party? Do you communicate better with some people than with others? It may surprise you to learn that some of you process information and make decisions based primarily on logic and others do so based on values and feelings."

Upon entering the auditorium, I'd heard several participants express skepticism at how answering a series of questions could correctly describe them. But when these same individuals read the description of their type that I provided them, I heard gasps of surprise. Many exclaimed that they couldn't believe how accurately the MBTI had depicted their personalities. I heard murmurs of approval throughout the audience. My efforts had the desired effect—teaching my audience something new and exciting about themselves and others.

"Would the two of you with ENFP (extroverted, intuitive, feeling, perceiving) preferences care to identify yourselves?" I asked, searching the audience for those with my same personality type.

Showing their hands wasn't mandatory but there seemed to be less inhibition to share after being through the two-hour experience together. The two Mexican teachers with ENFP preferences were good friends and sat side by side. There was no time to do the required added verification. Based on research at that time, the expected percentage of ENFPs for a group of businessmen in the States would have been around 5 percent, not the .01 percent of the teachers here.

"Likes often find one another," I told them, "just like those with some opposite traits form good partnerships because they have complementary strengths and weaknesses. My husband likes to have all the facts before making a decision, whereas I tend to be more impulsive and go with my gut. Using a combined approach usually results in better decisions."

"How can the result of filling in little bubbles," another participant asked, so excited she could hardly talk, "describe so well who I am?"

My Spanish vocabulary didn't allow for a detailed explanation of how Katherine Briggs and her daughter Isabel Briggs Myers developed the MBTI based on Carl Jung's theory of the existence of universal types. Nor did I have time to answer every question.

Cross-cultural research with the MBTI, at that time, had predicted my test results, but still surprised me. Fifty-three percent of my mostly female teacher instrument-takers fell into the STJ (sensing, thinking, judging) category and another 18 percent into the SFJ (sensing, feeling, judging) category for a total of over 71 percent in the SJ grouping. SJ types are broadly defined as systematic, factual, and conservative. The US population falls around the 40 percent level for SJ types. The difference may be partly attributed to the Mexican education system, which in 1994, tended to emphasize facts and "one correct" solution or what an authority says instead of many possible outcomes. I understood how Antonio with INTP (introverted, intuitive, thinking, perceiving) preferences felt out of place in his country.

I enjoyed my hosts' tour of their bustling city following the convention. However, I couldn't say I liked the evaluations of my presentation. Quite a few of the attendees criticized the mistakes I'd made in Spanish. However, many wrote that they now had new information about why people are different. I felt pleased to have facilitated new knowledge. However, I wouldn't attempt such a bold teaching venture again any time soon. I preferred to spend more time looking deeper inside myself.

∾

"I need to become more introspective," I said to my friend, Richard, as we drove down the freeway, two years after my Mexico presentation.

He had offered to give me a ride home from a June 1996 BAAPT executive board meeting. Richard had been a founding member of our regional organization for understanding the Myers-Briggs Type Indicator. I'd gotten to know and trust him at our monthly planning meetings. Being older and wiser, he knew more than me about type dynamics. I could confide in him the dissatisfaction I felt with my life.

"I'm sometimes afraid of not being busy all the time," I said. "I seem to need constant mental stimulation and entertainment."

"I highly recommend a program I'm involved in," he said. "They'll be having another weekend basic training in a few weeks in San Francisco. These spiritual awakening programs can help you develop deeper, more intimate connections to yourself and others."

I paid several hundred dollars and signed up for the weekend. On a Friday evening, I sat in a circular arrangement in a San Francisco hotel ballroom with 115 adults of all ages and ethnicities. We sat in silence, captivated by the conversation going on between the leader and a participant who had been braver than I to say why he'd come to this new age retreat. It was like a big group therapy session. The audience sat spellbound, identifying with the emotional pain of the father who'd come to learn how to relate to his estranged son. Never before in the US had I seen grown men express such vulnerable feelings so openly. Witnessing the outpouring of others' emotions stimulated my mind and heart. I felt more alive than I'd been in a long time. Then, I too had a chance at deeper emotions when we met in pairs, with instructions to reveal some intimate detail about our lives.

"I'm trying to figure out whether to stay in a three-year relationship," said Angel, who I'd paired up with. "I want to commit to my boyfriend, but he doesn't want marriage."

"I've been in a thirty-year marriage," I said, "but am questioning my commitment because my husband is from Peru and wants us to return there to live."

Antonio had begun missing his home country. I loved how much we enjoyed life whenever we visited Peru, but I couldn't imagine living there for the rest of my life. Yet, I felt obligated. My husband had lived where I had chosen for thirty years. Maybe my turn had come to live where he wanted. I wished he'd come to this workshop to explore these incongruities in our desires, but he'd refused.

Later, in a small group, I heard more stories of people dealing with far more serious problems than mine. Two seemed so full of self-doubt that they spoke in soft voices I could barely hear. Two had long histories of drug abuse. Many, like me, after two days of meditation, communication, and self-examination, came away vowing to live more satisfying lives.

By Sunday evening's finale, I'd experienced such a myriad of healing therapies that I wanted others to benefit from the workshop. I convinced my older son, two of my sisters, and some twenty other workmates and acquaintances to take the group's basic course. Antonio refused to join me in this "touchy-feely" activity but never objected to my involvement. Most of those I referred said they had benefited from participating. Enthusiastic after this first venture, I threw myself into the group's other activities.

I volunteered five times to be a facilitator at basic workshops. Between 1996 and 1998 I participated in the majority of the group's advanced programs. I spent a week in Arizona where I fasted and performed spiritual rituals designed to open my heart to greater emotion. In 1998, I traveled to Maui, Hawaii, for the group's program called "The Dark Side." There, with a group of thirty fellow soul-seekers, I subsisted on a vegan diet, meditated, viewed films, and appreciated the beauty of the land and ocean.

One of the first days, the group drove with our two leaders from our cabins in the forest out to the lava cliffs of Maui's shore. We were enjoying the perfect sunny morning when an unexpected big wave grew up from the Pacific Ocean and washed over four people from our group. As it receded, it swept Jose off the cliff and down into a watery cove. Those who'd not seen what happened, like me, soon heard others' shouts.

"I don't think he can swim," shouted Paul, looking down the craggy lava precipice at the flailing Jose far below. In a moment, Paul dove into the cove to save Jose. He gathered the agitated man in his arms and looked for a way back up the sharp lava rocks. The spiky, hardened ridges would tear the skin of anyone trying to climb out to safety.

"Over here!" several of us shouted rushing to the edge. We frantically tied our beach towels together and threw them over the edge of the cliff for Paul to grab. The ten-towel lifeline only reached half the distance to the churning waters. The strong undertow pushed Paul, holding Jose, farther and farther out to sea and away from us and solid ground.

"Don't give up!" we yelled over and over as we saw Jose thrashing to keep his head above the rough waters.

Jose became frantic. Big gulps of water entered his mouth every time he opened it to gasp for air. Paul began to lose the strength needed to keep a hold on the struggling man. He tried with all his strength to maneuver Jose toward solid ground. His efforts were useless against the strong ocean current. Both men drifted out into the ocean.

At some point, one of the leaders realized the desperate situation and headed off to find a phone and call the Coast Guard. The twenty-eight of us on the sea cliff shouted encouragement until we were hoarse. Despite our efforts, Jose stopped all movement and turned as white as my towel. He was dead. I could barely breathe. I'd never before witnessed a death.

Someone told Paul to let go of Jose or he'd also drown. Exhausted, Paul reluctantly let go and Jose's body floated out to sea. The Coast

Guard helicopter arrived and lowered a basket to Paul. Back at the camp, one of the leaders called Jose's family.

The group had a serious discussion in the aftermath of the tragedy. One of the leaders led us in the Jewish Kaddish prayers for the dead. She offered a total refund to anyone who wanted to leave the workshop. No one did. But a dark cloud hung over the remainder of the week's activities. We had truly seen "The Dark Side."

I didn't participate in more of their programs. Antonio made no arrangement for us to move to Peru. I switched to evaluating my problems in individual therapy and marriage counseling.

The Ins and Outs of In-Laws

The morning of September 26, 1994, I applied lipstick and glanced in the mirror. I hoped my cherry red lips would retain their color after pursing them during the tense hour-long drive to my new administrator's job in Brentwood. My route to work passed by Pleasanton where Antonio worked, so we commuted together.

Antonio finished brushing his teeth and said he'd be ready to leave in a minute. We were almost out the door when the phone rang. I considered ignoring it. I didn't want us to be late. Who would be calling at seven thirty? It might be one of our sons now living in Los Angeles on their own. I had to answer.

"Is this the Antonio LaTorre residence?" an unfamiliar female voice said.

"Yes," I said. "This is Antonio's wife."

"Does he have a father named Frank?" The voice sounded tentative.

I hadn't heard from Antonio's biological father, Frank, in over a year. My last two letters sent to Frank's Ohio address had been returned, stamped, "Addressee Unknown." Maybe he had married, and his wife was calling.

Antonio's father, Frank, had lived in Ohio ever since he left Peru in 1952. In 1965, Antonio and I were both twenty-two and knew my Peace Corps commitment would end the next year. We began thinking of ways we might make a life together in the United States. I'd encouraged Antonio to ask Frank for help to come to the country his father had called home for the past thirteen years. Antonio and I wrote letters pleading for Frank to sponsor his son in the US, but to no avail. We managed Antonio's immigration without Frank's help by marrying in Peru in 1966.

After Tony and Tim were born, I sent Frank photos of our growing family inside Christmas cards and occasional letters about our lives. I wanted him to feel proud of his intelligent son and thought he ought to know that he had grandchildren.

Frank wrote back a few polite, hand-printed letters in English stating that he worked as a computer programmer-analyst for the National Cash Register Company. The only emotion I ever detected from Frank came in 1972 when he wrote that his mother, Rosa, had passed away. He suggested Antonio send condolences to the surviving relatives in Lima. Antonio responded by tearing up the letter. He had no affection for his absent father. I couldn't comprehend the father and son's lack of affection for one another. After all, they were blood relatives.

Once, in 1975, when we'd recently returned from a visit to Peru, I wrote to Frank, concerned about his sister Haydee's mental state. Antonio's paternal grandfather had just been run over and killed by a bus. Haydee had lived with her parents all her life and cared for both as they aged. During our short visit, Haydee was distraught with grief. I thought her brother should know. But Frank didn't come to the aid of his sister any more than he'd helped his son.

In 1987, when Antonio had completed his college computer classes, he couldn't find work in that field. I wrote Frank to ask what he knew about possible computer program employment. He responded by sending ten pages of computer programmer job listings accompanied by $50 in cash. Antonio threw the letter in the trash. I confiscated the $50 and let the matter drop. However, I thought a reunion might clear the air between father and son. But neither one ever attempted to get in touch with the other. Now here was a phone call from a woman, possibly with news of Frank.

"I'm Jackie, a dear, close friend of Frank," the woman said. "I've known him since 1968 when he rented a room from me. I copied your address from the letters you sent. Frank hid them under the cushions of his sofa where I found them. I got your phone number from Information."

I looked at the clock. Though curious about my mysterious father-in-law, we had to start our drive to work. We'd both arrive tardy now. But Jackie's tone said I should listen to what she had to say. She explained the reason for her call.

"Six months ago, on March twenty-fourth, Frank fell during the night and couldn't get to a phone. I found him the next morning and got him to the hospital. Tests showed he'd had a heart attack. He regained consciousness in the ICU, but his health was compromised because of his diabetes. He didn't take care of himself very well. Frank passed away on May 1 without a will. I had him cremated and buried in my family plot. He left around thirty-three thousand dollars in AT&T stock and the lawyer says I'm entitled to three thousand as executor of his estate if I can find Frank's next of kin. Antonio would be his closest living relative."

"Here, I'll let you speak with him," I said, and handed Antonio the phone. He provided Jackie his date of birth and social security number. Then we left for work.

A couple months later, Antonio received a package from Jackie with Frank's personal effects. Along with a well-used clipboard and Frank's Peruvian passport, there were duplicates of thirteen years of alien address cards that he'd filed as a permanent resident. He never became a US citizen. Jackie included old letters from Antonio's grandparents, his aunt Haydee, and me. She wrote a note on one of the envelopes I'd sent to Frank that she kept the photographs of our children. She never explained why. Maybe she, not Frank, felt like my boys' grandparent.

A few weeks later, Antonio banked the $30,000 proceeds from

the sale of the AT&T stock. I hoped he might treat me to a restaurant dinner, but he used all of his inheritance to purchase a house in Cusco—in the country that his father had abandoned.

He moved his mother and stepfather into our four-bedroom house located in one of the better areas of Cusco. No longer would they have to move each time they couldn't pay their rent. Antonio had used his father's inheritance money to provide a permanent place for his mother to live—compliments of the man who had deserted her decades before.

In the summer of 1988, during his three-week vacation, Antonio had returned to Peru as he did every few years to visit his family. He brought his mother, Livia, back with him so she could relax and reacquaint herself with our sons. Our boys were now twenty-one and seventeen. She'd last seen them when we visited Arequipa in 1975. Antonio thought his mother would enjoy being with us in California where he had lived for twenty-two years. Adolfo obtained the required six-month visitor's visa for Livia and saw her off to the States with her son. A few days later, I welcomed my humble, sweet, and unassuming mother-in-law to my home.

That year, I worked in San Jose, and Antonio worked in Milpitas. Tony, away now at UCLA, only saw his Peruvian grandmother during his school vacations. Tim, a senior in high school, had a busy social life but saw his grandmother each evening. Our house was empty during the day. We needed a place for Livia to be while we worked at our offices so she wouldn't be lonely. My generous, outgoing mother stepped in.

Mom included Livia in her social circle. Communication proved difficult, however, because Livia spoke no English and Mom spoke no Spanish. Mom had tried to learn the foreign language for years because, living in the Bay Area, she heard it often.

Mom had taped cards with Spanish words on them throughout her house. *Puerta* was on the door, *estufa* on the stove and the card on Mom's table, said *mesa*. But Mom had never progressed to where she could use those Spanish words in a sentence. With Livia as a companion, Mom hoped she might finally master the Spanish language.

Our devout Catholic mothers attended Sunday Mass together. Mom found Spanish speakers in her church-based crafts and sewing groups who could converse with my mother-in-law. Our mothers enjoyed the church activities and one another. My mom didn't become fluent in Spanish but benefited from my mother-in-law's visit in other ways.

A prolific and accomplished knitter, Livia knit Mom a gorgeous mint green sweater. She produced sweaters, socks, vests, and gloves for all of us. When Tim's high school drama class needed armor costumes for the soldiers in their play, Livia knit some. Her handmade tunics looked as if they were made of chains.

Livia cooked Antonio's favorite meals, and the two of them spent hours reminiscing about people they had known. Antonio ushered his mother around the area like a tour guide. They went from the beaches of Santa Cruz to the capital buildings in Sacramento. I took my mother-in-law shopping for yarn and gifts to take back for her family in Cusco. I searched for activities I thought she'd enjoy. Once, I learned there would be a condor at a local wildlife museum. The condor is Peru's national bird, so I assumed Livia would like to see one up close. However, the bird we saw was a California condor— small by her standards—not a large Peruvian one. My mother-in-law wasn't impressed.

We enjoyed her stay so much that, in early January, Antonio applied to the US Immigration Service to extend his mother's six--month visitor's visa that would soon expire. We waited, then called the immigration office, but received no answer regarding the request. Not wishing her to be in violation of US immigration laws, a few days after her visa expired, we reluctantly put Livia on a flight back to Lima. Two months later, a letter arrived at our house from the immigration department extending Livia's visa by three months. Too late. She'd already bid us a sad farewell.

Antonio returned to Peru for a month in mid-November 1994. He planned to bring his mother back with him as he'd done six years before. I remained stateside working in my new job with Contra Costa County and couldn't accompany him. From Cusco, Antonio called to say that his stepfather was packing Livia's duffle bag with gifts for my parents and other family members.

In between my administrative responsibilities at work, I planned activities that my mother-in-law might enjoy during her stay. I purchased tickets for the Rose Bowl Parade in Pasadena. Livia would love all the flowers on the floats.

Antonio and his mother traveled from Cusco to Lima where Adolfo applied for Livia's visitor's visa, as he'd done in 1988. Then, I received a strange phone call from Antonio.

"Do you still have that letter," Antonio asked, "that the immigration service sent us back in 1989 extending my mother's visa?"

"No, I threw it away years ago," I said, "since she'd already returned to Peru when it arrived."

I wondered what that had been about. With my new work responsibilities, I couldn't worry about the details of Livia's visa. I waited for my husband and his mother to arrive back in California.

On a Saturday in mid-December, I made room for two sets of luggage in the trunk of my car. Antonio and his mother would arrive at the San Francisco International Airport that afternoon. I hummed along with the radio as I sped toward the airport to pick up the mother and son. I spotted Antonio waiting for me in front of the American Airlines International terminal. I looked behind him for another head of black curly hair. I didn't see his mother.

"Welcome home," I said, after pulling to the curb and kissing my husband hello. "I don't see your mother. Is she able to find her own way to the car?"

"She's not here," Antonio said, looking happy to see me but a bit unsettled. "The embassy wouldn't give her a visa. They said she'd overstayed her last visa so wouldn't issue her one now."

I was disappointed she hadn't come. Livia wouldn't be flying with us to Pasadena to attend the Rose Bowl Parade on the first day of 1995. In her place, I invited a niece. New Year's Day was overcast, like our mood. The flowers on the floats looked heavenly and smelled like perfume. We'd have to wait another three years before my mother-in-law would return.

Antonio hoped to bring his mother back to the US again to stay with us for longer than the six months her visitor's visa had permitted in 1988. So, after Antonio became a US citizen in 1997, he sponsored Livia for a US permanent resident's visa. Adolfo completed the paperwork, and I waited, eager to see my mother-in-law again. In December 1998, Antonio returned to his homeland to check on our house in Cusco and bring his mother to stay with us.

She wouldn't see our boys very often this time. Both now lived in their own places—Tony in Los Angeles and Tim usually in New York, when he wasn't traveling in Europe. We had our four-bedroom house to ourselves so there was plenty of space for a guest.

Livia settled into one of the bedrooms the boys had vacated. On her own TV set she watched her daily *telenovela* soap operas in Spanish and, like before, accompanied my mother to her church craft and sewing circles. I was pleased to be eating the delicious Peruvian dishes she made. I made arrangements for Livia to enjoy her stay.

In place of the trip to the 1995 Rose Bowl Parade she'd missed, I arranged for our two mothers and us to stay at the newly built Bellagio Hotel in Las Vegas in March 1999. Over and over we watched the large dancing water fountain in the hotel's eight-acre lake where fifty-foot plumes of water danced in time to music. The glittering lights and the Cirque du Soleil "O" show in water left us breathless and amazed. We tried to ride the "people mover" sidewalks between casinos. But it was the first time either of our mothers had witnessed sidewalks that moved, and they hesitated to get on them. Neither Mom nor Livia had ever experienced anything like this bustling show-off city.

Back home, I had to leave the house earlier now for a longer commute than I'd had when Livia last visited. Most mornings she caught me as I hurried out the door to ask what she should make for dinner. I appreciated having another person doing the cooking but found it difficult to plan our meals ahead of time. Often I couldn't find ingredients like beef hearts, tripe, and Peruvian spices in the local supermarket. I definitely couldn't decide what Livia should cook when I was in a hurry to get on the road.

As the months went by, travels and activities Antonio and I had previously enjoyed together, such as going to movies or concerts, had to be curtailed. His mother wouldn't enjoy them, and we didn't want to leave her alone. We had to consider the interests and stamina of the third person in our household. I had fewer conversations with my husband than he had with his mother. He was preoccupied with taking care of her.

When he could get off work, Antonio took his mother to places he'd never invited me. They toured the Bay Area from the Monterey Aquarium to Muir Woods. He took Livia to restaurants when I was at work. He'd never gone to that much planning for me. I'd always had to make the arrangements when we went to the zoo, a park, the planetarium, or a restaurant. Now I felt left out. No one made plans that included me.

Though I'd married Antonio, in part, because of how he revered his mother, neither my sons nor my husband treated me like someone to be watched over. Probably because I'd always been so independent, no one thought that I needed looking after. I wasn't needy like Livia. However, sometimes I secretly yearned to be taken care of.

Tensions

I sat in the therapist's office across from my husband in October 1999. My fingers gripped the arms of the sea green overstuffed chair. My insides churned. Antonio, sat stern and unsmiling in the chair across from me. A wide rift had formed between us. He'd been reluctant to seek help for our problems, but I had insisted. The love and passion we'd discovered in Peru thirty-three years before had diminished.

When we'd married in Cusco, Peru in June 1966, at the end of my Peace Corps commitment, we had little money, only our love to share with one another. In the years of living and working, we'd attended graduate schools, raised two sons, and acquired ample material goods. We had succeeded in achieving the American dream. But, over time, our deep affection for one another had lessened. My heart ached for the love and passion we'd once had. We were in an emotional whirlpool.

"I don't need you," I said, heat coursing through my body.

"Well, I don't need you either," Antonio said with equal agitation.

I hoped the bespectacled woman in the chair between us could help with our marital woes. I wanted her to bridge our communication gap. I yearned for our past happiness.

"That's good that you are both independent," the marriage counselor said. "It means you can make your own decisions about your lives. I think that is a healthy place for a marriage to be."

I wasn't convinced that this marriage, with our differences and our conflicts, was healthy. My nerves were on edge, and I no longer looked forward to coming home after work. Most evenings, I'd find my husband and his mother, heads together, laughing about the lives they'd had forty years before when they'd lived with Livia's parents on their hacienda below the Machu Picchu Inca citadel. My mother-in-law had been with us now for ten months, and no one had said how much longer she'd be staying.

Livia was her humble, sweet self, so I shouldn't have wanted her to leave. But I'd become weary of so many things. I had to direct my mother-in-law's activities, or she didn't know what to do. Her self-effacing, deferential ways irritated me. I found it odd that she never mentioned returning to her husband in Peru, even after Antonio's brother reported that Adolfo had undergone prostate surgery. She seemed unconcerned about him. I guessed neither one missed the other. Adolfo rarely wrote or called. Our situation caused me to take another look at our marriage.

Long ago I'd stopped reading the *Ladies Home Journal*. The column I'd once consulted, "Can This Marriage be Saved?" had never held the answer to a happy marriage for my circumstances. Instead, I'd looked for answers in type theory and in therapy.

Maybe Antonio and I were too different. He was passive, introverted, unambitious, and pessimistic. I was active, extroverted, ambitious, and optimistic. Did we fail to understand one another because of male–female differences, different personality types, or our diverse cultures? His sensitivity, once so endearing, often prevented my usual forthrightness, a quality that had first attracted him. Still, we had found ways to maintain a relatively happy marriage most of the time.

We stopped seeing the therapist and began planning the late November trip to Brazil we'd always wanted to take. Antonio finally told his mother that she'd have to return home because we'd be traveling. Livia said that the past year living with us had been the happiest of her life. Nevertheless, she had to resign herself to returning to her husband and not living with us forever.

I arranged our air flights so Antonio, his mother, and I could fly together to Miami. Livia's plane to Lima left twenty minutes after ours departed for Rio. Antonio checked on his mother every few minutes to make certain she knew how to board her plane. He didn't relax in Brazil until his stepfather reassured him in a phone call that his mother had arrived safely in Peru. Then, we both enjoyed the color, sambas, and art that surrounded us—and one another. Our lives were back to normal and we were free to travel the world together.

A Marriage of Countries

My early life in Montana pushed me to acquire a horse and a husband—in that order—by age eighteen. But I'd rejected both in favor of a life of travel and adventure. My world changed when I fell in love with Antonio, got pregnant, and married in Peru. Antonio loved me and left all he'd known to begin a new life with me in California.

We were as different as our countries. Antonio reflected his Latin heritage—generous, considerate, unassuming, and family-oriented with a strong love ethic. I mirrored my US culture—extroverted, forceful, confident, and goal-oriented with a strong work ethic. Marrying a man from a different culture resulted in a bigger challenge than I'd expected. We had the same desire for higher learning, but not the same ability to support our family. So, in the late '60s, a period when middle-class women with husbands and children seldom held down full-time, demanding jobs, I became a reluctant working mother. At first, I resented having to work full-time and my husband's seeming lack of ambition.

Despite the "accident" that began our union, I married the kind of man I thought I wanted—an affectionate husband who would be a good father. Antonio respected me as a capable individual with my own identity, not an appendage. I loved the warmth and caring of my husband and his Latin culture. And though our different customs and beliefs puzzled me and strained our relationship at times, our strengths and weaknesses complemented one another. We adapted and changed.

Marriage slowed me down and forced me to focus on family and career earlier than I'd intended. I believed my spouse should adhere to my society's expected norms and support our family. Though he quickly acquired English, he couldn't provide for us at the level I wanted, so I tore myself away from the job of full-time mother and became a full-time wage earner. We both opted for higher education, but Antonio's schooling continued for years past mine. Through all the disappointments, stresses, and joys, we made our marriage work. We weathered the marital storms and, over time, realized we didn't need to change the other person to fit our expectations.

We reared two gentle, compassionate sons who value the multitude of linguistic and cultural differences they live among in California and New York. Tim spent a year living with Antonio's family in Cusco. Tony is in the second decade of his marriage. Both perform daily household duties and do more cooking than their father. They are loving sons and upstanding citizens.

Many, like me, justify our lives and our past decisions. In summing up over five decades of marriage, I ask myself: Would I have been happier and achieved more had I married someone from my own country or agreed to live in Peru? As I sit here near my eighth decade, I think not.

Maybe the marriage therapist we saw, when Antonio's mother had lived with us too long, was wrong. Antonio and I did need each other. He needed me to provide him a permanent family and forge a path of economic security. I needed him for his dedication, calm problem-solving manner, and love. Together, we'd thrived. We complemented one another. Where I was eager, he was patient; when I was impulsive, he thought things through. Together we'd survived disagreements that had sunk the marriages of others we knew. Our lives have been fulfilling and meaningful by helping one another in our own ways.

My husband was the biggest cheerleader of my work. With Antonio holding the scaffolding, I became the architect of my life. In my marriage I had more voice and control over household decisions than my mother had over hers. Antonio and I furthered our educations and created a bridge between parenthood and work. My mind, career, and confidence blossomed. With my Peruvian husband's encouragement and my parents' help, I excelled. Antonio never saw my success as diminishing his value. This is what I have always loved about him and still do.

Had we remained in Peru, we might have had more relaxed and colorful lives with a greater number of close friendships, a busier social life, and more flavorful cuisine. Our children would have been bilingual. But the pursuit of education and our individual interests would not have been as accessible. We found a satisfactory compromise by residing in the US and visiting Peru.

All married couples make adjustments and compromises, but culture adds another layer to the process of understanding and developing the relationship. Our values aligned better than our personalities. Through study and reflection, I saw how our personalities, like our cultures, balanced one another. Antonio had what I often lacked. Where I had the ambition to sustain us financially, Antonio had the quiet sensitivity that sustained us emotionally. I drove in the fast lane and Antonio drove in the slow lane. But we traveled together to keep our family functioning. Each of us offered equal parts to sustain our marriage. We gradually learned to recognize and appreciate what we each brought to our relationship.

Anthropologists say that one must immerse oneself in another world to understand oneself. Marrying someone from another culture gave me the gift of seeing myself and my country through my husband's eyes. Over the years, our similarities and differences became clear. I tempered my impulsivity with my husband's patience and made better decisions. I learned to compromise and be more open to another's point of view. In time, I listened to and respected Antonio's opinions.

Paulo Coelho, in *The Alchemist,* writes, "When we love, we always strive to become better than we are. When we strive to become better than we are, everything around us becomes better too."

Sitting on a bench in Abancay, Peru on a spring 1966 evening, Antonio and I agreed that our union would be impossible. He asked me to give him one of my US dollars. I wondered why he wanted the currency not useable in Abancay's stores. I pulled out a crinkled dollar bill from among the Peruvian *soles* in my purse. Antonio took it and tore it in half.

"You keep one half," he said with tears in his eyes, "and I'll keep the other half. Maybe one day the two halves will come together, maybe not. If not, they'll be reminders of what once was possible."

I took my half, and my eyes watered too. The symbolism of his act struck me. We'd each have half of something of value that was worth nothing by itself. The only way the paper dollar would be worth anything was if the two parts were put together. We have put the two halves together, and today in our home, the bill and our lives are whole.

Acknowledgments

I owe much gratitude to the programs in the early years that made it financially possible for me to support our family. I received child-care on a sliding scale, food stamps, stipends, and low-priced housing and college tuition when most needed. How I wish those advantages were available to all who need them.

Thanks go out to those in the school districts who employed me and treated this working mother with compassion and allowed flexibility with my work schedule. Their humane decisions about part-time work, shared jobs, and time off to care for a sick child, allowed me to put my family's welfare first and still do the job I was hired for.

The assistance of my parents, Charles and Ila Kohl, may they rest in peace, who stepped in to help care for my boys when I couldn't, was invaluable.

I thank those who encouraged me throughout the writing of this book. Members of my Night Writers critique group Tish Davidson, Joyce Cortez, and Jan Salinas suggested ways to improve the book's readability. My online writing group Rikki West, Julie McGue, and Kim Fairley hurriedly edited the several critical chapters I struggled to revise prior to my submission deadline. Their ideas made my sentiments clearer. I so appreciate my developmental editor, Charlotte Cook, who patiently coached me through essential rewrites of the first half of the book. Her unflagging efforts set me on the path toward a more engrossing book and my writing life.

My son Tony improved the quality of my photographs, and son, Tim, designed the map of the San Francisco Bay Area. Thanks to all for their support.

About the Author

© Bejay Photography

Evelyn Kohl LaTorre's award-winning first book, *Between Inca Walls: A Peace Corps Memoir,* is about her adventures growing up in Montana, volunteering in Mexico, and coming of age in Peru. She holds a doctorate in multicultural education from the University of San Francisco and a master's degree in social welfare from UC Berkeley. She worked as a bilingual school psychologist and school administrator for 32 years in public education in California until her retirement in 2002. She and her Peruvian husband have been married since 1966 and have traveled to close to 100 countries. Their travel adventures will be the subject of her next book.

The couple have two grown sons. More of her stories and photos are available on her website, https://www.evelynlatorre.com. Her writing has appeared in *World View Magazine, The Delta Kappa Gamma*

Bulletin, the *California Writers Club Literary Review,* the *Tri-City Voice, Dispatches, Conscious Connection,* and *Clever Magazine.* Evelyn lives in Northern California but frequently visits Peru to work with the Peruvian American Medical Society (PAMS).

Please consider writing a review of this book on Amazon.com and/or Goodreads.com. Evelyn's website is: www.evelynlatorre.com. Evelyn is active on Facebook at EvelynKohlLaTorre, Author; on Instagram under evelynkohllatorre; and Pinterest at emlatorre42.

SELECTED TITLES FROM SHE WRITES PRESS

She Writes Press is an independent publishing company founded to serve women writers everywhere. Visit us at www.shewritespress.com.

How Sweet the Bitter Soup: A Memoir by Lori Qian
$16.95, 978-1-63152-614-5
After accepting an exciting job offer—teaching at a prestigious school in China—Lori found herself in Guangzhou, China, where she fell in love with the culture and with a man from a tiny town in Hubei province. What followed was a transformative adventure—one that will inspire readers to use the bitter to make life even sweeter.

Jumping Over Shadows: A Memoir by Annette Gendler
$16.95, 978-1-63152-170-6
Like her great-aunt Resi, Annette Gendler, a German, fell in love with a Jewish man—but unlike her aunt, whose marriage was destroyed by "the Nazi times," Gendler found a way to make her impossible love survive.

Fire Season: A Memoir by Hollye Dexter. $16.95 978-1-63152-974-0
After she loses everything in a fire, Hollye Dexter's life spirals downward and she begins to unravel—but when she finds herself at the brink of losing her husband, she is forced to dig within herself for the strength to keep her family together.

Brave(ish): A Memoir of a Recovering Perfectionist by Margaret Davis Ghielmetti $16.95, 978-1-63152-747-0
An intrepid traveler sets off at forty to live the expatriate dream overseas—only to discover that she has no idea how to live even her own life. Part travelogue and part transformation tale, Ghielmetti's memoir, narrated with humor and warmth, proves that it's never too late to reconnect with our authentic selves—if we dare to put our own lives first at last.

This is Mexico: Tales of Culture and Other Complications by Carol M. Merchasin $16.95, 978-1-63152-962-7
Merchasin chronicles her attempts to understand Mexico, her adopted country, through improbable situations and small moments that keep the reader moving between laughter and tears.